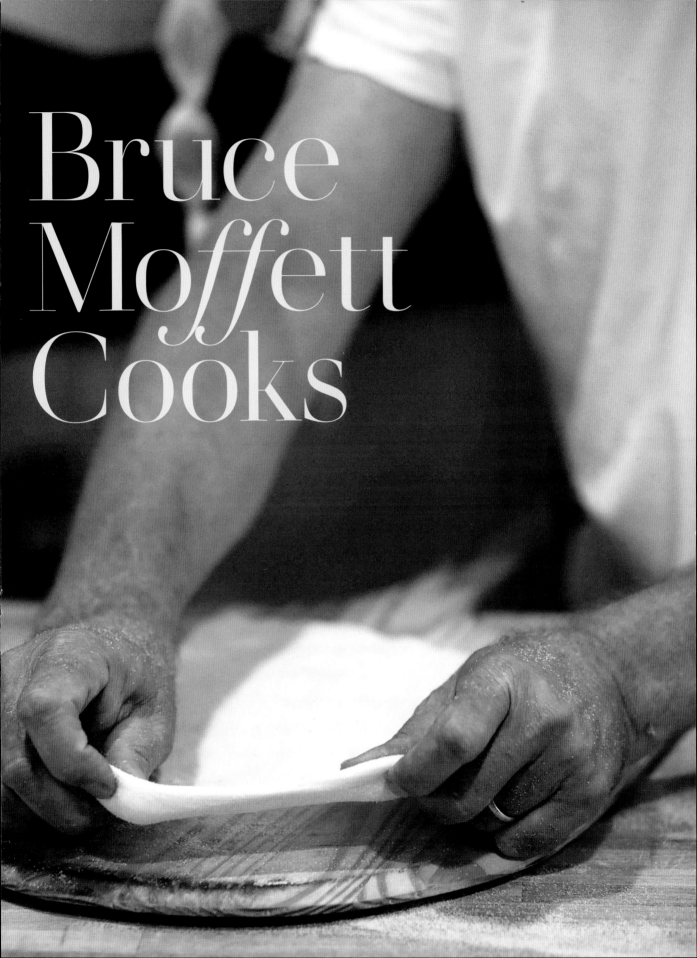

# Bruce Moffett Cooks

# Bruce Moffett Cooks

# A New England Chef in a
# New South Kitchen

## Bruce Moffett

Written with KEIA MASTRIANNI    Photographs by STEFANIE HAVIV

THE UNIVERSITY OF NORTH CAROLINA PRESS    *Chapel Hill*

*Publication of this book was supported in part by a generous gift from Vicki and Porter Durham.*

Manufactured in the United States of America

Designed by Kimberly Bryant

Set in Whitman by Rebecca Evans

The University of North Carolina Press has been a member of the Green Press Initiative since 2003.

Cover illustration courtesy of Stefanie Haviv

Library of Congress Cataloging-in-Publication Data

Names: Moffett, Bruce, author. | Mastrianni, Keia, author.

Title: Bruce Moffett cooks: a New England chef in a new South kitchen / Bruce Moffett, written with Keia Mastrianni; photographs by Stefanie Haviv.

Description: Chapel Hill: The University of North Carolina Press, [2019] | Includes index.

Identifiers: LCCN 2018042305| ISBN 9781469651125 (cloth : alk. paper) | ISBN 9781469651132 (ebook)

Subjects: LCSH: Cooking, American.

Classification: LCC TX715 .M755 2019 | DDC 641.5973—dc23

LC record available at https://lccn.loc.gov/2018042305

TO MY MOTHER,

Jane Moffett,

AND MY GRANDMOTHER,

Betty Perkins

# Contents

# Meat, 163

# Birds, 189

# Pasta and Pizza, 207

# Bruce Moffett Cooks

# Introduction

I was raised in New England by a fiercely independent mother and one strong-willed grandmother. From them, I first learned about the communal nature of food. It was a complicated love language, not the warm and fuzzy kind. To know me is to know the matriarchs in my life.

I grew up in Barrington, Rhode Island, a fairly idyllic coastal town not far from the state capital of Providence. Although Barrington is predominantly a preppy New England town with stately homes and manicured lawns, my family did not enjoy such status. We lived in a small ranch on a quiet middle-class street. Barrington is full of green trees, and the water is never more than fifteen minutes away in any direction. The fall brings brilliant orange, gold, and crimson leaves, and the winters are biting, though that never stopped us from playing hockey on the iced-over ponds. Being raised by a single mom made me self-sufficient. While my mother worked and attended school, I retreated to the kitchen to cook for my sister and myself. Nothing James Beard–worthy in those days, but I could make a mean scrambled egg and an exceptional coffee cake, and I loved to experiment with strange concoctions in the toaster oven.

As a shy kid who struggled in school, I lived for the weekend, when my mother would be off work. Some of our best times together happened in the kitchen, where she would take the day to slowly simmer red sauce on the white electric stove and charged me with browning the meat for her braised stews and chicken cacciatore. I took great pride in my abilities as her efficient sous chef.

Both my mother and grandmother were avid gardeners. They grew tomatoes, zucchini, eggplant, squash, and beans. My sister and I were expected to clip fresh herbs, harvest the vegetables, and weed the garden. We kicked and screamed, but fresh food was always available to us, a reality that I treasure more as an adult.

Some of my fondest memories and most formative experiences took place in the summertime when we would head down the coastline, along Route 1, to Matunuck, Rhode Island. About forty-five minutes south of Barrington, Matunuck was my retreat, the place where I could forget the stresses of childhood. In the early 1900s, my great-grandfather had purchased a large piece of property that loosely became a family compound known as Wilderness Farms. My grandfather Charles Perkins inherited the land and lived in a house on the other side of the property.

My grandmother, his ex-wife, lived close by in East Matunuck. Wilderness Farms is where I would run unsupervised with my gang of cousins. It was where I felt the most carefree. Still is.

Home base in Matunuck was the Lawton House, a rustic old place that always felt one year removed from falling down. Originally built in the 1700s, my grandfather bought the house from the Lawton family in the 1950s and added on to its original structure. The Lawton House sits on a large front yard overlooking Round Pond, a crystal-clear spring-fed pond. A rickety wooden dock stretches out on the placid water. Every summer we piled into the Lawton House with all my cousins, aunts, and uncles. It's where we would cook fish or have lobster boils. Anything with the potential for a mess was done here at "camp," as we called it.

Ten minutes away was my grandmother's house, done in the style of Frank Lloyd Wright, with clean, refined lines as orderly as the woman who lived in it. Her name was Betty Perkins, but we called her Craig, a nickname given from an old radio show she loved. Let's be clear: no one called her Grandma for risk of losing your life.

Craig was well traveled, educated, and opinionated to a fault. Though she was perceived as mean, she was an incredible cook. She always made it clear where you stood with her. Craig spent a lot of time in Europe, particularly Paris, Italy, and Romania, where my grandfather was stationed while working for the U.S. Foreign Service. On her bookshelf, you could find *The Joy of Cooking* (which she read like the Bible) and titles by James Beard, Julia Child, and Fannie Farmer. Her cooking style evolved through her travels. It was simple, classic, and always fresh. She wore Gucci loafers and wool pants, a silk shirt overlaid with a cardigan, and often a silk scarf tied taut around her neck. Her salt-and-pepper hair was short and tidy, and she donned a red and white gingham apron in the kitchen. She believed in using real silverware and adhered strictly to the philosophy of "everything in its place."

Everything in Craig's house was precise, almost militantly so. When you finished your meal, you did the dishes. When you woke up, you made your bed. When you went into the garden, you shut the gate, lest the deer and rabbits get into the vegetable patch. Of course, when she needed to get the gun, Craig was a pretty good shot.

Craig introduced me to stews made with offal, revealed the secret to soft-boiled eggs, and showed me how to use all my senses. She taught me how to blanch and shock vegetables; and she was more than particular about the doneness of a green bean. We exalted in trips to Skip's Dock, where we would buy fresh fish just off the boat, and to Carpenter's farm for sweet corn. Cooking was an act of love that transferred, even past family dysfunction. I took these things into my adulthood, although it would take a while for them to surface.

Cooking wasn't my first career. I dabbled in political communications in college and briefly afterward to no avail. I wandered for some time and made my first sojourn to Charlotte in the early nineties as co-owner of a pizza shop. The place didn't make it, but the experience helped me decide that I wanted to cook for a living. I sold the shop and attended culinary school, funded by Craig and my mother.

I entered the Culinary Institute of America in Hyde Park, New York, in 1994. After school, the industry took me to Atlanta and back to New England, specifically Boston, where I worked my way up to head chef at a restaurant called Metropolis Cafe. Besides the responsibilities of cooking, I learned to manage the day-to-day happenings, from staff shortages to broken dishwashers. By this time, too, I had a son, Christian, who lived in Charlotte. He's one of the main reasons I chose to make a home in the South.

I arrived back in Charlotte in 2000, a New Englander in a southern city that was just beginning to find its voice. In a way, the city and I were on equal footing. The culinary scene was very different back then, as you'll soon see when you read this book. What happened to me was ultimately what was supposed to happen, I guess. My first restaurant practically fell into my lap (page 10). Barrington's more or less materialized

before I knew what I was getting myself into. From there, I began my citizenship in the Queen City and in the South. I learned how to navigate the seasons (page 20), met my community of peers, acquainted myself with farmers' markets (page 121), opened two more restaurants (pages 42 and 226), and continued the journey that began all those years ago in Rhode Island. This book connects those dots and tells the story of my culinary life in Charlotte. For me, the city of Charlotte contains the meat and potatoes of my culinary experience. It is where I've built a life for my family and where I discovered my restaurant family. Charlotte is where I became part of a community of chefs, farmers, producers, and customers who have all contributed to my evolution and that of a growing city.

In these pages, you'll find recipes from my three restaurants—Barrington's, Good Food on Montford, and Stagioni—along with stories from my childhood, inspiration for certain dishes, and peeks into important moments in Charlotte's culinary evolution. You will meet the producers who have meant so much to me over the years and gather a sense of how I approach food from a personal and technical sense. My hope is that you take away new tips and tricks to enhance your own experiences in the kitchen. I hope that you find nourishment in these pages, both new and familiar, and that whatever you learn here will enrich the pleasures of your table.

# How to Use This Book

Whether you come to this cookbook a seasoned cook or a curious beginner, I'd like you to find useful ways to incorporate the recipes and techniques in your own kitchen routines.

This cookbook is a compilation of my own experiences, acquired over my culinary career. It contains a heavy dose of restaurant-style dishes and technique-driven recipes. Though some of the composed dishes could be called "cheffy" (they are, after all, dishes served inside my restaurants), I have worked hard to distill each recipe into approachable steps with clear instructions and helpful explanations. My hope is to expand your culinary knowledge by sharing my experience and to share culinary techniques that have been handed down to me along the way.

In every case, all the techniques inside these pages have a purpose. If you are asked to take an extra step, it's because that step will yield superior results. Below are some helpful tips on how to get the most out of this cookbook along with a few kitchen staples that will find good use in your kitchen as you work your way to your next meal.

### READ EACH RECIPE CAREFULLY
Reading each recipe before cooking familiarizes you with the steps, ingredients, and equipment involved. Does a dough need to rest for an hour before proceeding? Do you have all the ingredients listed? Will you need a special tool for this recipe? All of these elements require preparedness, and preparation is key to kitchen success. Which brings me to the next tip . . .

### MIND YOUR MISE EN PLACE
*Mise en place* is a French culinary term that means "everything in its place." It's something I learned from my grandmother and again in culinary school. In the kitchen, it means organizing your ingredients, kitchen tools, and equipment before proceeding with the recipe. If a recipe calls for "1 tomato, diced," be sure to cut the tomato as instructed before diving into the recipe. Proper mise en place breeds efficiency in the kitchen and ensures a smooth workflow. I like to set my ingredients in separate small bowls or other containers in front of me so I can easily reach for them while I cook. Once you make mise en place a habit, you will see that it's more than just a way of working in the kitchen.

### CHOOSE YOUR OWN ADVENTURE
While there are many ways to make a restaurant-worthy plate from start to finish in this book, there are just as many ways to tailor each recipe to your preference as it relates to your time and skill level. In many of the recipes, a store-bought alternative is offered. Perhaps you want to make the lobster rolls (page 57) but don't want to make the brioche buns or fingerling potato chips from scratch. Or maybe you'd like to make the bri-

oche on a different day for a completely different recipe. The recipes in this book are made for you to mix and match. The goal in every kitchen is to be creative, pick up a new technique, and use it as it suits you. Recipes are not law; rather, they are a tool for learning and shaping your culinary voice.

The bottom line is: enjoy the process. Cooking well requires all of the senses. It asks you to be present and prepared. Follow these few simple guidelines and you will be well on your way.

## HAVE THESE KITCHEN TOOLS AVAILABLE

Besides a well-made chef's knife, there are a few tools that make kitchen work easier. Some are used so often they feel like another appendage. Below are some of the ones that my kitchens couldn't do without. You may have some of these in your kitchen, or tools similar to those listed. The ones below are recommended for their ease of use and workhorse qualities. They appear a number of times in the recipes in this book.

*High-powered blender*: In our kitchens, a high-powered blender (we recommend Vitamix) is used to make soups, dressings, purées, and condiments. Find one that suits your price range. It is one of the best investments you can make for a functional kitchen.

*Food processor*: The food processor is handy for making pasta dough, simple condiments, and chopping ingredients.

*Stand mixer*: This versatile tool can be used for baking, grinding meats, and even making pasta. Invest in a high-quality brand and splurge on the attachments that will serve your kitchen interests.

*Japanese mandoline*: There may be mandolines with more bells and whistles, but the Benriner Japanese mandoline is the standard in most kitchens, and it is sharp as hell. Use it to shave uniform vegetable slices for salads, pickles, and garnish.

*Y-peeler*: Although there are many fruit and vegetable peelers in the world, the Y-peeler is the most ergonomic and efficient one I've found, especially in kitchens where it's normal to peel twenty pounds of carrots in a day.

*Cake tester*: Most home cooks think of a toothpick as a cake tester, but there's an actual tool that works for baking purposes and checking meat temperatures. It's a simple investment.

*Digital scale*: Precision is the key to many dough recipes, especially pizza dough and specialty breads. A digital scale is a minimal investment that removes the guesswork.

*Pastry brushes*: Find these anywhere cooking tools are sold. They are inexpensive and useful when making pasta, pastries, and breads.

# Pantry Basics

Customers often ask me if I cook at home. Unfortunately, I don't much. On the rare occasion when I do, I'm often reminded that I have neglected my pantry and simply do not have any of my go-to's. A well-stocked pantry is essential to building flavor and executing a successful meal. I find that pantry items are key to creating balance and adding a final flourish. I often use sweet to balance salty, use texture for added mouthfeel and interest, and add acidic elements to counter rich and fatty components. These considerations work together to form a skill set, a consciousness, that can be brought into any kitchen for a dish that's restaurant worthy, even at home.

This chapter, full of pickles, condiments, and other flavor-packed items, is where we begin. They are a collection of staples that we use time and again in my restaurants, recipes we couldn't do without. At home, they can be an arsenal for your creations. These recipes are multifunctional: they can enhance a dish, add an unexpected note, or bind together specific flavors.

The condiments here range from a simple lemon vinaigrette that adds life and brightness to any salad or garnish to a roasted garlic that infuses dressings and adds depth to soups. I lean toward herbaceous or deeply savory condiments that can punctuate a dish's main component. Here you'll discover specialty items such as Bay Oil (page 12): its brilliant green droplets add verve to soups and fish dishes like Grouper with Creamy Grits and Tomato Vinaigrette (page 142). Salsa Verde (page 9) is versatile: you'll find it tossed with the butternut squash in Duck Confit Pizza with Butternut Squash and Gorgonzola (page 236) and mixed into the bread crumbs that crown Seafood Cannelloni with Lobster Sauce (page 214).

The discovery of pickles—tart, vinegary, spiced, and sometimes sweet—as part of a complete meal represents a significant chunk of my southern food education. Down here, whole jars full of last season's dilly beans or this summer's green tomatoes will grace a table as part and parcel of the dining experience. I began experimenting with pickles as elements of the dishes I create at my restaurants. The options are endless. Red Wine Pickled Onions (page 23) cut through the richness of a thick-cut pork chop, and I have learned that Ramp Pickles (page 24) are a North Carolina mountain delicacy that is not to be missed.

Make these recipes to keep on hand in your pantry. You can use them in the recipes in this book or to add flavor and depth to your creations. I hope you will land on a few revelatory finds to enhance your home pantry.

# Salsa Verde

This bright condiment improves the flavor of everything it touches. We use it all the time, including atop Chicken Cacciatore (page 197) and in the crunchy garnish that crowns Seafood Cannelloni with Lobster Sauce (page 214). It would also work well on a rack of lamb or a whole roasted fish. Use it liberally. We certainly do.

**MAKES 2 CUPS**

Mix all the ingredients together. Use the salsa immediately or store it, tightly sealed, in the refrigerator for 1 week. Allow the refrigerated contents to come to room temperature before using.

2 tablespoons finely chopped fresh parsley

2 tablespoons finely chopped fresh chives

1 tablespoon finely chopped fresh oregano

1 tablespoon finely chopped fresh rosemary

Zest of 2 lemons

3 garlic cloves, peeled and finely grated

1 ½ teaspoons kosher salt

1 teaspoon black pepper

1 ½ cups extra-virgin olive oil

1 teaspoon Aleppo pepper (or crushed chili flakes)

# Barrington's Story: A Man Walks into a Restaurant . . .

I arrived in Charlotte knowing few people, but I had been here before. Seven years earlier, I spent a year living in the city running a pizza place, of all things. Charlotte was different back in the early nineties. Places like Harper's and Village Tavern, a meat-and-three staple and casual pub with food to match, passed for dining.

When it came to finding a job, I knew one person: Fran Scibelli, owner of the Metropolitan Café. My last post as executive chef in Boston was at a restaurant called Metropolis Cafe, so I bet my luck on finding work at her restaurant. Go figure.

My luck, as it turns out, was better than I expected (although I probably didn't think so at the time). Instead of offering me a job, Fran told me that she'd rather give me the entire restaurant. She was selling, and she needed a buyer.

The decision was terrifying. *If I threw my life savings into a restaurant, would it go over well in Charlotte?* I surveyed the dining culture to see if the concept I had in mind—interesting, composed plates driven by the seasons and my New England roots—was viable. There were glimmers of hope: a handful of chefs and restaurants pursuing cuisine past the predictable steak and potatoes fare. My peers were chefs like Tom Condron, Gene Briggs, and Tim Groody. Restaurants like Upstream, Bonterra, the Lamplighter, Toscana, Dakota's, and Sonoma were on the scene trying to raise the bar in a city that seemed slow to respond to chef-driven approaches.

I considered the plusses. My son, Christian, lived in Charlotte. I wanted nothing more than to be closer to him. Since graduating from the Culinary Institute of America, I had bounced around, working in kitchens in both Atlanta and Boston. When I lived in Atlanta, I got to visit my son every few weeks, but once I got to Boston and took on an executive chef position, I was lucky if I saw him every three months.

## Peggy Gibouin  GENERAL MANAGER, BARRINGTON'S

When I first opened Barrington's, I put a word out to hire a manager. I received five responses, but only Peggy Gibouin bothered to show up. A French native who had landed in the United States to work for the America's Cup, Peggy is a direct, matter-of-fact woman with an affinity for organizing messes, like me.

When she arrived, she asked a few simple questions in her unmistakable French accent. "What is the name of the restaurant?" she said. I told her I was still working on it. "Can I see a menu?" "Not yet," I said, "it's only halfway done."

Peggy's husband, who is a great friend of ours today, tells me that when Peggy returned home that day, she commented on the disarray of the restaurant but promptly stated, "I will take this job, and I will organize him." Nineteen years later, Peggy still answers the phones at Barrington's, curates our wine program, and handles day-to-day operations. She is one of the anchors of our restaurant family.

I was optimistic that I could handle the business side of a restaurant. My experiences in Boston at high-end places like L'Espalier and Metropolis Cafe prepared me for the inevitable hiccups of small business ownership—broken dishwashers, maintaining sustainable food costs, staffing issues, and personnel management.

Plus, something about the space felt like home. I made up my mind, gave Fran the money for the place, and moved to Charlotte. I enlisted my brother Kerry to "help out for a few months" while I got the still unnamed place off the ground.

I tossed around names for the restaurant with an old college friend who lived in Charlotte—"Table? Home?" I floundered. My friend said, "What about Barrington's? It's the name of your hometown." I thought he was on to something. I did feel at home in the space.

Next up was staffing. I had my brother, who was willing to work with me, but he was the only one. Then I hired a manager, Peggy Gibouin, and together we assembled a small staff. For the first few months, we ran a lean operation. There were times when I worked in the kitchen seven days a week with just my brother. We cooked all the food, plated everything, and washed all the dishes. It was stressful and exhausting.

Back then, we served a small audience. More than once, diners told us that we didn't "get" the Charlotte food scene. Composed plates were just not common. Sysco trucks still took precedence at the back doors of most kitchens. Local sourcing wasn't a thing.

In the early days, Peggy would pull a barstool to the front door and stare longingly out the window, silently summoning customers. I paced back and forth waiting for guests to arrive, firmly convinced that I'd be back in Boston in two months. By the time these words are printed, Barrington's will have been open for eighteen years.

## Jason Newman
### CHEF DE CUISINE, BARRINGTON'S

The tiny kitchen inside Barrington's has seen the arrival and departure of many a chef. Over the years, my post has morphed into varied roles, including mentor, chief employment officer, and babysitter. But one chef stands out. He's the one who stepped in and allowed me to grow professionally.

Jason Newman, the chef de cuisine at Barrington's, has been with me for almost a decade. He came to us as a line cook and worked diligently from the start. When Barrington's underwent a changing of the guards—our sous chef departed and took another employee with him—Jason seamlessly filled the gaps and stepped into his newfound role. Besides being a great cook, our chief forager, and a dedicated culinarian, Jason has allowed me to step away from the kitchen and into my role as a restaurant owner. Without his leadership in the kitchen, and frankly, without him covering my ass, I wouldn't be able to do what I do. Jason knows every station in the kitchen, intimately understands my food, and humbly leads the tiny kitchen where it all started.

# Bay Oil

**1 ½ cups (2 ¼ ounces) packed fresh bay leaves, divided**
**6 cups neutral oil, such as grapeseed or canola, divided**
**Pinch kosher salt**

Three ingredients and a few minutes in the kitchen will yield a bright, herbaceous oil that adds an interesting element to your cooking. You can use Bay Oil on just about anything, but it goes especially well with fish, soups, pastas, and such dishes as Chicken Cacciatore (page 197).

*Note*: This recipe requires fresh bay leaves and will not produce the same result with dried leaves. If you do not have access to a bay laurel plant, look for fresh leaves at specialty supermarkets or online.

**SPECIAL EQUIPMENT**: high-powered blender, coffee filter, rubber band, 2 sterile quart-size Mason jars (or other nonreactive containers) with lids

**MAKES ABOUT 4 CUPS**

Add 1 cup of the bay leaves, 4 cups of the oil, and the salt to a blender and blend on high speed for 5 minutes. Add the remaining bay leaves and oil and continue blending for 4–5 minutes more, or until the blender emits wisps of steam from the top.

Place a coffee filter over the opening of a jar and secure it in place with a rubber band. Carefully pour the bay oil (it will be hot) into the coffee filter to strain out the leaf particles. Seal the jar tightly with a lid. Use the second jar if needed. This oil will keep in the refrigerator for 6 months.

# Garlic Confit

We make roasted garlic in large batches to add to sauces, dressings, and sautés. It adds depth of flavor to most any dish.

**2 cups garlic cloves, peeled**
**4 cups vegetable oil**

**MAKES 2 CUPS**

Preheat the oven to 350°.

In a small cake pan, cover the garlic cloves with the oil, and seal the pan tightly with foil. Roast the garlic for 45–60 minutes, or until the cloves are golden brown. Separate the cloves from the oil. Place the oil in one container and the garlic in another, and cover both tightly. Refrigerate the oil and use it within 3 days. The cloves will keep in the refrigerator for 10 days.

# Fermented Hot Sauce

**1 pound Fresno (or red
jalapeño) peppers**

**3 garlic cloves, peeled**

**4 teaspoons kosher salt**

**½ cup distilled white vinegar**

**½ cup fresh lime juice
(from about 3 limes)**

**4 teaspoons sugar**

This hot sauce is a staple at Stagioni. We use it when we want to elevate dishes with a touch of heat and acid. We drizzle it on Biscuit Breakfast Pizza (page 242).

This is a fermented product, so give yourself four days' lead time before using it. Remember that temperature plays a factor in the process. Fermentation thrives in warm environments, so if you are working in a cooler setting, the time may vary. This hot sauce has a thick consistency, similar to sriracha.

**SPECIAL EQUIPMENT:** food processor, sterile 16-ounce Mason jar (or other nonreactive container) with lid, cheesecloth, rubber band

**MAKES 2½ CUPS**

Pulse together the peppers, garlic, and salt in the bowl of a food processor until the ingredients form a fine paste.

Transfer the contents to the jar, cover the opening with a cheesecloth, and secure the cheesecloth with a rubber band. Let the contents sit at room temperature (preferably between 65°–72°) for 2 days.

After 2 days, the paste may have separated and risen to the top; this is normal. Transfer the contents of the jar to a blender, and add the vinegar, lime juice, and sugar. Purée until smooth. Place the purée in the jar, cover the lid tightly with cheesecloth, and secure the cheesecloth with a rubber band. Let the purée sit on the countertop for 2 more days.

Remove the cheesecloth, cover the jar with a tight-fitting lid, and refrigerate for up to 1 month.

# Lemon Vinaigrette

We use a neutral vinaigrette at the restaurants to help balance savory fish dishes, pizzas, and more. Lemon and mustard cut through the richness of certain elements and offer a balancing counterpoint.

**MAKES 2 CUPS**

In a small bowl, combine the lemon juice, mustard, and honey. Whisking vigorously, slowly drizzle in the oil and emulsify. Season with salt and pepper. Add more mustard or honey, if desired. You can store the vinaigrette in the refrigerator for up to two weeks.

**½ cup fresh lemon juice (from 3–4 lemons)**
**1 teaspoon Dijon mustard**
**1 tablespoon honey**
**1 ½ cups vegetable oil**
**Kosher salt and ground white pepper**

# Basil Pesto

A basic pesto recipe is handy in many ways. The savory combination of Parmesan and pine nuts with fresh basil and lemon zest adds flavor to a host of recipes throughout this book. We mix it into a savory cannoli filling paired with a colorful tomato salad (page 99), toss it with a summer squash salad that accompanies charred octopus (page 51), and stir it into a warm summer succotash (page 140). Toss vegetables with pesto before roasting them in the oven or add a dollop to a bowl of soup. Pesto takes just a few minutes to create, and its versatility makes it a workhorse in our kitchens.

**MAKES 2 CUPS**

Prepare an ice bath. Boil a pot of water and add the basil. Blanch the leaves for a few seconds, then immediately plunge them into the ice bath. This will keep the vibrant color of the basil. Drain the leaves, then add them to a blender with oil and purée on high speed. Add the pine nuts, Parmesan, lemon zest, and garlic, and blend on medium speed until they are incorporated. If the pesto is too thick, add water, 1 tablespoon of at a time, until the mixture blends smoothly. Season with salt and pepper. Use immediately or, in order to maintain the vibrant color, store in the freezer for up to 1 month.

**½ pound fresh basil leaves**
**½ cup extra-virgin olive oil**
**¼ cup toasted pine nuts**
**¼ cup freshly grated Parmesan**
**Zest of 1 ½ lemons**
**2 Garlic Confit cloves (page 15) or plain garlic cloves**
**Kosher salt and black pepper**

# Seven-Day Sauerkraut

1 head green cabbage,
    approximately 2 pounds
1 heaping tablespoon
    kosher salt
4 tablespoons (½ stick)
    unsalted butter
½ large yellow onion, sliced
3 ounces country ham,
    cut into ¼-inch dice
3 fresh bay leaves
1 teaspoon chopped fresh
    thyme
1 cup Riesling
Pinch ground white pepper

Sauerkraut is the wonderful result of salt, cabbage, and time. We ferment ours for seven days, but many can go for a month or two: the longer the ferment, the more piquant the flavor. We soften the traditional tang of sauerkraut by finishing it on the stovetop with onions, country ham, butter, Riesling, and herbs. Sauerkraut is a natural fit with pork and sausages like bratwurst. For a twist on German tradition, try it alongside the Tilefish Schnitzel on page 152.

**SPECIAL EQUIPMENT:** ceramic crock (or other nonreactive container) with lid

**MAKES 1 HALF-GALLON**

Remove the outer leaves from the cabbage. Slice off the root stem and remove the core. Slice the cabbage into quarters, thinly slice the quarters, and place the slices into a large mixing bowl. Add the salt, massaging it into the cabbage with your hands.

Place the salted cabbage in a ceramic crock (or a nonreactive container) and pack the leaves tightly. Use a lid that's slightly smaller than the opening of the container to cover the leaves, and then weigh them down with something heavy, such as a stack of plates, to submerge the cabbage in its own liquid. Store in a cool, dark place for 7 days. Every other day, check the sauerkraut and skim off any impurities that have accumulated. Don't be deterred by a little green or white mold. Simply skim it off and discard it. Keep the cabbage submerged.

After 1 week, skim off any impurities once more. Melt the butter in a large saucepan over medium-high heat. Reduce the heat to medium, then add the onions, ham, and herbs. Cook until softened, about 5 minutes. Avoid getting color on the onions. Add the sauerkraut and its juices. Add the Riesling and white pepper. Bring everything to a simmer, cover the pan loosely, and cook for 30–45 minutes. Enjoy the sauerkraut immediately or refrigerate it and use within 2 weeks.

# Pickled North Carolina Shrimp

Fresh shrimp arrives from the Carolina coast in midsummer and is readily available through the fall. Pickled is just one of the many ways we enjoy this popular crustacean in the South. These shrimp, blanched and marinated in a flavor-packed blend of vegetables, spices, and citrus, make a nice addition to fresh summer salads or atop a flatbread pizza.

To find seasonal availability for your region, visit seafoodwatch.org and download a consumer guide for your state.

**SERVES 4**

In a large pot, combine 1 teaspoon of the salt and all remaining ingredients except the shrimp. Simmer on medium heat until the vegetables become tender, about 5 minutes. Remove the pot from the stovetop and let it cool to room temperature.

Meanwhile, fill a medium saucepan halfway with water and add the remaining salt. Bring to a simmer, then add the shrimp; gently simmer, but do not boil, for 3 minutes, until just cooked. The shrimp should remain tender. Transfer the shrimp to a sheet pan with a slotted spoon and chill it in the refrigerator for 30 minutes. Transfer the chilled shrimp to a bowl, add the cooled pickling liquid, and mix thoroughly. Cover and refrigerate immediately. Eat within 2–3 days.

2 tablespoons plus 1 teaspoon kosher salt, divided

1 small white onion, thinly sliced

1 jalapeño, seeded and thinly sliced

1 small fennel bulb, thinly sliced

1 small red bell pepper, seeded and thinly sliced

10 fresh bay leaves

1 cup extra-virgin olive oil

6 garlic cloves

4 sprigs fresh thyme

1 teaspoon white peppercorns

1 teaspoon celery seeds

1 teaspoon yellow mustard seeds

1 teaspoon red pepper flakes

1 teaspoon coriander seeds

½ cup fresh orange juice

½ cup fresh lemon juice (from about 3–4 lemons)

¼ cup white wine vinegar

1 pound large fresh shrimp, tails on

# Adapting to the South

I must admit that it took me some time to acclimate to the New South. Things work a little differently here. But I also knew that as a restaurant owner, I needed to plant roots and learn as much as possible about my new home city. I was eager to explore the South, its cuisine, and its traditions. My hope was that my integration into the city—as a chef, business owner, and newly minted Charlottean—would inspire my food. But first, I had to reset my internal clock.

My seasonality was way off. I was on New England time, so in my mind, the arrival of fresh produce was a month past the southern reality. Tomatoes should arrive in August, right? Wrong. Tomatoes come to Carolinas in early July, sometimes earlier. Becoming a regular at the farmers' markets was imperative to learning the cycles of seasonality. Just as one develops muscle memory through repetition in the kitchen, one develops a keen sense for the arrivals of each season. I anticipate peach season with the eagerness of a child every year.

Southern ingredients were a conundrum, too. There were some I had never used before, like okra and kohlrabi. I had to learn from my peers, see what they were doing on the plate, and taste everything. Sweet potatoes, North Carolina's most prolific crop, was not in my repertoire for composed dishes. Until I moved to Charlotte, they were reserved only for sweet applications. Funny to think of that now.

Smoking meat was a technique that I picked up with regularity here. Exposure to southern barbecue, especially the Boy Scout barbecues that take over church parking lots in Charlotte every fall, indoctrinated my sensibilities and got me thinking about all the ways that smoke can impart flavor.

And then there were the pickles. My early chef friends showed me the way. In New England, our preservation techniques leaned more toward jams and preserves. In the South, the pickle is almost its own food group. This was a revelation to me, and it became a key element for balancing dishes. Pickles added acidity and cut through the richness of meats and savory sides. Where had pickles been all my life?

As I learned about the South and ate its celebrated foods—banana pudding, coleslaw, pulled pork—I began to incorporate certain signature flavors, or specific techniques, into my arsenal. Inevitably, the South began to influence my work in the kitchen.

Southerners are in tune with the rhythms of life, in a way that northerners eschew. There is a warmth that exudes from them. They say hello and make eye contact in the streets. They have an of-the-earth quality that feels more communal, more prone to gathering, and more apt to welcome you to the table. Southern hospitality is a real thing, and it expanded my purview. This place has made me a better chef and restaurant owner.

# Pickled Butternut Squash Ribbons

1 large butternut squash,
    peeled (3–4 pounds)

2 cups sugar

2 cups white balsamic vinegar

1 tablespoon yellow mustard
    seeds

1 fresh bay leaf

1 tablespoon kosher salt

In this recipe, bright orange ribbons of butternut squash are pickled in a sweet brine made with white balsamic vinegar. We use this on Duck Confit Pizza with Butternut Squash and Gorgonzola (page 236), but you can try these ribbons in your own salad creations, atop pizzas, or stuffed inside a sandwich.

**SPECIAL EQUIPMENT:** mandoline, Y-peeler

**MAKES APPROXIMATELY 1 QUART PICKLED SQUASH**

Slice the ends off the squash. Cut the bottom lobe off so that you are left with the neck portion. Peel the neck of the squash with a Y-peeler, then slice off the rounded sides to form a solid rectangle. Using a mandoline, shave the butternut block into thin, rectangular slices about ⅛ inch thick, then cut the slices into 1-inch ribbons.

Combine the sugar, vinegar, 1 cup water, mustard seeds, and bay leaf in a saucepan and bring to a boil. Stir with a wooden spoon to dissolve the sugar. Add the squash ribbons and return to a boil, then turn the heat off and let the squash rest for 2 minutes. Add the salt, stirring to combine, and let the mixture cool to room temperature before covering tightly and refrigerating. These pickles are best when they sit for a few days, but 6 hours will do. They will keep in the refrigerator for up to 1 month.

# Red Wine Pickled Onions

As a chef, I'm always trying to achieve balance. Contrasting flavors, like sweet and sour, is one way to offer a nice counterpoint to the rich mouthfeel of fatty proteins. That is why we regularly make pickles like these onions, which the Italians call *agrodolce*. Try them with roast pork, salmon, or a well-marbled rib eye. It's best to give the onions a full day to absorb the aromatics.

**SPECIAL EQUIPMENT**: mandoline, cheesecloth, butcher's twine, 2-quart Mason jar (or other nonreactive container) with lid

**MAKES 2 QUARTS**

2 small red onions, peeled
2 cups red wine
1 cup red wine vinegar
1 tablespoon kosher salt
½ cup sugar
4 fresh bay leaves
4 sprigs fresh thyme
1 tablespoon black peppercorns
1 tablespoon coriander seeds
4 garlic cloves

Trim the sides of the onions to help them fit on the mandoline with ease, then slice the onions into thin rounds. Place the onions in a small saucepan and cover them completely with the wine, vinegar, and 1 cup water. Add the salt and sugar. Using the cheesecloth, make a sachet of the remaining ingredients. Place the herbs and spices in the center of the cheesecloth, tie the cloth into a secure pouch with butcher's twine, and submerge it in the pickling liquid. (For easy retrieval, tie the sachet to the handle of the saucepan.)

Bring the contents to a rolling boil. Boil for 1 minute, then remove from the heat. Pour the contents, including the sachet, into the jar. Cover and refrigerate. Pickled onions will keep in the refrigerator for 1 month.

# Ramp Pickles

2 cups apple cider vinegar

¾ cups sugar

1 cinnamon stick, broken
   in half

1 tablespoon coriander seeds

¼ teaspoon crushed chili
   flakes

1 teaspoon yellow mustard
   seeds

1 teaspoon fennel seeds

2 fresh bay leaves

1 tablespoon kosher salt

1 pound ramps, leaves
   separated from bulbs and
   papery skins removed

Ramps—wild onions that grow in the nearby mountains of western North Carolina—are a taste of Appalachian spring. Jason Newman, the chef de cuisine at Barrington's, is an avid hiker and loves to forage for wild ingredients. He says to be sure to wash ramps well because they tend to hold a lot of soil sediment. In this recipe, we pickle the bulbs only, but don't discard the leaves. They can be used for pesto, sautéed as a green, or chopped up into a salad. If you cannot get ramps where you live, this recipe also works well with scallions.

**SPECIAL EQUIPMENT:** cheesecloth, butcher's twine, 2-quart sterilized Mason jar (or other nonreactive container) and lid

MAKES 1 POUND RAMP PICKLES

Add the vinegar, ½ cup water, and sugar to a small saucepan. Wrap the cinnamon sticks, coriander seeds, chili flakes, mustard seeds, fennel seeds, and bay leaves in the cheesecloth, and tie the cloth securely into a sachet with butcher's twine. Add the sachet to the pot and bring to a boil, then reduce to a simmer over low heat. Meanwhile, prepare an ice bath.

Add the salt to a medium pot filled with water and bring to a boil, then add the ramp bulbs. Blanch the ramps for 3 minutes, or until they are tender. Transfer the bulbs immediately to the ice bath. Drain and transfer the bulbs to a 2-quart jar and pour the hot pickling liquid (with sachet) over the top. Cover tightly and refrigerate at least 24 hours before serving. Remove the sachet after 24 hours. Pickled ramps will keep in the refrigerator for 1 month.

# Giardiniera

1 head cauliflower

1 jalapeño, seeded, ribs
    removed, and thinly sliced

2 medium red bell peppers,
    seeded, ribs removed,
    and julienned (cut into
    2 × 1/8-inch pieces)

3 celery ribs, sliced on the
    bias into 1-inch pieces

2 large carrots, peeled

3/4 cup kosher salt

1 3/4 cups distilled white
    vinegar

1 1/2 cups extra-virgin olive oil

4 garlic cloves, sliced

1 teaspoon crushed chili flakes

2 teaspoons celery seeds

2 teaspoons dried oregano

Another favorite in our pantry is *giardiniera*, an Italian pickled relish. Unlike chowchow (page 86), a southern relish that is finely minced, the vegetables in giardiniera are cut into bite-size pieces. A colorful combination of cauliflower, carrots, celery, and peppers, giardiniera adds visual appeal along with a zesty, robust kick. We toss it in salads for an acidic pop and slice it thinly to garnish dishes like calamari. This recipe requires an overnight brine, so plan ahead.

**SPECIAL EQUIPMENT:** 4 sterile, quart-size Mason jars (or other nonreactive containers) with lids

MAKES 4 QUARTS

Trim and core the cauliflower, then cut it into quarter-size florets. Add the florets to a large mixing bowl with the jalapeños, bell peppers, and celery. Cut the carrots in half lengthwise, then slice them into 1/4-inch pieces; add them to the bowl. Add the salt and mix well. Submerge the vegetables completely with cold water, then wrap the bowl in plastic and refrigerate it overnight. This denatures the vegetables enough so that they will more readily absorb the aromatics.

The next day, drain the water from the vegetables and rinse them well. Transfer the vegetables to a mixing bowl and add the vinegar, olive oil, garlic, chili flakes, celery seeds, and oregano. Mix until the vegetables are evenly coated. Pack the giardiniera into the jars, cover each one with a tight-fitting lid, and refrigerate. Because the vegetables will not be completely covered with marinade, mix them every few days to ensure consistent flavor. The vegetables will keep in the refrigerator for 1 month.

# Refrigerator Pickles

1 pound Kirby cucumbers

1 cup distilled white vinegar

½ cup apple cider vinegar

½ cup white wine vinegar

¼ cup kosher salt

10 garlic cloves

1 tablespoon black
    peppercorns

1 tablespoon coriander seeds

1 tablespoon fennel seeds

2 teaspoons gochugaru
    (Korean chili flakes)

3 fresh bay leaves

1 bunch dill

½ bunch thyme

¼ bunch parsley

Every summer our farmers bring us some of the best cucumbers that I have ever tasted. I love the crunch and silky texture of the variety known as Kirby. When combined with a brine of vinegar, garlic, spices and herbs, the result is a bright pickle with a surprising crunch and depth of flavor. We use Korean chili flakes, called *gochugaru*, to add a unique spice. You can find them at a grocery with a good Asian section or online. Try these pickles in New South Beef Carpaccio with Fried Pickles and Pimento Cheese (page 37), on top of a cheeseburger, or by themselves as a welcome addition to any southern table.

SPECIAL EQUIPMENT: mandoline, 2 sterile, quart-size Mason jars (or other nonreactive containers) with lids

MAKES 2 QUARTS

Slice off the rounded ends of each cucumber. Using a mandoline, slice the cucumbers into ¼-inch rounds. Set aside.

Bring the vinegars, salt, garlic cloves, peppercorns, coriander seeds, fennel seeds, and Korean chili flakes to a boil in a large pot. Turn off the heat and let the liquid steep for 10 minutes. Pour the pickling liquid into a heatproof container. Add 2 cups of ice and stir, then allow the liquid to cool completely.

Meanwhile, pack the cucumber slices into the jars. Divide the fresh herbs evenly among the jars, then pour the cooled pickling liquid over the cucumbers until they are submerged. Cover the jars tightly and refrigerate. The pickles will be ready in 2 days and will keep for 2 weeks.

# Bacon Jam

Bacon jam is a condiment made for fatty cuts of meat and fish dishes. Although bacon is the star ingredient here, the jam also incorporates acid and sugar to cut through the richness of certain foods. I love this jam on a grilled pork chop and use it on barbecued salmon at my flagship restaurant, Barrington's. I prefer a chunkier bacon jam to one that is more like a paste. This recipe yields a jam with noticeable texture, as well as a signature tang that's different from the sweeter versions you may already have tried.

*Note*: Freeze the bacon a day ahead, then let it thaw at room temperature for 30 minutes before slicing. Also, be patient while the bacon renders. To render is simply to cook the fat out of something. In this case, we cook the bacon until it is crispy and make use of its flavorful fat.

1 pound smoky, thick-cut bacon (such as Benton's), cut into ¼-inch pieces
4 large shallots, thinly sliced
1 tablespoon chopped fresh thyme
2 cups red wine
1 cup red wine vinegar
2 tablespoons sugar

**MAKES 2 CUPS**

Cook the bacon in a medium sauté pan over medium-high heat until crispy. Add the shallots and continue to cook, stirring occasionally, until they brown slightly. Remove the bacon mixture and drain the fat through a colander. Return the bacon to the pan, along with the thyme, wine, vinegar, and sugar. Bring the mixture to a boil, then lower the heat to a simmer. Reduce until most of the liquid has evaporated and the jam has thickened, about 30–35 minutes. Serve warm. The jam will keep stored in the refrigerator for 1 week.

# Apple Chutney

2 tablespoons unsalted butter

2 medium shallots, cut into
⅛-inch dice

1 teaspoon grated fresh ginger

4 green apples, peeled, cut
into ½-inch dice

½ teaspoon ground cinnamon

¼ teaspoon ground allspice

¼ teaspoon freshly grated
nutmeg

1 cup apple cider

½ cup apple cider vinegar

2 tablespoons light brown
sugar

1 teaspoon kosher salt

1 sprig fresh thyme

This warmly spiced apple chutney offers a soft acidity for balancing out rich dishes. The play between sweet and sour in this fruity condiment creates a nice accompaniment to pork, lamb, and rich stews.

**MAKES 3 CUPS**

Melt the butter in a saucepan over medium-high heat. Add the shallots and ginger and sweat them until they are translucent, about 3 minutes. Add the apples and spices and gently stir for 1 minute. Reduce the heat to medium. Add the remaining ingredients and simmer, uncovered, stirring occasionally, until the liquid is nearly gone, about 15–20 minutes. The chutney should be thick and the apples glazed. The chutney can be served immediately or kept in the refrigerator for up to 7 days.

# Gremolata

1 teaspoon fresh thyme leaves

½ cup fresh parsley

1 tablespoon fresh rosemary

1 tablespoon fresh oregano

Zest of 2 lemons

4 tablespoons (½ stick)
unsalted butter

1 teaspoon minced garlic

2 cups panko

1 teaspoon kosher salt

This gremolata is a bright, textural pop that we add to pasta specials at Barrington's and Stagioni. It also works well atop osso buco, a braised pork shank, or a beautiful piece of seared fish. Fresh herbs and lemon zest add an aromatic element to awaken the palate, and the buttery crunch of toasted, garlicky bread crumbs provides an addictive savory bite. Fresh herbs are best for this recipe if you can find them.

**MAKES 3 CUPS**

Combine and finely chop the herbs. Add the lemon zest to the chopped herbs and mince them together, then set the herbs aside. Melt the butter in a large pan over medium-high heat, then add the garlic, panko, and salt. Using a small spatula, move the bread crumbs around the pan, stirring constantly. Toast the panko until it is golden brown and all the butter has been absorbed. Remove the bread crumbs from the heat and toss in the herbs. Store the gremolata, covered, in the refrigerator for 1 week.

# Chipotle BBQ Sauce

Sauces are a great way to add concentrated flavor to an already tasty dish. We use this sauce to finish Pecan-Crusted Lamb with Chipotle BBQ Sauce, Sweet Potatoes, and Green Beans (page 171), but it also works well with other meats, especially chicken and pork. At Barrington's, we vary it by adding veal stock and reducing the sauce to create a smoky demiglace.

**MAKES 3 CUPS**

Heat a large pot with the vegetable oil over high heat. When the oil begins to shimmer, add the onions, celery, and carrots; cook until the vegetables are caramelized, about 6 minutes, stirring frequently.

Add the chipotle pepper, wine, vinegar, ketchup, and molasses to the caramelized vegetables. Stir to incorporate and reduce by approximately two-thirds, about 8 minutes. Once reduced, add the chicken stock, decrease the heat to medium low, and simmer for 40 minutes.

Pour the warm mixture carefully into a blender and purée. Pass the sauce through a strainer, cover, and chill. The sauce will keep in the refrigerator for 1 week and in the freezer for 1 month.

3 tablespoons vegetable oil

1 small yellow onion, sliced

2 celery ribs, sliced

1 large carrot, roughly chopped

1 chipotle pepper (from 1 can of chipotle in adobo)

1 cup dry white wine, such as Chardonnay

⅔ cup apple cider vinegar

½ cup ketchup

¼ cup blackstrap molasses

6 cups good chicken stock

# Ricotta

Homemade ricotta is relatively easy and the flavor is miles above the store-bought version. This recipe produces a soft, milky cheese that is a blank canvas for herbs, citrus zest, and spices. We use it in Savory Cannoli with Tomato Salad (page 99), Ricotta-Stuffed Delicata Squash with Roasted Pepitas (page 129), Seafood Cannelloni with Lobster Sauce (page 214), and on pizzas. You can also simply pair it with salt and black pepper on toast or drizzle it with honey.

Cheesemaking yields whey, the liquid that remains after the curds separate. We use this whey regularly in soups and stocks for adding depth and flavor to dishes. Try it in White Bean Soup (page 91) or any place where you would normally use stock. As with all recipes that have only a few ingredients, aim for the best possible quality when purchasing.

**SPECIAL EQUIPMENT:** cheesecloth

**1 gallon whole milk**

**1 cup heavy cream**

**½ cup distilled white vinegar**

**MAKES 4 CUPS**

Combine the milk, cream, and vinegar in a large pot over medium-low heat, stirring occasionally with a wooden spoon. When the liquid reaches a simmer, turn off the heat, cover the pot, and rest it for 20 minutes. After this period, the curds (solids) should separate from the whey (liquid), and the ricotta is ready to be strained.

Line a fine-mesh strainer with cheesecloth. Using a large slotted spoon or a skimmer, transfer the curds to the strainer. Let the curds drain for 10 minutes. Use the ricotta immediately or refrigerate it in a container with a tight-fitting lid for up to 3 days. Reserve the whey for other uses; it can be stored, refrigerated, for 1 week.

# Small Plates

When I lived in Boston I had a group of friends who shared my interest in food. We always challenged ourselves to find out-of-the-way spots that offered dishes we could enjoy together. We would often meet up after our shifts, or on our days off, and head to Chinatown, where we dove into dim sum, as well as Japanese and Korean foods. Other nights we would head across the Charles River to our favorite Spanish tapas spot. We loved these restaurants because the plates were shareable and we could sample the entire menu in one sitting.

Fast-forward to 2006, and I was sitting with my wife at a small plates restaurant in Chicago, and she asked if I thought the concept could work in Charlotte. I told her I loved the idea but wasn't sure. All that changed when I laid eyes on the space that was to become Good Food on Montford (see sidebar on page 42). When it finally opened in 2008, some customers were confused by the concept. Accustomed to a typical three-course meal, the idea of sharing all the food felt foreign to them.

Fortunately, the food was really good. My brother Kerry, who opened Barrington's with me, and Larry Schreiber, whom I knew from Boston, excelled with this concept. We developed a menu of globally inspired small plates, and once the restaurant gained its footing, we began to have fun. Small plates have always been a place where we can play—with composition, texture, ingredients, and modern technique. At Good Food, we get to color outside the lines and dip into an array of global flavors.

In this chapter you'll find many of the small plates that have gained notoriety over the years—our greatest hits, if you will. Items like Green Curry Mussels (page 64), Steamed Buns with Spice-Rubbed Pork Belly, Hoisin, and Daikon Salad (page 55), and Korean Beef with Crispy Rice and Scallion Kimchi (page 67) are mainstays that exit the kitchen in droves. These constitute some of our more composed and technical plates, the ones with an identifiable flourish.

These recipes contain techniques to learn and techniques to master: all can be taken piecemeal. I hope you'll enjoy playing with these dishes and pioneering your own parade of plates.

# New South Beef Carpaccio with Fried Pickles and Pimento Cheese

Inside the kitchen at Good Food on Montford, we like to take traditional southern foods and make them new. This can mean pairing them with unlikely ingredients, as we do in this appetizer. Here, we take fried refrigerator pickles (page 28) and pimento cheese (two very southern items) and serve them atop beef carpaccio, delicately seared. The result is a dish that impresses yet still feels comfortably familiar.

**SPECIAL EQUIPMENT:** food processor

**SERVES 4 GENEROUSLY**

Trim all the fat from the meat. Slice the steak in half so that it makes two logs roughly 2 × 2 inches and season with salt and pepper. Add the oil to a skillet over high heat. When the oil starts to smoke, add the steaks and sear them for about 45 seconds on each side in order to evenly brown the meat. Chill the steak in the refrigerator for 1 hour.

### TO MAKE THE RANCH DRESSING

Bring a pot of salted water to a boil. Prepare an ice bath and set aside.

Add the garlic to the boiling water and cook until the cloves are soft, about 7–10 minutes. Add the scallions and parsley and blanch for 15 seconds until bright green. This will help maintain the vibrancy of the herbs. Drain the vegetables immediately, then plunge them into the ice bath. When they have cooled, drain them again. Transfer the contents to a blender and add the buttermilk. Blend on high speed until the buttermilk is incorporated.

Lightly whisk the mayonnaise in a bowl to loosen it up. Add the buttermilk mixture and whisk to combine. Season with salt to taste. Cover and chill until use.

1 pound New York strip steak, about 2 inches thick
Kosher salt and black pepper
2 tablespoons neutral oil, such as grapeseed or canola

**FOR THE RANCH DRESSING**
Kosher salt
5 garlic cloves, peeled
½ cup roughly chopped scallions (green tops only, from about 6 scallions)
½ cup fresh parsley leaves and tender stems
¼ cup whole-milk buttermilk
½ Duke's mayonnaise

## TO MAKE THE PIMENTO CHEESE

Pulse the cream cheese in a food processor until smooth. Add the mayonnaise and pulse to combine. Add ½ cup of the cheddar, the Worcestershire sauce, the hot sauce, and the spices. Pulse a few more times. Transfer the mixture to a bowl, and fold in the remaining cheddar and the pimentos. Add salt and pepper to taste. Cover and chill until use.

## TO FRY THE PICKLES

Fill a pot one-third full with oil and heat to 350°.

Place ¼ cup of the flour in a bowl and set aside. In a separate bowl, whisk together the remaining flour, cornstarch, baking powder, and salt. Add the beer and whisk again until no lumps remain. (If the batter is too thick, add a little more beer.) Pat the pickles dry, then toss them in the reserved flour. Shake off the excess flour, transfer the pickles to the beer batter, and coat the slices. Remove the pickles 1 slice at a time and allow the excess batter to drip off, then carefully drop each slice into the hot oil. Fry the slices until golden brown, flipping them after 1 minute, and cooking for about 3 minutes total. Transfer them to a plate lined with paper towels and set aside.

## TO ASSEMBLE THE CARPACCIO

Use a sharp knife or meat slicer to cut the chilled beef into paper-thin slices. Arrange the meat in an overlapping pattern on a platter, then drizzle the slices with olive oil and sprinkle them with salt and pepper. Top the carpaccio with about a dozen small spoonfuls of the pimento cheese. Drizzle the platter with ranch dressing, then top each pimento cheese mound with a fried pickle. Serve immediately.

**FOR THE PIMENTO CHEESE**
½ cup (4 ounces) cream cheese, softened
¼ cup Duke's mayonnaise
1 cup grated cheddar, divided
1 dash Worcestershire sauce
2–3 dashes Frank's RedHot sauce
1 teaspoon garlic powder
1 teaspoon onion powder
1 teaspoon paprika
½ teaspoon cayenne pepper
1 (4-ounce) jar diced pimentos
Kosher salt and black pepper

**FOR THE PICKLES**
Neutral oil, such as grapeseed or canola
¾ cup all-purpose flour, divided
¼ cup cornstarch
1½ teaspoons baking powder
¼ teaspoon kosher salt
6 ounces beer (½ bottle)
12 Refrigerator Pickle slices (page 28) or store-bought pickle slices

# Tuna Tartare with Cornmeal-Fried Oysters and Lemon-Chive Mayo

½ pound fresh tuna

1 tablespoon celery, cut into
⅛-inch dice

1 tablespoon red onion,
cut into ⅛-inch dice

1 tablespoon red bell pepper,
cut into ⅛-inch dice

½ teaspoon kosher salt

¼ teaspoon black pepper

2 teaspoons fresh lemon juice

1 teaspoon minced fresh
parsley

1 teaspoon finely chopped
fresh chives

Dash Tabasco sauce

1 large egg yolk

1 teaspoon extra-virgin
olive oil

2 teaspoons Dijon mustard

1 slice thick-cut bacon

FOR THE MAYONNAISE

Zest of 1 lemon

2 teaspoons fresh lemon juice

1 teaspoon finely chopped
fresh chives

½ cup Duke's mayonnaise

Pinch kosher salt

Tartare is a dish typically made with finely chopped raw beef or fish and mixed with a binding agent such as mustard or mayonnaise. Rich egg yolks are a standard accompaniment, as are herbs and finely diced vegetables. In this dish we explore temperatures and textures. The soft and cooling tartare is paired with fried oysters for a warm, briny crunch.

Fresh tuna is essential for good tartare, so find a trusted seafood source to purchase a high-quality cut. To save time, look for shucked oysters at your local grocer. They come ready for use in 8–12-ounce plastic containers.

SPECIAL EQUIPMENT: thermometer, skimmer (optional)

SERVES 4

Dice the tuna into ¼-inch pieces, then mince it by passing the knife over the tuna several times in a rocking motion. Transfer the minced tuna to a bowl and add the remaining ingredients except the bacon; mix until they are evenly incorporated. Cover the tartare and refrigerate until use.

Cook the bacon in a frying pan until crispy, drain the fat, and then set the bacon aside.

TO MAKE THE MAYONNAISE
In a small bowl, whisk together the lemon zest and juice, chives, mayonnaise, and salt. Refrigerate until use.

## TO COOK THE OYSTERS

Fill a large pot halfway with oil, leaving 4–6 inches of space between the oil and the top of the pot. Heat the oil to 350°. Be safe! Oysters contain water, which can cause the oil to spit. While the oil heats, mix the flour, cornmeal, and Old Bay Seasoning together. Toss the oysters in the flour mixture, coating well. Shake off any excess flour. When the oil reaches temperature, gently submerge each oyster into the hot oil. Fry the oysters for 1–2 minutes, or until they are golden brown and crispy. Remove the oysters from the oil, drain them on a plate lined with paper towels, and sprinkle them with salt.

## TO ASSEMBLE

For each serving, brush the lemon-chive mayonnaise on a plate in the shape of a comma. Decoratively sprinkle the plate with the chives, black pepper, and Old Bay Seasoning. Add a scoop of tartare and top with 3 fried oysters and the reserved bacon. Serve immediately.

**FOR THE OYSTERS**

**Neutral oil for frying, such as grapeseed or canola**
**1 cup all-purpose flour**
**½ cup fine-grind cornmeal**
**1 tablespoon Old Bay Seasoning**
**12 raw oysters**
**Kosher salt**

# The Good Food on Montford Story

The words still ring in my ears. The year was 2007 and I was conversing with a barista friend in my regular coffee shop. I told her, "I'm thinking about opening a restaurant on Montford Drive." She looked at me, incredulous, and replied, "You can't open a restaurant on Montford, it's not a destination street. There is no good food on Montford. There will never be good food on Montford."

Jokingly I said, "Just to prove you wrong, I'm going to name it Good Food on Montford when it opens."

She was right about the location. At the time, Montford Drive was a rather seedy place lined with a beat-up bowling alley and beer-soaked taverns—the Press Box, Moosehead Grill, Angry Ales—that hosted heavy drinkers and industry folks.

Its merit (and I use the term loosely) was that it was sandwiched between a few really great Charlotte neighborhoods: Dilworth, Myers Park, and South Park. So, when a Vietnamese restaurant on Montford shuttered its doors, one of my servers who saw the "For Lease" sign apprised me of its availability.

A year before this happened, my wife, Katrina, and I were in Chicago at a restaurant whose concept revolved around beautiful, composed small plates. Katrina was enamored and asked if I thought a concept like that could work in Charlotte. I told her she was out of her mind.

But when I saw the vacant space on Montford, I knew it had to be small plates. The unique architecture of the building was vastly different than its street-side neighbors, and it begged for something novel.

Of course, there were a few hiccups along the way. The landlord was cautious to rent to me for fear of creating unsustainable competition with another restaurant moving into the neighborhood. I wrote a long letter to counter his argument. I talked about the potential I saw in this shadowy strip of road. *It could become something*, I wrote. Think about Franklin Street in Chapel Hill. In Montford Drive, I saw a place that could become a vibrant destination with the addition of a few great food and beverage tenants. The landlord finally agreed to let me have the space. When I told Katrina about my idea, she told me I was out of my mind.

By this time, the climate in Charlotte warmed to accommodate more sophisticated chef-driven establishments in the city. Restaurants like Ratcliffe on the Green, Noble's, Rooster's, Las Ramblas, Sonoma, and Blue were serving innovative foods, and market ingredients started to appear on menus more regularly. Still, aside from Las Ramblas and its Spanish-style tapas concept, no one had attempted composed small plates in the Queen City.

In the beginning, my brother Kerry helmed the kitchen along with Larry Schreiber, a cook I had lured from Boston who is now the executive chef today. We decided that Good Food would impart a global touch to all the plates, plus modernity and a good helping of playfulness.

When the restaurant opened, people absolutely did not get it. Diners wanted their meal served in courses, they did not want to share plates with their companions, and they certainly didn't appreciate the barrage of small plates that seemed, in their eyes, to arrive haphazardly to the table. The whole concept felt very foreign to Charlotte's dining set, and they let us know it.

It took almost three years for Good Food to find its footing. We fought daily against the rigid expectations of diners before finding our groove. We had to trust ourselves, and we had to make undeniably good food. By 2010, we had accomplished our goals in a big way. Good Food was nationally recognized by the James Beard Foundation and garnered a semifinalist nomination for Best New Restaurant.

Today, a line out the door is not unusual. Of course, now there's plenty to do along the vibrant strip of Montford Drive. That beat-up bowling alley got a makeover, and the dreary strip diversified to include more restaurants and pedestrian-friendly traffic. Across the main thoroughfare that connects Montford Drive to Park Road lies the Park Road Shopping Center, another booming destination with retail shops, restaurant peers, and activities. This area is one of the definitive pockets of Charlotte where one can easily gauge the pulse of the city. What a difference a decade makes.

## Larry Schreiber
### EXECUTIVE CHEF, GOOD FOOD ON MONTFORD

Besides my brother Kerry, only one other person has been with me so long it feels as if we're related. I've known Larry Schreiber since my days in Boston. A fellow CIA alumnus, I enlisted him to the South when I opened Barrington's. It was during a time when I needed good professional help, and Larry was a sure bet. From there, he has been an essential part of our restaurant family. Larry has worked inside every restaurant and led the team in crucial times. At Barrington's, he was the extra set of hands we needed when the restaurant took off. He was a member of the inaugural team at Good Food on Montford, working directly with Kerry to develop the menu and forge a new path in the city. When I opened Stagioni, Larry stepped in as executive chef and guided the opening team. Today, he's back at Good Food on Montford, the place that allows him the most creative freedom, as executive chef. Larry did try to leave once, and it never stuck. In this journey, Larry has become a valued friend, and my restaurants are better for having him.

# Classic Mussels with Crushed Tomatoes, White Wine, and Garlic

2 pounds mussels

¼ cup extra-virgin olive oil

4 garlic cloves, shaved

1 teaspoon chopped fresh
   thyme

Pinch crushed chili flakes

½ cup white wine

¼ cup clam juice

Pinch kosher salt

4 whole Roma tomatoes,
   peeled, with juice

Crusty bread, for serving

Mussels are abundant on the jetties that line the New England shore. As kids, we'd go out with our buckets and rakes to pick clams and mussels. When we collected enough for a meal, we would head back to the Lawton House and steam the mussels and clams as a start to a summer meal. Mussels were a distinct part of my childhood, which is probably why they appear twice in this book (see page 64 for Green Curry Mussels). At Barrington's, we serve a classic Italian version—plump mussels steamed in tomatoes, white wine, and garlic. This recipe takes almost no time to make and works as a quick lunch, a light dinner, or an appetizer for two.

Mussels may require a process called debearding that removes a wiry membrane on the shell's exterior. You can purchase mussels already debearded, but in case you need to take this step, there are instructions below.

SERVES 2 GENEROUSLY

Rinse the mussels under cold running water to remove any sediment. If necessary, use your fingers to pull off the beard, the wiry excess protruding near the hinge of the shell. Scrub the mussels once more under cold running water and place them in a colander to drain until use.

Heat a sauté pan with olive oil over high heat and add the shaved garlic. Toast the garlic until it is golden brown, then add the thyme and chili flakes, shaking the pan to incorporate the flavors. Add the mussels, wine, clam juice, and salt. Crush the tomatoes and add them to the pan with their juices. Simmer, covered, for 4 minutes, or until the mussels open. Transfer the mussels to a wide, shallow bowl, discarding any that have not opened. Serve immediately with crusty bread.

# Foie Gras with Fig Jam and Toaster Pastry

**FOR THE TOASTER PASTRY**

2 cups all-purpose flour

1 cup (2 sticks) cold unsalted
   butter, diced

1 tablespoon sugar

1 teaspoon kosher salt

2 large eggs, divided

2 tablespoons whole milk

1 (8-ounce) jar fig jam

3 tablespoons coarse sugar

Fig season is an exciting time at Barrington's. When Fergus the Fig Tree (the name given to the fig tree that lives in my backyard) bears fruit in late summer, we collect the ripened figs to use at the restaurant. Our customers have caught on to this tradition and share their backyard harvests with us.

This dish is a whimsical play on the old-school toaster pastry, made decadent by the addition of foie gras, which marries perfectly with sweet fig jam. We make our jam in-house, but I recommend purchasing a jar from a gourmet grocery to save time.

**SPECIAL EQUIPMENT**: ruler, pastry brush

**SERVES 4**

**TO MAKE THE TOASTER PASTRY**

Process the flour, cold butter, sugar, and salt in a food processor until it resembles coarse cornmeal. Add 1 of the eggs and pulse until it is incorporated. Slowly add the milk and pulse again until the mixture comes together. Transfer the mixture to a clean work surface and bring the dough together into a cohesive disc. It will be soft and slightly tacky. Wrap the dough in plastic and refrigerate for at least 1 hour.

Make an egg wash by beating the remaining egg; set aside.

On a floured work surface, roll the chilled dough into a rough rectangle about ¼ inch thick, and then it cut into 8 (2 × 4-inch) rectangles. Use the tines of a fork to poke holes (also called docking the dough) in 4 of the rectangles.

Line a baking sheet with parchment paper and preheat the oven to 350°.

Brush the edges of an undocked rectangle with egg wash, then place a scoop of fig jam in the center, top the pastry with a docked rectangle, and seal it. Crimp the edges with a fork and set the pastry on the baking sheet. Repeat this process for the rest of the toaster pastries, then brush the tops with egg wash and sprinkle them with coarse sugar. Bake the pastries for 20 minutes, or until they are golden brown. Keep the oven set to 350°.

## TO MAKE THE FOIE GRAS

Score the foie gras with a crosshatch pattern and season it generously with salt and pepper. Heat a cast-iron pan over high heat until scorching hot, then add the foie gras and sear for 2 minutes, or until it is deep brown. Flip the fois gras and sear it for another minute. If the foie gras is still firm in the middle, place it in the preheated oven and cook it until it is soft and warm in the middle, about 2 minutes, depending on the thickness.

## TO ASSEMBLE

Place 1 tablespoon of fig jam on the upper third of each plate. Cut the toaster pastry diagonally into 2 triangles and stack them on the fig jam. Gently lean the foie gras on the triangles and finish the dish with a drizzle of aged balsamic vinegar.

**FOR THE FOIE GRAS**

**8 ounces foie gras, cut into 4 (2-ounce) portions**
**Kosher salt and black pepper**
**1 teaspoon vegetable oil**
**Aged balsamic vinegar (5–10 years), optional**

# Falafel with Hummus and Tzatziki

This famed Israeli street food, often stuffed into soft pita, has a permanent home on our global small plates menu at Good Food on Montford. We have maintained the traditional ingredients—chickpeas, garlic, and cumin—but have created a patty with a softer, moister core. The falafel is served with two likely companions: creamy, cool tzatziki and hummus.

Removing excess moisture is critical to achieving the texture you'll want for the falafel and the tzatziki. You can use a folded cheesecloth for this job, but we recommend a clean tea towel, which allows you to remove more moisture with greater ease.

**SPECIAL EQUIPMENT:** food processor, clean tea towel or cheesecloth, 1½-inch circle cutter

**SERVES 8**

TO MAKE THE FALAFEL

Place the rinsed chickpeas on a rimmed baking sheet lined with paper towels to remove excess moisture. Process the cilantro, onions, and garlic in a food processor until the mixture is pulpy in texture. Scrape the mixture into a tea towel or cheesecloth draped over a bowl. Squeeze out excess moisture, discard the liquid, and set aside.

Add the chickpeas to the food processor and pulse several times, until they resemble chopped peanuts. Transfer them to a large mixing bowl. Add the cilantro mixture and lightly toss with your hands to combine.

In a separate bowl, combine the dry ingredients, then add them to the chickpea mixture. Lightly toss the ingredients using your hands until everything is evenly mixed, then press the mixture down several times to compress it into a dough.

Turn the dough on a clean work surface and press it into a rectangle about 1 inch thick. Use a circle cutter to cut the falafel patties. Reshape the leftover dough and continue cutting until all of it is used, placing the patties on a large sheet pan or plate. Set aside.

**FOR THE FALAFEL**

2 (15½-ounce) cans chickpeas

½ cup packed cilantro, tender stems and leaves

½ medium yellow onion, cut into ¼-inch dice

2 garlic cloves, peeled

1 teaspoon baking powder

¼ cup all-purpose flour

2 teaspoons kosher salt

1 teaspoon ground cumin

**FOR THE TZATZIKI**

1 European cucumber, peeled,
    seeded, and sliced
2 teaspoons kosher salt
1 cup whole-milk yogurt
¼ teaspoon ground cumin
¼ teaspoon fresh lemon juice

**FOR THE HUMMUS**

1 (15 ½-ounce) can chickpeas,
    drained and rinsed
1 tablespoon fresh lemon juice
1 teaspoon kosher salt
1 tablespoon Garlic Confit
    (page 15) or finely minced
    garlic
1 teaspoon sriracha
1 teaspoon ground cumin
½ cup extra-virgin olive oil

## TO MAKE THE TZATZIKI

Toss the cucumbers in a bowl with the salt. Rest for 30 minutes. Transfer the cucumbers and their liquid to a blender and blend on medium-low speed until they are pulpy (but not puréed). Scrape the contents into a tea towel or cheesecloth and squeeze out excess liquid.

In a mixing bowl, whisk together the strained cucumbers with the yogurt, cumin, and lemon juice. Add salt to taste. Refrigerate until use.

## TO MAKE THE HUMMUS

Add all of the ingredients except the olive oil to a blender and mix them on high speed. With the motor running, add the olive oil and blend until smooth and creamy. (If the hummus is too thick, add a little water to loosen the mixture.) Taste and adjust the seasoning.

## TO FRY THE FALAFEL

Fill a large pot halfway with oil and heat to 350°. Working in batches, carefully lower the falafel into the oil and fry the patties for 4 minutes, or until they are golden brown. Transfer the patties to a plate lined with paper towels, and lightly season them with salt. Allow the oil to come back to temperature before continuing to fry.

## TO ASSEMBLE

Spread a generous spoonful of hummus on a plate. Top with falafel (3 per guest for individual portions) and spoon tzatziki over the top. Garnish with cilantro leaves and serve immediately.

# Charred Octopus with Squash Salad and Roasted Tomato Vinaigrette

Octopus can fall into the category of "intimidating things to cook," but when done right, it has the power to impress. A tender braise followed by a quick sear creates memorable texture and flavor in this recipe. The octopus is then paired with a roasted tomato vinaigrette and a shaved summer squash salad for a light Mediterranean meal or an intriguing starter.

The key to a nicely charred piece of octopus is to remove as much moisture as possible before cooking it. We do this by pressing it for 24 hours, so plan accordingly. Make the tomato vinaigrette early the next day and then finish the recipe just before serving.

**SPECIAL EQUIPMENT:** cheesecloth, potato ricer, mandoline

---

**SERVES 6–8**

·····························································································

## TO PREPARE THE OCTOPUS

Preheat the oven to 300°. On a clean work surface, place the octopus in front of you and slice the head off right below the eyes. Remove the beak, which can be found at the center point of all the tentacles. Turn the lower part of the octopus inside out and cut into the doughnut-like hole in the center to create a half-circle, then push the beak out. Slice off all the tentacles and lay them in a large roasting pan, fully stretched out. Add the herbs to the pan.

In a separate pan, heat the olive oil over medium heat. Add the onions, celery, and carrots, and season with salt and pepper. Cook for about 5 minutes; you are not looking for color on the vegetables, just trying to wake them up. Pour the vegetables over the octopus. Add the wine to barely cover. Wrap the pan tightly with foil and place it in the oven for 70 minutes, or until tender. To test for doneness, use a cake tester (or a toothpick) to pierce the octopus. If is the tester meets with no resistance, the octopus is done. If it resists, cook it longer. Let it cool to room temperature.

Place the cooled octopus between 2 sheets of cheesecloth and on a baking sheet. Place another baking sheet on top and weigh the pan down with something heavy, such as a large can of food or a bag of flour. Refrigerate for 24 hours.

**FOR THE OCTOPUS**

1 (4–6 pound) octopus

1 sprig each fresh thyme, rosemary, and oregano

1 fresh bay leaf

2 tablespoons extra-virgin olive oil

1 medium yellow onion, sliced thin

5 celery ribs, sliced into ¼-inch pieces

3 medium carrots, sliced into ¼-inch pieces

Kosher salt and black pepper

4 cups white wine

## TO MAKE THE VINAIGRETTE

Preheat the oven to 500°. Combine the tomatoes, garlic, bell peppers, onions, sugar, salt, and olive oil in a roasting pan. Roast for 90 minutes, stirring every 20 minutes to help the liquid evaporate. Once the liquid has reduced and the tomatoes are deep red, add the vinegar, stir, and cook 5–7 minutes more. Immediately pass the vegetables through the ricer. Set aside.

## TO MAKE THE SALAD

Thinly shave the zucchini, squash, and carrots on a mandoline, then julienne them (cut into 2 × ⅛-inch pieces) with a sharp knife. Julienne the red bell peppers. Set aside.

Prepare the pesto. Season with salt and pepper. Toss the julienned vegetables with 2 tablespoons of the pesto. Squeeze ½ a lemon over the top. Set aside until ready to use. Reserve extra pesto for plating.

## TO SEAR THE OCTOPUS

Place a large cast-iron skillet in the oven and preheat to 500°. Separate the thicker sections of the octopus tentacles and cut them in half lengthwise. Season all the portions with salt and drizzle them generously with olive oil, tossing to coat. Carefully remove the preheated skillet from the oven and sear the octopus over high heat for 4 minutes. Flip the tentacles and sear them for 1 minute more.

## TO ASSEMBLE

Spread more pesto on a large serving platter. Top with the squash salad and then arrange the octopus on top. Drizzle with additional olive oil and serve immediately.

### FOR THE VINAIGRETTE

8 medium Roma tomatoes, cut into ½-inch dice

3 garlic cloves, peeled and sliced

1 large red bell pepper, cut into ¼-inch dice

½ large yellow onion, cut into ¼-inch dice

2 tablespoons sugar

1 tablespoon kosher salt

¼ cup extra-virgin olive oil

1 tablespoon red wine vinegar

### FOR THE SALAD

1 medium zucchini

1 medium yellow squash

1 medium carrot

2 small red bell peppers

1 recipe Basil Pesto (page 17)

½ lemon

# Steamed Buns with Spice-Rubbed Pork Belly, Hoisin, and Daikon Salad

The steamed buns at Good Food on Montford are one of our most popular items. To make them, we braise pork belly in a blend of Asian aromatics until the meat is tender and rich. We serve the pork inside pillow-soft steamed buns, known as *bao*, and crown them with a sweet-sour daikon salad and hoisin sauce. At the restaurant, we make our bao from scratch every day, but to save time after a long braise, we suggest that you pick up a package of premade buns from an Asian market.

Serve these as a heavy hors d'oeuvre at your next gathering. Since braising is a worthy but time-consuming technique, we recommend doing it a day ahead. And don't throw away that rich braising liquid. Save it to braise something else, add to a bowl of ramen, or use as a stir-fry liquid.

**SPECIAL EQUIPMENT:** mandoline with julienne blade

**SERVES 8–12**

### TO COOK THE PORK BELLY

Combine the sugar, salt, and five-spice powder and mix them with your hands. Rub the mixture over the pork belly, coating all sides.

In a 10-inch skillet over medium heat, add the oil and pork belly. Cook for 5 minutes, or until the meat is golden brown. Flip the pork belly and cook it for 3 minutes more. Turn off the heat.

Combine the scallion whites, garlic, ginger, star anise, soy sauce, brown sugar, and 4 cups water in a deep braising pan. (This is the braising liquid.) Place the pan in the oven and set the temperature to 350°. You want the liquid to heat up as the oven heats. Once the oven comes to temperature, carefully add the pork belly to the braising liquid and cover the pan tightly with foil. Return the pan to the oven for 2 hours and 45 minutes.

If braising a day ahead, cover and refrigerate the cooked pork belly in its liquid until use. If braising on the same day you are serving, make the daikon salad and the sauce in the second half of the cook time.

**FOR THE PORK BELLY**

- 2 cups light brown sugar
- 1 tablespoon kosher salt
- 2 teaspoons five-spice powder
- 3 pounds pork belly
- 3 tablespoons neutral oil, such as grapeseed or canola
- 2 bunches scallions, white and green parts separated
- ½ cup garlic cloves (about 20–25), peeled
- ½ cup ginger, peeled and sliced into ¼-inch rounds
- 6 whole star anise
- 4 cups soy sauce
- 1 cup light brown sugar
- 1 package (12 count) Chinese sandwich-style steamed buns, or bao (can be found at Asian groceries)

**FOR THE SALAD**

5 medium carrots, peeled

1 medium daikon radish,
    peeled

1 tablespoon kosher salt

1 tablespoon sugar

¼ cup plus 1 tablespoon
    rice vinegar

**FOR THE HOISIN SAUCE**

1 cup hoisin sauce

2 teaspoons sriracha

1 tablespoon rice vinegar

TO MAKE THE SALAD

Cut the carrots into 2-inch pieces, then use a mandoline with a julienne blade attachment and slice them lengthwise. Work carefully, and slice only about two-thirds of the way down to avoid injury. Slice the ends off the daikon and julienne it lengthwise with the mandoline.

Combine the julienned vegetables in colander and rinse them under cold water. Drain the vegetables well, transfer them to a bowl, and toss them with the salt and sugar. Cover the vegetables tightly and let them sit for 1 hour. Drain the excess liquid, then add the vinegar and toss well. Chill until ready to serve.

TO MAKE THE HOISIN SAUCE

Whisk together all the ingredients. Set aside.

TO ASSEMBLE

Warm the buns according to the package instructions. Meanwhile, get a sauté pan hot over high heat. Slice the pork belly into 3-ounce portions and sear each portion for 1–2 minutes per side, or until the meat is lightly caramelized and warmed through. Place a portion of pork belly in the center of each bun. Top with the daikon salad and finish with a drizzle of hoisin sauce. Serve immediately.

# Lobster Rolls on Brioche with Fingerling Potato Chips

I remember visiting the mansions of Newport, Rhode Island, as a child. They were the summer "cottages" for wealthy New Yorkers in the Gilded Age. One of the mansions retained letters from the service staff posted in the basement. In one, a maid complains about having to walk down to the beach after a big storm to grab the lobsters that had washed ashore. In those days, lobsters were in abundance and, for a time, deemed servant food.

Today, lobster isn't quite as plentiful and its status has risen considerably. Almost every shoreline restaurant boasts that it has the best lobster roll in the Ocean State. Not to be outdone, even from afar, here's my entry. Mine has a tarragon mayonnaise and is served with fingerling potato chips.

*Note*: You will have extra brioche. Use it for making sandwiches, croutons, or French toast.

**SPECIAL EQUIPMENT:** lobster cracker, kitchen shears, mandoline, skimmer

---

**SERVES 4**

.........................................................................................................

## TO PREPARE THE LOBSTER FILLING

Fill a large stockpot halfway with water, add 2 tablespoons of the salt, and bring to a boil. Prepare an ice bath and set aside.

Once the water comes to a rolling boil, add the lobsters and boil them for 8 minutes. Remove the lobsters and plunge them immediately in the ice bath. Let them cool for 5–10 minutes.

Meanwhile, combine the peppers, onions, and celery in a medium bowl. Mince the tarragon, parsley, and chives together in a separate bowl, then add them to the bowl with the vegetables. Add the lemon juice, mayonnaise, Tabasco, and remaining salt, and mix. Taste and adjust seasoning.

1 recipe Brioche rolls (page 246) or store-bought brioche rolls

**FOR THE LOBSTER FILLING**
2 tablespoons plus ½ teaspoon salt, divided
2 (1-pound) lobsters
1 tablespoon red bell pepper, cut into ⅛-inch dice
1 tablespoon red onion, cut into ⅛-inch dice
1 tablespoon celery, cut into ⅛-inch dice
½ teaspoon fresh tarragon
1 teaspoon chopped fresh parsley
½ teaspoon fresh chives
1 teaspoon fresh lemon juice
½ cup Duke's mayonnaise
Dash Tabasco sauce
4 tablespoons (½ stick) unsalted butter

Remove a lobster from the ice bath. Place the tail on a clean dish towel, then hold one side of the tail in each hand and push upward to crack it open. Pull out the tail meat and coarsely chop it. Crack the claws near the joint and remove the meat. Remove any remaining lobster meat with kitchen shears. Repeat with the remaining lobster. Add the lobster meat to the bowl with the dressing and gently incorporate it. Chill until ready to use.

### TO MAKE THE POTATO CHIPS

Heat a large pot filled halfway with oil to 300°. Meanwhile, use a mandoline to shave the fingerlings on the bias to $\frac{1}{16}$ inch. Soak the slices in water for 5 minutes to remove excess starch, then place them in a colander and rinse them until the water runs clear. Shake the colander vigorously to remove excess water; this helps prevent oil splashes when frying.

When the oil is hot, fry the potatoes, moving them around with a skimmer. The oil will bubble vigorously, but the bubbling will subside when the potatoes are nearly finished. Once the chips are golden brown, transfer them to a plate lined with paper towels and season them with salt.

### TO ASSEMBLE

Heat a sauté pan over medium heat and melt 2 tablespoons of butter. Slice 2 brioche rolls and toast them in a pan until they are golden brown, about 2 minutes. Fill the rolls generously with the lobster mixture. Repeat the process with the remaining rolls. Serve the rolls immediately with a side of potato chips.

**FOR THE POTATO CHIPS**
**Neutral oil for frying, such as**
**grapeseed or canola**
**8 ounces fingerling potatoes**
**Kosher salt**

# Pastrami-Cured Salmon with Rye Crackers, Sauerkraut, and Russian Dressing

## FOR THE CURED SALMON

1 (3-pound) salmon fillet

4 cups sugar

4 cups kosher salt

½ bunch cilantro, about
    ½ cup packed

½ bunch parsley, about
    ½ cup packed

Zest of 1 lemon

1 teaspoon crushed chili
    flakes

1 ounce bourbon

## FOR THE PASTRAMI GLAZE

1 teaspoon cumin seeds

1 teaspoon fennel seeds

1 teaspoon caraway seeds

1 teaspoon yellow mustard
    seeds

1 teaspoon celery seeds

1 cup blackstrap molasses

¼ teaspoon cayenne pepper

I love Reuben sandwiches. I'm always experimenting with different ways to make them. This is one attempt that I thought worked well. I serve it as an appetizer or a small bite.

The process for this recipe takes four days. The salmon is cured twice over three days and then rests for a day with a pastrami-style glaze. At Barrington's, we achieve the Reuben effect by pairing it with Rye Crackers (page 253), Seven-Day Sauerkraut (page 18), and Russian dressing. This recipe generously serves a crowd.

---

**MAKES 3 POUNDS CURED SALMON**

................................................................

### TO CURE THE SALMON

Place the salmon fillet on a baking sheet. Combine the sugar and salt in a bowl. Reserve half of the mixture and rub the other half on the salmon fillet, covering it completely. Refrigerate the salmon, uncovered, for 6 hours, then rinse the cure off it and pat the fillet dry.

In the bowl of a food processor, pulse the reserved cure with the cilantro, parsley, lemon zest, chili flakes, and bourbon. Rub the cure all over the salmon. Return the salmon to the baking sheet and stack another baking sheet on top. Weigh it down with a heavy plate or something similar. Return the salmon to the refrigerator for 2 days. When the second cure is complete, rinse the salmon well and pat it dry. Refrigerate until ready to use.

### TO MAKE THE PASTRAMI GLAZE

Toast the spices over medium heat until they release their oils. The mixture will become aromatic. Add the molasses and simmer for 3 minutes. Add the cayenne, stir to incorporate, and remove from the heat. Let the glaze cool to room temperature and then brush it on salmon fillet, coating it generously so that it looks like black lacquer. Cover and refrigerate for another 24 hours.

## TO MAKE THE DRESSING
Fold together all the ingredients.

## TO ASSEMBLE
Remove the finished salmon from the refrigerator and rinse off any excess pastrami glaze under a faucet running slowly with cool water; pat dry. Slice the salmon as thinly as possible and serve the slices on a platter with the crackers, sauerkraut, and Russian dressing. Pat yourself on the back for a patient job well done.

**FOR THE DRESSING**

**2 cups Duke's mayonnaise**

**½ cup chili sauce**

**¼ cup minced Ramp Pickles (optional, see page 24)**

**¼ cup minced cornichons**

**2 tablespoons fresh lemon juice**

**2 tablespoons minced shallots**

**1 tablespoon Worcestershire sauce**

**1 tablespoon sriracha**

**1 teaspoon finely minced fresh tarragon**

# Pork Meatballs with Marinara

At Stagioni, we take our meatballs seriously, which is why we go the extra step to grind our pork. Meatballs should have a crisp crust and a tender, juicy interior. Fresh herbs, garlic, Parmesan, and lemon zest make each bite balanced and full-flavored. We serve meatballs as a small plate with Ciabatta (page 254). You can also go classic with pasta and red sauce.

**SPECIAL EQUIPMENT:** stand mixer fitted with meat grinder attachment and large die

**SERVES 10**

Chill all the grinder components in the freezer as you prepare the ingredients. Trim the pork of sinew, excess fat, and silver skin, then cut the meat into ¼-inch cubes. Set aside.

Cut the bread into small cubes and soak the cubes in the milk, pressing down to moisten them completely. In a separate bowl, combine the pork with the onions, garlic, and parsley. Add the lemon zest and toss again. In another bowl, mix together the Parmesan, salt, and pepper; set aside.

Attached the chilled parts to the meat grinder. Grind the pork mixture and bread directly into the bowl of a stand mixer. Switch to the paddle attachment, then add the Parmesan mixture to the ground pork mixture. Paddle together on medium speed for 3 minutes. This helps emulsify the meat, which will yield a juicy meatball.

Preheat the oven to 450° and line a baking sheet with parchment paper.

Portion the pork into 2-ounce meatballs and set them on the baking sheet. Bake the meatballs in the oven until they have browned, about 20 minutes. Remove them from the oven and transfer them to a deep roasting pan. Reduce the oven temperature to 400°. Pour the marinara and chicken stock into the roasting pan. Cover the pan with foil, return it to the oven, and braise the meatballs for 30 minutes.

Serve the meatballs (about 3 per person) with sliced ciabatta. Extras will keep in the refrigerator for 1 week or in the freezer for 3 weeks.

3 pounds boneless pork shoulder

4 slices day-old bread (sourdough or something similar)

¾ cup whole milk

1 medium yellow onion, cut into ¼-inch dice

3 garlic cloves, peeled

½ cup fresh parsley, packed

Zest of 1 lemon

¼ cup freshly grated Parmesan

2 tablespoons kosher salt

2 ½ teaspoons black pepper

1 quart store-bought marinara sauce

1 pint chicken or vegetable stock

1 recipe Ciabatta or store-bought ciabatta

# Green Curry Mussels

**FOR THE GREEN CURRY**

2 jalapeños, seeded and
    chopped

½ medium shallot, minced

1 tablespoon minced ginger

5 garlic cloves, minced

2 tablespoons fish sauce

2 tablespoons green curry
    paste

2 tablespoons vegetable oil

1 bunch cilantro, washed
    and chopped (include
    the stems)

**FOR THE COCONUT CREAM**

1 medium shallot, minced

1 tablespoon minced ginger

1 tablespoon minced garlic

⅓ cup white wine

½ cup clam juice

¼ cup light brown sugar

1 tablespoon fish sauce

2 cups heavy cream

2 cups coconut milk

**FOR THE MUSSELS**

1 tablespoon vegetable oil

3 pounds mussels, cleaned
    and debearded

We use one of my favorite seafoods in this popular curry dish served at Good Food on Montford. Here, the mussels are swimming in a curry so delicious that it's tempting to drink the leftovers straight from the bowl. We suggest serving it to your guests with ample grilled bread slices or naan for soaking up the broth.

The curry can be prepared ahead and refrigerated until you're ready to cook the mussels.

**SERVES 4**

**TO MAKE THE GREEN CURRY**
Place all the ingredients in a blender and purée until smooth.

**TO MAKE THE COCONUT CREAM**
Sweat the shallots, ginger, and garlic in the wine for 2 minutes. Stir in the clam juice, sugar, and fish sauce and simmer another 2 minutes. Add the cream and coconut milk. Bring the liquid to a boil, then remove the pan from the heat and let it cool.

**TO COOK THE MUSSELS**
Heat a large, heavy-bottomed pot over high heat. Add the green curry mixture, followed by the oil. If the pan is hot and the oil is added first, it can flare up, so *always* add the curry first, then the oil. Sauté the curry for a few seconds, then add the mussels and toss them before adding the cream mixture. Cover the pot and cook until the mussels open, about 2 minutes. Discard any unopened mussels. Serve immediately with plenty of grilled bread or naan.

# Korean Beef with Crispy Rice and Scallion Kimchi

My brother Kerry was the executive chef when we opened Good Food on Montford. He had an endless fascination with Asian food and culture: I remember, growing up, that Kerry always wanted Peking Duck for his birthday dinner. So I was not surprised when he started experimenting with Asian food at the restaurant. The Korean beef at Good Food on Montford is Kerry's version of *bulgogi*, a classic dish of grilled marinated beef. We have added kimchi scallions and crispy rice to round out the dish.

*Note*: The beef in this recipe should be marinated overnight, and the scallions need to rest as well. You can make the *gochujang* sauce ahead of time to lighten your load on the second day. *Gochugaru* is tough to find at a conventional grocery store; try an international market. It is usually sold as flakes or as a powder. Alternatively, you can mix smoked paprika with coarsely ground chili powder to mimic the flavor, although Korean chili flakes are smokier than regular chili flakes.

**SPECIAL EQUIPMENT:** 2½-inch square cutter (or a round cutter of similar size)

**SERVES 6**

### TO MAKE THE BULGOGI

Place all the ingredients for the marinade (except the sesame seeds) in a blender and mix on high speed until smooth. Pour the contents into a medium-size bowl. In a dry pan, toast the sesame seeds over medium-high heat, 3–5 minutes. Immediately (and carefully) whisk the hot seeds into the marinade mixture. Let cool.

Cut the steak into 6 equal portions, about 4 ounces each. Place the steaks on a piece of plastic wrap. Cover them with another piece of plastic wrap and pound them to ½-inch thick.

Transfer the beef to a plastic storage bag and cover it with all but 1 cup of the marinade. Refrigerate overnight. Store the remainder of the marinade in a separate container.

**FOR THE BULGOGI**

- **½ cup garlic cloves (about 20–25), peeled**
- **1-inch nub fresh ginger, peeled**
- **1 small yellow onion**
- **4 scallion stalks**
- **1 kiwi, peeled**
- **½ Fuji apple, peeled and cored**
- **1 cup soy sauce**
- **4 slices pineapple rings in heavy syrup, plus ⅓ cup juice (from 20-ounce can)**
- **¾ cup sugar**
- **2 teaspoons gochugaru (Korean chili flakes)**
- **2 teaspoons black pepper**
- **3 tablespoons sesame oil**
- **6 tablespoons black sesame seeds**
- **6 tablespoons white sesame seeds**
- **1 ½ pounds New York strip steak**

## FOR THE KIMCHI SCALLIONS

2 bunches scallions

⅓ cup kosher salt

½ cup gochugaru

1 ½-inch nub ginger, peeled
   and sliced

⅛ cup garlic cloves, peeled

## FOR THE CRISPY RICE

2 cups short-grain sushi rice

Nonstick spray

¼ cup neutral oil, such as
   grapeseed or canola,
   plus more as needed

## FOR THE GOCHUJANG SAUCE

⅓ cup sugar

⅓ cup hot tap water

⅓ cup rice vinegar

2 cups gochujang (Korean
   chili paste)

### TO MAKE THE KIMCHI SCALLIONS

Remove the papery skins from the scallion bulbs. Trim off the roots and trim the green tops to an equal length. Massage the salt into the scallions and spread them on a rimmed baking sheet. Cover the scallions with another baking sheet and weigh the sheet down with something heavy. Allow the scallions to sit at room temperature for 1 hour.

Combine 1 cup water and the gochugaru in a saucepan over medium heat; gently bring the liquid to a simmer, mixing it into a loose paste. Remove the sauce from the heat and let it cool slightly. In a blender, combine the ginger, garlic, and ¼ cup water. Combine the mixture with the gochugaru and set the mixture aside.

Brush off excess salt from the scallions, draining any excess liquid. Add the scallions to the gochugaru mixture and toss (with gloved hands or tongs) to combine. Store and refrigerate the scallions until use.

### TO MAKE THE CRISPY RICE

Rinse the rice under cold water until the water runs clear. Bring the rice and 2 cups water to a boil, stirring occasionally while it comes to temperature. Reduce the heat to low, cover, and cook for 15 minutes, then turn the heat off completely. Let the rice stand, covered, for 10 minutes.

Spray a baking sheet and the inside of a square (or round) cutter with nonstick spray. Place the cutter on the baking sheet and scoop enough rice into the cutter to form a cake about 1¼–1½ inches tall. Lift the cutter carefully and repeat this process of making cakes until all the rice has been used. You should have 6 portions. Cover the rice cakes and keep them at room temperature.

### TO MAKE THE GOCHUJANG SAUCE

Whisk the sugar and hot water until the sugar dissolves; add the vinegar and stir to combine. Place the gochujang in a separate bowl; slowly add the sugar-vinegar mixture and whisk until it is incorporated. Set aside.

## TO COOK AND ASSEMBLE

Coat a large nonstick skillet with oil and place it over medium-high heat. Carefully add the rice cakes and cook them for 4–6 minutes on one side, until they are golden and crispy. Transfer the cakes to a plate; set aside.

Heat a grill pan over high heat. Grill the marinated steak for about 3 minutes, then flip it and grill for 2 minutes more. (You can use a weight to get a better sear and cook the meat evenly.) Medium rare is best. Transfer the steak to a cutting board and let it rest before slicing thin, keeping portions together for easy assembly.

Add the kimchi scallions to the hot grill pan, maintaining the high heat. Place a weight on the white parts to char them. Grill the scallions for 2–3 minutes, then flip them and grill 1 minute more. Transfer them to a cutting board or plate. Twist several scallions around a fork to form a nest; continue with the remaining scallions to form 5 more nests.

For each serving, spread a little gochujang and the reserved bulgogi marinade on a plate. Add 1 rice cake, crispy-side up, then top each cake with one portion of the sliced beef. Place a scallion nest on top of the beef and serve.

# Sticky Rice Cakes with Pork Belly and Kimchi Stew

This dish is inspired by one of my favorite places to eat in Charlotte. Musashi is a small Japanese restaurant in a nondescript strip mall south of town. There isn't much ambiance, but the food is really good. We often hold Sunday "staff meetings" there while enjoying a variety of small plates and sushi.

One of our favorite dishes at the restaurant is a simple bowl of pork and kimchi. We usually order two servings. At Good Food on Montford we put our twist on this dish by preparing the pork and kimchi as more of a sauce, pairing it with a chewy rice cake for a surprising contrast. It's a hearty, satisfying meal with a strong kick.

A trip to your local Asian grocery or international market should yield the special ingredients needed for this dish. We use the Kikkokin brand of jarred kimchi. If you would rather not make the rice cakes, you can find packaged rice cakes in the aisle where fresh noodles are found.

**SPECIAL EQUIPMENT:** food-grade disposable gloves, stand mixer, bench scraper

**SERVES 10**

### TO MAKE THE RICE CAKES

Bring a large stockpot of water to a boil. Meanwhile, combine the flour, both starches, and salt in the bowl of a stand mixer fitted with a paddle attachment. Carefully ladle out 5¾ cups of boiling water into the mixture.

Mix the ingredients on low speed until the dough comes together in a loose ball, then increase the speed to medium and continue mixing for 1 minute, or until the dough is uniformly smooth.

Return the water in the stockpot to a boil. Meanwhile, put on the gloves and lightly coat a work surface (and the gloves) with cornstarch. Turn the dough out onto the work surface. Portion the dough and roll it into logs about 1 inch in diameter and 6 inches long.

Drop the logs into the boiling water, stir, and maintain a boil. Cook, stirring occasionally, until the rice cakes float. Drain them in a large colander, rinsing them with cold water to remove excess starch. When completely cooled, gently slice the logs into ¼-inch-thick discs. Toss them with the oil. Set aside.

**FOR THE RICE CAKES**

1 cup rice flour

1 cup wheat starch

7 tablespoons tapioca starch

1 teaspoon kosher salt

3 cups water

Cornstarch, for dusting

2 tablespoons neutral oil, such as grapeseed or canola

## FOR THE STEW

1 ½ pounds slab pork belly,
   frozen

1 (32-ounce) jar kimchi, plus
   liquid

4 tablespoons neutral oil, such
   as grapeseed or canola,
   divided

1 large yellow onion, sliced

1 quart chicken stock

¼ cup soy sauce

1 tablespoon sesame oil

1 bunch scallions, thinly sliced

## TO MAKE THE STEW

Remove the pork belly from the freezer and allow it to thaw slightly. (Keeping it cold will make it easier to slice.) Cut the belly in half so that there are 2 slabs, each about 4–5 inches thick, then slice the slabs into super-thin slices with a sharp knife.

Strain the liquid from the kimchi into a bowl; reserve.

Heat 2 tablespoons of the oil in a large pot or Dutch oven over high heat. When the oil starts to shimmer, layer the pork belly in the pan and render it on both sides for 3 minutes, or until the meat starts to brown. Add the onions and cook, stirring the mixture occasionally, until they start to get soft, about 4 minutes. Drain the excess fat and return the pan to the heat.

Reduce the heat to medium and add the reserved kimchi liquid, chicken stock, and soy sauce. Simmer until the pork belly is tender, about 15 minutes (this will vary depending on the thickness). Reduce the heat to low, add the kimchi and sesame oil, and return to a gentle simmer.

## TO ASSEMBLE

Heat a large, nonstick pan over medium heat. Add the remaining neutral oil and a single layer of rice cakes and cook until they begin to brown. Agitate the pan so that the rice cakes brown all over. Transfer them to the kimchi stew and stir; repeat with the remaining rice cakes.

Ladle the stew into bowls and garnish with fresh scallions. Serve immediately.

# Soups

Making a good soup doesn't require a laundry list of ingredients, just fresh ones. I believe in soup for all seasons, mainly because I love to make it. In soup, there is a simplicity that I appreciate—the gentle coaxing of flavor from vegetables and the reward of a finished product bearing a heightened version of a single ingredient that needs little more than a few complimentary touches, technique, and time.

Each recipe in this chapter contains soups that taste like themselves. The sweet corn soup tastes deeply of corn; the warm mushroom soup has a rustic earthiness representative of the season's forage. At the restaurants we elevate our simple soups by paring them with a worthy garnish. Atop a silky cauliflower soup, you'll find a truffle mascarpone with sweet crab folded into it. The English pea soup features flavorfully poached North Carolina shrimp and a drizzle of lemon-infused olive oil. Prepare a large batch to serve your family throughout the week, or create a warm evening at home when the temperatures begin to drop. Soups make use of surplus and are a wonderful way to enjoy the wealth of each season.

# Soup on Sundays

The essence of soup is communal. One giant pot and a ladle is enough to draw a crowd and feed the masses. Soup is a meal for gathering, for coming together.

Besides that, making soup speaks to my biggest cooking mantra: less is more. My goal is to use as few ingredients as possible with minimal manipulation. Soup is an exploration in texture—from silky, velvety versions to delightfully chunky. Grab a couple loaves of crusty bread, and you've got a worthy meal.

The first charitable event I participated in after moving to Charlotte was in 2003 for Soup on Sunday, a regional annual fund-raiser for hospice and palliative care. I was invited to join in by Catherine Rabb, owner of Fenwick's (a Charlotte institution three decades strong) and culinary instructor. Soup on Sunday was on a day the restaurant was closed, and that was a plus. It was rare, back then, for me to be out of the kitchen and among fellows. For Soup on Sunday, various chefs each prepare a five-gallon batch of soup to serve to community members who show up to eat. I've done the event every year since. It always feels good to give back, but Soup on Sunday holds a special place in my heart as the communal gathering that first truly connected me to the city at large.

# Sweet Corn Soup with Poached Lobster, Radish, and Truffle Oil

I learned to make this soup from my executive chef at Metropolis Café in Boston. I have always loved its simplicity, studded with fresh lobster and peppery radish. This soup shaped my philosophy of highlighting a singular ingredient. Corn is the star here. For some reason, this dish takes me back to summers in Matunuck, Rhode Island, when I would eat fresh corn on the cob loaded with butter and black pepper.

**SPECIAL EQUIPMENT:** lobster cracker, kitchen shears, immersion blender, mandoline (optional)

**SERVES 10–12**

### TO MAKE THE SOUP

Place a clean dish towel on work surface and hold an ear of corn upright on the towel. (This will prevent the corn from slipping.) Slice the corn off the cob and place the kernels in a bowl. Reserve the corn cobs.

Add the onions, potatoes, wine, and 1 cup water to a large soup pot. Cover and cook over medium heat for 10 minutes, or until the potatoes and onions soften. Uncover the pot and add the reserved corn cobs and 8 cups water. Simmer for 30 minutes, then remove and discard the corn cobs. Next, add the corn kernels and simmer, uncovered, for 25 minutes. Remove the soup from the stovetop and add the salt, cream, and sugar and blend the liquid with an immersion blender. Start with small pulses to prevent splashing. Blend for about 5 minutes. Alternatively, use a standing blender and work in batches. Begin on low speed, then increase the speed, and blend the soup to the desired texture. Strain the soup through a colander using the bottom of a ladle or a rubber spatula to push out all the liquid. Discard the remaining hulls. Keep the soup warm while you poach the lobster.

**FOR THE SOUP**

8 ears fresh corn, shucked

1 medium Vidalia onion, sliced

1 large russet potato, peeled and sliced

1 cup white wine

2 tablespoons kosher salt

1 cup heavy cream

1 tablespoon sugar

Truffle oil, for drizzling (optional)

3 watermelon radishes, for garnish

## TO POACH THE LOBSTER

Fill a large stockpot halfway with water and the salt. Bring to a boil. Prepare an ice bath and set aside.

Once the water comes to a rolling boil, add the lobster and boil for 8 minutes. Transfer the lobster immediately to the ice bath and let it sit 5–10 minutes. Meanwhile, slice the radishes paper thin using a mandoline or a very sharp knife.

Remove the lobster from the ice bath. Place the tail on a clean dish towel, then hold one side of the tail in each hand and push upward to crack it open. Pull out the tail meat and coarsely chop it. Crack the claws near the joint and remove the meat. Use kitchen shears to reach additional lobster meat.

## TO ASSEMBLE

Ladle 1–2 cups of soup into each serving bowl. Add 1 ounce of lobster to the center of the bowl and garnish with the thinly shaved radishes and a drizzle of truffle oil. Leftover soup can be covered and refrigerated for 1 week.

**FOR THE LOBSTER**
**2 tablespoons kosher salt**
**1 (1-pound) live lobster**

# English Pea Soup with Poached Shrimp

**FOR THE SHRIMP**

1 lemon, quartered

1 medium yellow onion, sliced

2 celery ribs, sliced

2 fresh bay leaves

2 sprigs fresh parsley

2 sprigs fresh thyme

4 garlic cloves

1 tablespoon whole black
   peppercorns

1 tablespoon coriander seeds

1 cup white wine

8 ounces fresh shrimp, 16–20
   count, peeled and deveined

I love fresh English peas; their arrival tells me that spring is here. One of my cardinal rules for soup is to preserve the integrity of the ingredients, particularly when it comes to vegetables. When I first made this soup, I had trouble maintaining the vibrancy of the peas.

To overcome this, I developed a neutral base made of potato and onions to serve as the canvas for the bright color and sweet flavor of the peas. This base makes a nice foundation for both flavor and texture, while tender poached shrimp add an attractive contrast in color and texture. We like to drizzle the finished soup with lemon-infused olive oil and garnish it with pea tendrils.

You can also use this neutral base for other vegetable soups. We especially like it for green soups including broccoli, spinach, and watercress.

**SERVES 6–8**

## TO POACH THE SHRIMP

Place 8 cups of water plus all the ingredients except the shrimp in a large stockpot and bring to a simmer. After 10 minutes, add the shrimp and return to a simmer for about 2 minutes. Turn the heat off and keep the shrimp in the poaching liquid for another 6–8 minutes. Check the shrimp for doneness by cutting one in half. It is done when the middle is opaque and white. If it is not white, leave it in the liquid for another minute or so. Drain the liquid and place the poached shrimp on a plate in the refrigerator to cool completely.

## TO MAKE THE SOUP

Add the potatoes, onions, wine, and 1 cup water to a large pot over medium-high heat. Cover and steam for 10 minutes to allow the onions to soften, then add another 6 cups of water. Bring the water to a boil, then reduce the heat and simmer for 15 minutes until the potatoes can be easily pierced.

Remove from the heat and stir in the salt, heavy cream, and lemon juice. Working in batches, carefully add the potato and onion mixture to a blender and purée. This is the base of the soup. Transfer the liquid to a container and set aside.

Prepare an ice bath and bring a medium pot of salted water to a boil. Blanch the fresh peas for about 2 minutes, or until they soften a bit and turn vivid green. Shock the peas in the ice bath, then add the peas, 2 cups of cold water, and sugar to a blender and purée on high speed until the mixture resembles a milkshake. Strain the purée by pressing with a ladle or rubber spatula through a fine-mesh colander.

Return the potato and onion soup base to the stovetop over medium heat. As it begins to warm, mix in the strained pea purée. Stir until blended, and allow the soup to warm up fully.

## TO ASSEMBLE

Ladle 1–1½ cups of soup into each bowl, top with poached shrimp, and drizzle with olive oil. Serve hot.

**FOR THE PEA SOUP**

2 large russet potatoes, peeled, halved, and cut into ½-inch slices

1 medium yellow onion, sliced

1 cup white wine

2 tablespoons kosher salt

1 cup heavy cream

1 tablespoon fresh lemon juice

4 cups fresh English peas

1 tablespoon sugar

Extra-virgin olive oil or lemon-infused olive oil, for drizzling

# Creamy Spring Onion Soup

At Good Food on Montford, we welcome spring with a delicate onion soup topped with roasted spring onions, asparagus, and smoked olive oil. Our method of making soup is simple yet precise: we coax flavor from the ingredients by cooking them slowly over low heat. If you cannot find spring onions for the garnish, you can substitute Vidalia onions. Lemon-infused olive oil can be purchased at specialty shops; it adds the brightness of lemon without the acidity.

**FOR THE SOUP**
**1 cup (2 sticks) unsalted butter**
**5 large Vidalia onions, sliced**
**2 cups white wine**
**2 tablespoons kosher salt**
**1 fresh bay leaf**
**1 bunch thyme**
**3 cups cream**

SERVES 10–12

TO MAKE THE SOUP

In a large pot over medium heat, combine the butter, onions, wine, salt, bay leaves, and thyme. Cover the pot and cook over low heat, about 30–40 minutes. You want the onions to be very soft. Stir the onions occasionally, and add a little water if they start drying out. Avoid getting any color on the onions. You want the soup to be ivory white.

After the onions have softened, remove the herbs, add the cream, and stir. Working in batches, purée the mixture in a blender on high speed until smooth. Avoid filling the blender more than halfway; this helps achieve a velvety texture (and prevents burns). Keep the soup warm until ready to serve.

Preheat the oven to 400°.

**FOR THE GARNISH**

3 tablespoons extra-virgin
    olive oil, divided

3 spring onion bulbs (or 1 large
    Vidalia onion), sliced into
    1-inch-thick rounds

3 fresh bay leaves

4 sprigs fresh thyme

Kosher salt and black pepper

½ pound asparagus, woody
    ends removed

Zest of ½ lemon

Lemon-infused olive oil or
    extra-virgin olive oil, for
    drizzling

TO MAKE THE GARNISH

Coat a cast-iron skillet with 2 tablespoons of the olive oil and place it over medium-high heat. Once the skillet is hot, add the onions and herbs, and season with salt and pepper. When the onions begin to take on some color, transfer them to the oven and roast them for 5 minutes. Flip the onion rounds and return them to the oven for another 5 minutes, or until the onions are tender and caramelized. Try to keep the rounds intact for even cooking.

Remove the onions from the skillet; discard the herbs but keep the skillet handy. Cut the onion rounds into 4 equal wedges. Place them in a bowl and set aside.

Toss the asparagus with the remaining olive oil and season with salt and pepper. Using the same skillet, cook the asparagus over high heat, turning frequently to char the spears on all sides. Transfer the asparagus to a cutting board and slice the spears into 2-inch pieces on the bias. Add the sliced asparagus and lemon zest to the chopped onions and toss to combine.

TO ASSEMBLE

Ladle 1–1½ cups warm soup into each bowl and garnish with the caramelized onions and asparagus. Finish with a drizzle of lemon-infused olive oil (or regular olive oil). Serve immediately.

# Cauliflower Soup with Crab Truffle Mascarpone

To make a soup that tastes most like cauliflower, this recipe relies on a French technique called *à l'étouffée*, where vegetables are covered and placed over moderate to low heat so that they steam and gently cook down in their own liquid. This process captures a great depth of flavor and creates a silky texture. We accent this warming soup with white wine and lemon, then finish it with a truffle crab mascarpone and truffle oil.

---

SERVES 10–12

............................................................................................

TO MAKE THE SOUP

Place the onions, cauliflower, wine, and 1 cup water in a large stockpot over medium heat. Cover the pot and cook for 20–25 minutes, until the cauliflower is tender. While the cauliflower cooks, make the mascarpone.

TO MAKE THE MASCARPONE

Mix all the ingredients together until they are evenly incorporated. Cover the mascarpone and refrigerate until ready to serve.

Return to the soup: Add 2 more quarts water, then bring the pot to a simmer over medium-low heat and cook for 30 minutes more. The cauliflower should be mushy and falling apart. Remove the pot from the heat and add the cream, salt, white pepper, lemon juice, and Tabasco; stir.

Working in batches, ladle the soup into a blender, leaving an air gap for any hot steam to escape. Start blending on the lowest setting and slowly increase the speed to high; purée until silky smooth.

TO ASSEMBLE

Ladle 1–1½ cups of soup into each bowl. Place a scoop of the truffle mascarpone in the center, then drizzle with truffle oil and a sprinkling of chopped chives. Serve immediately. The leftover soup will keep in the refrigerator for 1 week.

FOR THE SOUP

1 medium yellow onion, sliced
2 large cauliflower heads, cored, halved, and sliced thin
1 cup dry white wine
1 cup heavy cream
2 tablespoons kosher salt
½ teaspoon ground white pepper
1 teaspoon fresh lemon juice
2 dashes Tabasco sauce
Truffle oil or extra-virgin olive oil
Fresh chives, for garnish

FOR THE MASCARPONE

1 cup mascarpone
4 ounces jumbo lump crab
Zest of 1 lemon
1 tablespoon fresh lemon juice
1 tablespoon truffle shavings or truffle oil
1 teaspoon finely chopped fresh parsley
1 teaspoon finely chopped fresh chives
Kosher salt and ground white pepper

# Mushroom Soup with Truffle Whip

**FOR THE SOUP**

2 pounds portobello
    mushrooms, gills on,
    sliced

1 medium yellow onion,
    sliced

1 cup white wine

1 cup water

1 tablespoon Garlic Confit
    (page 15) or finely
    minced garlic

1 cup heavy cream

2 tablespoons kosher salt

1 teaspoon black pepper

**FOR THE TRUFFLE WHIP**

1 cup heavy cream

¼ teaspoon kosher salt

1 teaspoon chopped
    fresh thyme

1 teaspoon truffle oil

This soup was on my menu when I opened Barrington's. About a month in, a couple came in for dinner and ordered it. They remarked to the server that it was one of the best mushroom soups they'd ever tasted and that it reminded them of a soup they ate in a tiny restaurant in Boston's South End. When I stopped by their table, they shared the name of the restaurant where they had eaten the soup. It just so happens that I was a chef at that restaurant and this was the same exact soup! To this day, I remain friends with that couple.

SERVES 6–8

TO MAKE THE SOUP

Place the mushrooms, onions, wine, water, and Garlic Confit into a large pot. Cover and cook over medium heat until the mushrooms release all of their liquid, about 12–15 minutes. Meanwhile, make the truffle whip.

Once the mushrooms have released their liquid, add 5 more cups water, bring the pot to a simmer, and cook, uncovered, for 10–15 minutes. Add the cream, salt, and pepper. Remove the soup from the heat and blend it with an immersion blender or in a standing blender, leaving a little texture.

TO MAKE THE TRUFFLE WHIP

Combine all the ingredients. Use a whisk to whip the cream until soft peaks form. (You can also use a stand mixer.) Refrigerate until ready to use.

TO ASSEMBLE

Ladle 1–1½ cups of soup into each bowl and top with the truffle whip. Serve immediately.

# Butternut Squash Soup with Chowchow

FOR THE CHOWCHOW

1 medium butternut squash
(2–3 pounds)

½ small yellow onion, cut into
⅛-inch dice

1 medium red bell pepper,
cored and seeded, cut into
⅛-inch dice

2 celery ribs, ends trimmed,
cut into ⅛-inch dice

¼ cup kosher salt

½ cup rice vinegar

½ cup apple cider vinegar

1 teaspoon curry powder

This recipe is a classic example of what we like to do at Good Food on Montford. To a well-balanced butternut squash soup, we add a tangy southern chowchow with a global touch. The addition of curry infuses this quintessential southern condiment with a traditional Indian spice. Use chowchow anywhere you would use relish; it's incredibly versatile.

Make the chowchow a day ahead. It requires patient knife work to perfect the brunoise, a ⅛ × ⅛-inch dice, and the chowchow needs to steep in its pickling liquid overnight.

**SPECIAL EQUIPMENT:** mandoline, blender

**SERVES 8–10**

TO MAKE THE CHOWCHOW

Slice off the neck of the squash. Reserve the wide, bottom lobe for roasting with the soup. Wrap and refrigerate it until use. Slice off the rounded edges of the neck to create a rectangular block. Peel off any remaining skin. The block should weigh about 8 ounces.

Using a mandoline, place the longest side of the squash block on the cutting surface and shave it into ⅛-inch-thick slices to create thin, wide strips. Stack a few strips on top of each other in order to cut your brunoise efficiently. Cut lengthwise and then horizontally to make a fine dice (it should yield about 1½ cups). Add the onions, peppers, and celery and toss together.

Place the prepared vegetables in a heatproof bowl and set aside. Heat 2 quarts of water in a large pot and dissolve the salt to make a brine. Pour the brine over the vegetables and let them sit for 30–60 minutes, then drain. Combine the vinegars and curry powder, then pour the liquid over the brined vegetables. Cover and refrigerate overnight.

## TO MAKE THE SOUP

Preheat the oven to 400°.

Slice the neck off the remaining intact squash. Cut the bottom lobe in half and scoop out the seeds. Do the same with the reserved lobe from the chowchow preparation. Place the squash in a roasting pan, skin-side up. Fill the pan with 1 inch of water. Cover the pan tightly with foil and roast for 90 minutes.

Once the squash is cool enough to handle, peel off the skin. Add the squash to a large pot, along with the apple juice, vinegar, salt, brown sugar, mustard, cream, and spices. Mix well over medium-low heat until warmed through, about 5 minutes. Ladle the contents into a blender, working in batches if needed, and purée. Strain the mixture for a smooth texture.

## TO ASSEMBLE

Ladle 1½ cups of soup into each bowl, then top with a dollop of chow-chow. Extra soup can be stored in the refrigerator for 1 week. Extra chowchow can be refrigerated for 1 month.

**FOR THE SOUP**

- **1 large butternut squash (2–4 pounds)**
- **¼–½ cup apple juice (depending on the sweetness of the squash)**
- **¼ cup apple cider vinegar**
- **2 tablespoons kosher salt**
- **2 tablespoons light brown sugar**
- **2 tablespoons whole-grain mustard**
- **2 cups heavy cream**
- **¼ teaspoon cayenne pepper**
- **¼ teaspoon ground allspice**

# Minestrone Soup with Farfalle

1 tablespoon extra-virgin
   olive oil
1 pound sweet Italian sausage,
   cut into 1-inch-thick rounds
1 large white onion, cut into
   ¼-inch dice
6 medium carrots, peeled and
   cut into ¼-inch dice
5 celery heart ribs, cut into
   ¼-inch dice
4 garlic cloves, minced
3 heirloom tomatoes, cut into
   1-inch dice
2 cups white wine
1 small head napa cabbage,
   sliced
4 quarts chicken stock
2 quarts vegetable stock
   (or whey, see page 33)
3 fresh bay leaves
2 (15-ounce) cans great
   northern beans, drained
2 (15-ounce) cans chickpeas,
   drained
2 cups freshly grated
   Parmesan
2 tablespoons chopped fresh
   parsley
2 tablespoons kosher salt
½ cup fresh spinach
1 pound farfalle, cooked
   al dente

This hearty soup is a warming meal made to feed a crowd or turn into multiple meals. Make a batch on a Sunday and let this minestrone—chock-full of sweet Italian sausage, cabbage, white beans, chickpeas, and farfalle—carry you well into the week. Parmesan, fresh parsley, and wilted spinach finish this nutritious and easy meal.

SERVES 10–12

In a large soup pot, heat the olive oil over medium heat. Add the sausage and fully cook. Remove the sausage, then add the onions, carrots, celery, and garlic; sauté the vegetables in the sausage fat until they are softened, 5–7 minutes. Return the sausage to the pot, add the tomatoes and wine, and simmer 3 minutes. Add the cabbage and both stocks. Bring the pot to a boil and add the bay leaves. Reduce the heat and let simmer 20 minutes. Add the beans and chickpeas and simmer 15 minutes more. To finish, discard the bay leaves and stir in the Parmesan, parsley, and salt. Taste and adjust seasoning if needed.

TO ASSEMBLE

Place the spinach and cooked pasta in individual bowls and ladle the hot soup over them. Drizzle with olive oil and sprinkle with extra Parmesan. Extra soup can be stored in the refrigerator for 1 week.

# Tomato Soup with Roasted Garlic, Basil, and Salsa Rosa

The merging of tomatoes, garlic, and basil give this soup its familiar and comforting flavor, while the addition of emulsified olive oil adds a wonderful creaminess without feeling heavy. Of course, the tomatoes shine the brightest (as they should), but a little dash of Tabasco and a fiery salsa rosa make for a bold finish. This soup is dairy free, making it a great option for vegan or lactose-intolerant guests.

SERVES 6–8

## TO MAKE THE SALSA ROSA
Slice the tomatoes into quarters, discarding the core and seeds. Cut the quarters into ¼-inch dice and set aside.

Place the olive oil, garlic, and chili flakes in a sauté pan over high heat. Cook until the garlic turns golden brown, about 3 minutes. (Tilting the pan will help to submerge the garlic and chili flakes in the hot oil.) Add the red onions and toss for 15–30 seconds, then add the tomatoes and toss for 30 seconds more. Reduce the heat to low; add the remaining ingredients and simmer for 5 minutes. Season with salt. Set aside.

## TO MAKE THE SOUP
Combine the tomatoes, wine, garlic, salt, sugar, Tabasco sauce, and basil in a soup pot over high heat. Bring to a boil, then reduce the heat to medium and simmer for 30 minutes. Remove from the heat.

Place the soup into a blender and blend on medium-high speed. With the blender running, slowly add the olive oil to the hot soup. Strain the soup through a fine strainer to remove seeds and basil leaves.

## TO ASSEMBLE
Ladle 1½ cups of soup into each bowl and garnish with salsa rosa and fresh basil.

**FOR THE SALSA ROSA**
- 4 Roma tomatoes
- ½ cup extra-virgin olive oil
- 4 garlic cloves, peeled and thinly sliced
- 2 teaspoons crushed chili flakes
- ½ medium red onion, cut into ¼-inch dice
- ¼ cup white wine
- 1 teaspoon chopped fresh parsley
- 1 teaspoon chopped fresh oregano
- ½ teaspoon chopped fresh thyme
- Zest of 1 lemon
- Kosher salt

**FOR THE SOUP**
- 8 cups peeled Roma tomatoes with juice
- 1 cup white wine
- 2 tablespoons Garlic Confit (page 15) or finely minced garlic
- 1 tablespoon kosher salt
- 2 tablespoons sugar
- 1 teaspoon Tabasco sauce
- 10–12 basil leaves, plus more for garnish
- 1 cup extra-virgin olive oil

# White Bean Soup

This is a late fall menu item at Stagioni. We introduce it when the cold winds start to nip, signaling winter. When we make it at the restaurant, we often use a toasted Parmesan broth made from whey (see page 33) and Parmesan rinds to achieve a rich, savory base.

The beans need to be soaked overnight, so plan ahead. Freeze extra soup for a quick, warming meal in the dead of winter.

**SERVES 10–12**

Add the olive oil to a large pot over medium-high heat. Add the pancetta and cook the cubes for 10 minutes, or until they are lightly caramelized. Add the garlic and toast it, stirring frequently, until it is light golden in color, about 3 minutes. Add the celery, carrots, and onions and cook until they are soft, about 3 minutes more. Add the soaked cannellini, stock, and greens and cook over medium heat, partially covered, for 90 minutes, or until the beans are soft. Stir occasionally. Add water or reserved bean liquid if the soup thickens too much. Cook longer if the soup is too thin.

Serve hot. Extra soup can be stored in the refrigerator for 1 week.

1 tablespoon extra-virgin olive oil

1 pound smoked pancetta, cut into ¼-inch cubes

1 head garlic cloves, peeled and sliced

1 bunch celery, cut into ½-inch dice

5 medium carrots, cut into ½-inch dice

3 small yellow onions, cut into ¼-inch dice

1 quart dried cannellini, soaked overnight, liquid reserved

1 gallon stock (chicken, pork, or whey)

2 bunches collards, stems removed, leaves torn into 1-inch pieces

# Lentil Soup with Saucisson

½ large yellow onion, sliced
    into ¾-inch-thick rings

2 cups beluga lentils, rinsed
    and debris removed

1 celery rib

1 medium carrot, peeled

¼ pound thick-cut bacon

1 quart stock (chicken or
    vegetable)

¼ bunch parsley

4 sprigs fresh thyme

2 fresh bay leaves

4 tablespoons extra-virgin
    olive oil, divided

1 large yellow (about 2 cups)
    onion, cut into ¼-inch dice

1 cup celery, cut into
    ¼-inch dice

1 cup carrots, cut into
    ¼-inch dice

1 tablespoon sliced garlic
    cloves

1 tablespoon chopped fresh
    thyme

4 teaspoons kosher salt,
    divided

½ teaspoon black pepper

8 tablespoons (1 stick)
    unsalted butter

1 quart water

½ pound saucisson à l'ail
    or mortadella

I associate this soup with winters in Rhode Island. We would spend hours at the local pond playing hockey until the sun went down. This soup would be waiting back home, if I was lucky. I felt that it was directly responsible for returning the feeling back to my fingers and toes. It was so satisfying.

In this recipe, we use beluga lentils, a caviar-like lentil that holds up well during the cooking process. They add texture but still maintain a delicate mouthfeel. The base of this soup is a fortifying purée of mirepoix (gently cooked celery, carrots, and onions), bacon, and butter. Bits of *saucisson*, a traditional French sausage, make the soup even heartier.

*Note*: We make our own sausage at the restaurants. Given how time-consuming that effort is, we suggest purchasing Les Trois Petits Cochons' Saucisson à l'Ail, a garlic sausage, which can be found online. You can also ask your deli department to provide a half-pound of mortadella cut into half-inch-thick slices, which you can then dice.

**SPECIAL EQUIPMENT**: blender, cheesecloth, butcher's twine

**SERVES 8–10**

Place the onion rings in a dry pan over medium-high heat; cook until they develop color on both sides, about 3–5 minutes per side.

Transfer the cooked onions to a large pot, and add the lentils, celery, carrots, bacon, and stock. Wrap the parsley, thyme, and bay leaves in cheesecloth, tie the cloth into a secure bundle with twine, and add the sachet to the pot. Add enough water to cover the lentils by 1 inch of liquid (about 1 quart). Cover the pot and bring to a boil. Reduce the heat to low and simmer for 55–60 minutes, or until the lentils are tender.

While the lentils cook, heat 2 tablespoons of the olive oil over medium-high heat. Add the diced onions, celery, and carrots, along with the garlic and thyme. Add 1 teaspoon of the salt plus the pepper, then cook for 4 minutes, or until the vegetables are tender. Remove the mirepoix from the heat and set aside.

When the lentils are done, discard the sachet. Transfer the vegetables and bacon used to season the lentils to a blender, along with 2 cups of the cooking liquid, the butter, and the remaining salt. Purée and strain the mixture, then return it to the pot. Stir in the reserved mirepoix.

Remove the casing from the sausage, pat dry, and dice it into ½-inch cubes. Heat a cast-iron skillet with the remaining olive oil. Cook the sausage until browned, stirring occasionally, about 5–7 minutes. Drain any excess fat and stir the sausage into the soup. Add more salt and pepper if needed, then serve with a good, crusty bread.

# Salads

Salads are the ultimate expression of seasonality. They are a colorful time stamp. Searching the markets for of-the-moment inspiration and building a plate around that ingredient is one of my simplest pleasures. With salads I explore the myriad combinations of sweet, sour, salty, and crunchy, a place to play with texture, flavor, and color.

I have but a few rules for salad composition. Be succinct. That is, have a thoughtful reason for pairing one ingredient with another. Each should serve a purpose. If the component doesn't have a purpose, discard it. Also, be gentle with salad greens. Don't overdress them. Allow the unique qualities of each—the sharp bitterness of arugula, the supple leaf of Boston lettuce— to shine on the plate. Don't dilute their characteristics. It's a disservice to the freshness of the season.

This chapter moves through the seasons beginning with the fruit-juicy produce of summer before landing on the comforting flavors of fall and winter, including roasted beets, kale, and butternut squash. But first, the salad that became my life lesson in technique: Craig's Summer Salad.

# Craig's Summer Salad

My grandmother, whom we called Craig, was a precise woman. Meticulous. When it was time to make a salad, she had very specific instructions. She would send me out to her garden with a pair of scissors and tell me to get two tomatoes, twelve green beans, and three heads of lettuce. Her method for making the dressing was just as specific. If it wasn't made in a wooden bowl, it wasn't right. Cooking the green beans was serious business, too. You wanted crunch but not a fibrous chew. And we were taught to always add the lettuce at the last minute, just before serving. I've never deviated from this method, and it has never let me down.

**SERVES 2–4**

Bring a large pot of water to a rolling boil. Meanwhile, prepare an ice bath. Using a paring knife, make an X on the bottom of each tomato. Place the tomatoes into the boiling water for 20 seconds, then remove them with a slotted spoon and plunge them into the ice bath. When they have cooled, gently remove the skins and cut each tomato into 6 wedges. Reserve the ice bath and return the water to a boil.

Generously salt the boiling water and add the green beans. After 3 minutes, check for doneness. You should be able to bite through the green bean with the slightest resistance, but it should still have structure and toothiness, like al dente pasta. Plunge the green beans into ice bath. When chilled, remove them from the water and pat dry.

In a large, wooden salad bowl, crush a clove of garlic with the back of a wooden spoon into 2 teaspoons of salt until it resembles a paste. Remove any large chunks of garlic. Add the vinegar, then slowly whisk in the oil and emulsify. Add the herbs, green beans, and tomatoes and mix together. Let the vegetables marinate at room temperature for 30–60 minutes.

Just before serving, add the lettuce and toss well. Season with salt and pepper to taste.

2 medium tomatoes

12–16 French green beans, cut in half

1 garlic clove

2 teaspoons kosher salt, plus more for seasoning

1 tablespoon white wine vinegar

3 tablespoons extra-virgin olive oil

4 basil leaves, thinly sliced

1 teaspoon chopped fresh tarragon

3 small heads of lettuce (such as Greenleaf), cored

Black pepper, to taste

# Savory Cannoli with Tomato Salad

Cannoli is a quintessential Italian pastry, one most often associated with dessert. Its crisp, golden tubes are typically filled with sweet cream, pistachios, and chocolate chips. At Stagioni, we use cannoli in a savory dish, filling its center with a creamy ricotta with pesto. We pair it with a fresh tomato salad made with pickled red onions, arugula, and basil.

Cannoli dough needs time to rest. Make it at least a day ahead and then fry the cannoli shells the day you wish to serve the dish.

**SPECIAL EQUIPMENT:** 15 cannoli form tubes (purchase online), 3-inch biscuit cutter, food processor, piping bag

SERVES 5

### TO MAKE THE CANNOLI DOUGH

In a food processor, combine the flour, sugar, and salt. Slowly add the olive oil and Marsala until a dough forms. Be careful not to overprocess the dough or it will become brittle when rolling out. Wrap the dough in plastic and refrigerate for 2 hours. While the dough rests, make the pesto and ricotta filling.

### TO MAKE THE FILLING

In a small mixing bowl, combine the pesto, ricotta, and salt. If the mixture seems too thick, add the milk or cream, 1 tablespoon at a time, until the mixture loosens. Transfer the filling to a piping bag and refrigerate it until use. (It's easier to work with a chilled filling.) Refrigerate the remaining pesto and reserve it for another use.

### TO MAKE THE CANNOLI

Remove the dough from the refrigerator and let it sit at room temperature for 10 minutes.

Lightly flour a work surface, or if using a pasta maker, dust the dough surface with flour. Roll the dough to a sheet 1/16 inch thick. Use a 3-inch biscuit cutter to cut rounds from the sheet. Place the rounds on a parchment-lined baking sheet and freeze them for 90 minutes.

Make the egg wash. Beat the egg and 2 tablespoons water together; set aside. Fill a large pot about halfway with oil and heat to 350°. Set a wire rack on top of a sheet pan or line the pan with paper towels.

## FOR THE CANNOLI

¾ cup all-purpose flour

½ tablespoon sugar

½ teaspoon kosher salt

½ tablespoon extra-virgin olive oil

¼ cup Marsala

1 large egg

Neutral oil, such as grapeseed or canola

Nonstick spray

1 recipe Basil Pesto (page 17)

## FOR THE FILLING

3 tablespoons pesto

1 cup whole-milk ricotta or fresh Ricotta (page 33)

1 teaspoon kosher salt

Whole milk or heavy cream, for thinning

## FOR THE SALAD

1 large heirloom tomato, cut into ½-inch dice

2 tablespoons Red Wine Pickled Onions, plus 1 tablespoon pickling juice (page 23)

1 tablespoon smoked olive oil (or regular extra-virgin olive oil)

¼ cup roughly chopped arugula

¼ cup rolled and thinly sliced basil leaves

2 teaspoons smoked salt (or kosher salt)

Aged (5–10 years) balsamic vinegar, for drizzling

Spray the cannoli tubes with nonstick spray. Place a tube horizontally across the top third of a dough round. Brush the bottom third with egg wash. Roll the tube toward you until the bottom of the dough round overlaps the top. The seam should be facing downward. Apply gentle pressure on the top of the tube to seal the cannoli. It should have the same thickness all the way around. Place the cannoli on the baking sheet and repeat this process with the remaining rounds.

Working in batches, drop the cannoli tubes into the hot oil and fry them for 2–3 minutes, or until they are golden brown. Use tongs or a skimmer to transfer the tubes to the wire rack. Cool the tubes completely, then separate the cannoli from the tubes by carefully pulling and twisting until they release.

Gently squeeze chilled filling into both ends of the cooled cannoli shells until they are full. Reserve additional filling for plating.

### TO MAKE THE SALAD

In a bowl, lightly toss the tomatoes, pickled onions, pickling juice, and olive oil. Add the arugula, basil, and salt, tossing again until just combined.

### TO ASSEMBLE

Pipe 3 dime-size dots of filling on each plate. (These hold the cannoli in place.) Place a filled cannoli on top of each dot, then spoon tomato salad over them, drizzle the dish with aged balsamic vinegar, and serve immediately.

# Sammy Koenigsberg, New Town Farms

A few years before I moved to the South, chef Tim Groody was the first Charlotte chef to form a meaningful relationship with a farmer at the market and the first to put the farmer's name on a restaurant menu. That farmer was Sammy Koenigsberg. Sammy and his wife, Melinda, started New Town Farms in 1991 on his family's land in Waxhaw, North Carolina, a town about twelve miles south of Charlotte. That same year, the Koenigsbergs were part of an instrumental gathering of citizens and municipal organizations who established the Matthews Community Farmers' Market, today a stalwart of Charlotte's local food scene.

In fact, it was Sammy's urging that drove the community decision to establish a growers-only market—a place where goods are grown or made within fifty miles of the market center and where you could find producers selling their own stuff every Saturday. That is the very signature of the market and why it's easy to find chefs in Matthews every Saturday morning.

I tell people that my introduction to the Market was my introduction to the food community. There I found people with common interests and causes, and it solidified my belief that food brings people together. I was touched by the generosity of the farmers who would set aside vegetables just for me. It was a revelation, a turning point, and Sammy's vegetables were some of the most pristine I had ever seen.

At first, my visits to market were fairly transactional. I'd come to find ingredients for the week and gather inspiration for specials. I'd make small talk with the farmers, Sammy included, and then I'd be on my way. But that changed. I began to engage more and more with the familiar faces I saw each week, and I looked forward to those interactions.

Before long, Sammy was delivering to the restaurant each week and we started talking about things other than vegetables, like the physical aches and pains of kitchen life. He told me about his passion for cycling, and before I knew it, I was cycling down the country roads of Waxhaw with my farmer. That relationship has deepened over the years. In a way, Sammy's work has helped me feed my family, and my work has helped him do the same. Our businesses have grown up together, and Sammy still sets the standard with his picture-perfect produce and genuine warmth.

My relationship with Sammy Koenigsberg and New Town Farms has been one of the defining relationships of my career, one that I cherish and one that got me excited to be a part of the South, no longer a fish out of water.

# Arugula Salad with Strawberries, Herbed Ricotta, and Strawberry-Champagne Vinaigrette

**FOR THE VINAIGRETTE**

1 cup strawberries, tops removed

1 cup champagne (or white wine) vinegar

¼ cup sugar

1 vanilla bean, scraped

¼ cup neutral oil, such as grapeseed or canola

**FOR THE HERBED RICOTTA**

1 (15-ounce) container whole-milk ricotta or fresh Ricotta (page 33)

½ cup chopped basil leaves

1 tablespoon chopped fresh chives

1 teaspoon lemon-infused olive oil or zest of 1 lemon

¼ teaspoon kosher salt

Pinch black pepper

**FOR THE SALAD**

10 ounces baby arugula

2 cups strawberries, hulled and sliced

¼ cup toasted sliced almonds

Black pepper

North Carolina's mild climate affords our farmers a long strawberry-growing season. This gives us more opportunities to enjoy this salad throughout the entire spring. The peppery bite of arugula plays nicely off the strawberries, which come both sliced and as part of a luscious vinaigrette. A sprinkle of sliced almonds at the end adds a crunchy texture that might otherwise be missed.

SERVES 5

**TO MAKE THE VINAIGRETTE**

Place the strawberries into a medium saucepan with the vinegar, sugar, and vanilla bean; bring to a boil and then simmer 10–12 minutes, or until the mixture reduces by three-fourths. Carefully transfer the sauce to a blender and purée on medium speed. With the blender running, slowly add the oil and emulsify. Refrigerate until use.

**TO MAKE THE HERBED RICOTTA**

In a medium bowl, gently fold all the ingredients together. Set aside.

**TO ASSEMBLE**

Toss the arugula with your preferred amount of dressing. Spread the herbed ricotta on a serving platter, then top it with the dressed arugula, followed by the sliced strawberries and almonds. Drizzle with more dressing, if desired, and finish with a few cracks of black pepper.

Extra dressing can be stored in the refrigerator for 1 week.

# Pickled Mushroom Salad with Arugula and White Balsamic Dressing

**FOR THE PICKLED MUSHROOMS**

12 ounces mixed mushrooms (such as oysters, shiitake, cremini, and beech), cleaned and stemmed

1 cup rice vinegar

1 cup sugar

3–4 sprigs fresh thyme

2 fresh bay leaves

**FOR THE VINAIGRETTE**

¼ cup sugar

½ cup white balsamic vinegar

2 Garlic Confit cloves (page 15) or plain garlic cloves

1 cup blended oil, such as canola and extra-virgin olive oil

1 teaspoon kosher salt

1 tablespoon chopped fresh parsley

1 tablespoon chopped fresh chives

**FOR THE CROUTONS**

1 cup cubed Focaccia (page 248 or store-bought)

2 tablespoons Salsa Verde (page 9)

**FOR THE SALAD**

5 ounces baby arugula

Parmesan, for shaving

Sweet and sour pickled mushrooms are the star of this salad, which includes peppery arugula and a white balsamic dressing with roasted garlic and herbs. Extra mushrooms can be used as a soup garnish, pizza topping, or layered into a sandwich.

SERVES 8

**TO PICKLE THE MUSHROOMS**

Stem shiitakes, if using. Slice or tear the other mushrooms into slices about ¼ inch wide, then place them into a heatproof container. Heat the vinegar, ½ cup water, sugar, thyme, and bay leaves on the stovetop. Stir until the sugar is dissolved, then bring to a boil. Strain out the herbs and pour the hot liquid over the mushrooms. Use a weight to submerge the mushrooms. Allow the mushrooms to cool to room temperature, then cover and refrigerate them overnight.

**TO MAKE THE VINAIGRETTE**

Combine the sugar, vinegar, and garlic in a blender and mix on medium speed. Increase the speed to high; slowly add the oil and emulsify. Add the salt and herbs and pulse a few times to gently incorporate them.

**TO MAKE THE CROUTONS**

Preheat the oven to 450°. Toss the focaccia cubes with the salsa verde and spread them on a baking sheet. Roast for 7–10 minutes, until crisp. Cool slightly.

**TO ASSEMBLE**

Toss the arugula with your preferred amount of dressing, then transfer it to a serving plate. Top with the pickled mushrooms and generously shower the salad with Parmesan shavings. Add croutons and serve.

# Arugula and Endive Salad with Honeycrisp Apples, Spiced Nuts, and Cranberry Vinaigrette

**FOR THE VINAIGRETTE**

3 cups fresh or frozen
    cranberries

½ cup fresh orange juice

½ cup port

½ cup sugar

1 tablespoon Dijon mustard

1 cup vegetable oil

**FOR THE SPICED NUTS**

¼ teaspoon kosher salt

1 tablespoon honey

Pinch cayenne pepper

Pinch ground cinnamon

½ cup walnut halves

1 tablespoon vegetable oil

**FOR THE SALAD**

1 Honeycrisp apple, cored
    and halved

5 ounces baby arugula

1 Belgian baby endive, sliced

½ cup blue cheese crumbles

2 tablespoons Lemon
    Vinaigrette (page 17)

Pinch kosher salt

This salad was on the first menu I wrote for Barrington's. The sweet-tart combination of apples and cranberries is fall friendly and balances the peppery sharpness of the arugula. To round out the flavor and create textures, we add savory blue cheese and warmly spiced nuts. When the leaves start to change color in North Carolina, it's our cue to seek out Honeycrisp apples from local orchards, but any sweet, firm variety will do.

**SPECIAL EQUIPMENT:** mandoline

---

SERVES 4

...........................................................................................................

TO MAKE THE VINAIGRETTE

In a medium pot over medium-high heat, combine the cranberries, orange juice, port, and sugar, and stir. Cook for 5–7 minutes, until the cranberries begin to burst. Remove the pot from the heat; using a slotted spoon, remove half of the cranberries and set them aside. Return the pot with the remaining cranberries to the stovetop over medium-high heat and cook until the berries break down, about 6 minutes.

Carefully pour the hot cranberries into a blender and add the mustard. With the blender running, slowly add the oil, then increase the speed to high and emulsify. Pass the dressing through a fine-mesh strainer and set aside.

TO MAKE THE SPICED NUTS

Preheat the oven to 350°. In a small bowl, mix together the salt, honey, cayenne, and cinnamon. In a separate bowl, toss the nuts with oil; add the spice mixture and toss to coat. Spread the nuts on a baking sheet and bake for 10 minutes. Keep an eye on them; nuts quickly go from toasty to burnt if left unattended. Let cool.

## TO ASSEMBLE

Shave the apple halves thinly using a mandoline.

Toss the arugula and endive in a large mixing bowl. Add the blue cheese crumbles, reserved cranberries, and spiced nuts. Toss the mixture with the Lemon Vinaigrette and a pinch of salt, then add the shaved apples and gently toss once more.

To serve, pile the salad high in the center of a plate. Using a squeeze bottle or a small spoon, dot the cranberry vinaigrette on the salad to form a circular pattern. Serve immediately.

# Mixed Greens with Bacon, French Fries, and Blue Cheese Dressing

**FOR THE VINAIGRETTE**

4 ounces slab bacon, cut into
 ¼-inch dice

3 medium shallots, sliced into
 rings

1 teaspoon chopped fresh
 thyme

2 tablespoons red wine
 vinegar

1 tablespoon Dijon mustard

¼ cup extra-virgin olive oil

**FOR THE DRESSING**

1 cup Duke's mayonnaise

¼ cup whole-milk buttermilk

1 teaspoon Worcestershire
 sauce

½ cup sour cream

4 ounces good blue cheese
 (we like Point Reyes),
 divided

I can't remember the exact day, but one staff meal we had chicken tenders, french fries, and a salad with bacon and blue cheese. I remember being busy and not having much time to eat, so I threw everything in a bowl and quickly shoved dinner in my mouth. Suddenly I stopped; this was a surprisingly good combination. I made everyone try it, and they all agreed.

Two weeks later, we did a modified version for the menu. In this recipe, we toss leafy lettuce with roasted shallots, bacon, and cherry tomatoes and serve it with not one but two dressings—a creamy blue cheese dressing and a tangy red wine vinaigrette. Then we double-fry our french fries for impeccable crispness and one unforgettable salad.

**SPECIAL EQUIPMENT:** candy thermometer, mandoline

**SERVES 4**

### TO MAKE THE VINAIGRETTE

Preheat the oven to 350°. Place the bacon into a small roasting pan and cook it in the oven, 15–18 minutes. Stir in the shallots and return the pan to the oven for 20 minutes more. (Meanwhile, make the blue cheese dressing.) Remove the pan from the oven, stir in the thyme, vinegar, mustard, and olive oil, and set aside.

### TO MAKE THE DRESSING

Whisk together the mayonnaise, buttermilk, Worcestershire, sour cream, and 2 ounces of the blue cheese. Set aside.

## TO COOK THE FRENCH FRIES

Fill a pot halfway with oil and heat to 300°. Rinse the potato sticks with cold water until the water runs clear (to remove the starch). Pat the potatoes dry with a towel, add them to the heated oil, and blanch for 2 minutes, then remove. Let them cool slightly. Heat the oil to 350° for the second fry. Meanwhile, fill a gallon-size storage bag with cornstarch and add the blanched fries. Toss them gently to coat, and tap off any excess. Return the fries to the hot oil and fry for about 8 minutes, or until they are golden brown. Remove them with a slotted spoon or skimmer to a plate lined with paper towels and sprinkle them with salt.

## TO ASSEMBLE

Using a mandoline, shave the onion into paper-thin rings; add the onions to a bowl with the remaining blue cheese, tomatoes, lettuce, and vinaigrette. Gently toss together.

For each serving, spoon the blue cheese dressing on a plate and mound with the dressed salad. Top with french fries and serve immediately.

**FOR THE FRENCH FRIES**

Neutral oil for frying, such as canola

2–3 large russet potatoes, peeled and cut into ½-inch sticks

¼ cup cornstarch

**FOR THE SALAD**

1 small red onion

½ cup cherry tomatoes, halved

6 ounces tender, leafy lettuce

Kosher salt and black pepper

# English Pea Salad with Cheddar-Ham "Croutons"

**FOR THE CROUTONS**

6 ounces sharp yellow
    cheddar, cubed

6 ounces ham, cubed

1 cup all-purpose flour

2 cups panko

½ cup freshly grated
    Parmesan

¼ cup chopped fresh parsley

4 large eggs

Pinch kosher salt

Neutral oil, such as grapeseed
    or canola

The star of this salad is most definitely the "croutons" that top it. Savory ham and cheddar are fried together, then tossed with tender lettuce, spicy radishes, fresh peas, and a sweet pea purée for a salad that hits almost every note.

**SPECIAL EQUIPMENT:** mandoline, stand mixer with large grinder attachment, food processor, candy or meat thermometer

**SERVES 4–6**

### TO MAKE THE CROUTONS

In a stand mixer fitted with a large grinder attachment, grind together the cubed cheddar and ham, alternating between adding cheddar cubes and ham while grinding. Use your hands to form the ground mixture into ½-inch cubes. Put the flour into a gallon-size storage bag, then add croutons and shake to coat. Pour into a colander and tap to remove excess flour. Set aside.

In a food processor, pulse the panko, Parmesan, and parsley together, then transfer the mixture to a bowl. In another bowl, thoroughly beat the eggs with a pinch of salt. Add croutons to the egg mixture and coat well. Using a slotted spoon, remove them and drop them directly into the bread crumbs. Toss to coat, then add the croutons back to the egg and bread crumbs a second time. This double-breading technique keeps the cheese intact as it cooks.

## TO MAKE THE PEA PURÉE

Place the peas, water, and sugar in a blender and purée on high speed until thick, like a milkshake. Strain the purée through a fine-mesh colander using the back of a ladle. Set aside until ready to plate.

## TO FRY THE CROUTONS

Fill a large pot one-third full with oil and heat to 350°. Fry the croutons until golden brown, about 3 minutes. Use a slotted spoon to transfer them to a plate lined with a paper towel.

## TO ASSEMBLE

Use a mandoline to shave the onions and radishes. For each serving, spoon some pea purée on a salad plate. Combine the lettuce, onions, radishes, and peas, then dress the vegetables with the lemon vinaigrette. Season with salt and pepper and mound on each plate. Garnish with the croutons.

### FOR THE PEA PURÉE

2 cups fresh English peas
(or thawed frozen peas)
1 cup water
1 tablespoon sugar

### FOR THE SALAD

1 small sweet onion, peeled
3 radishes
½ cup fresh English peas
(or thawed frozen peas)
6–8 ounces tender lettuce
1 recipe Lemon Vinaigrette
(page 17)

# Baby Arugula with Pickled Beets, Pumpernickel, and Creamy Horseradish

When my wife's Ukrainian mother comes to visit, she always brings a jar of beets pickled with horseradish. I've come to love the taste of earthy beets spiked with sour vinegar and assertive horseradish. It's the inspiration for this recipe. Consider it my homage to my mother-in-law.

You can make the beets up to five days ahead of serving. They get better every day, so give them at least a couple of days to soak.

**SERVES 4**

## TO MAKE THE PICKLED BEETS
Place the sliced beets in a medium saucepan and fill it three-quarters full with water. Add the vinegar, salt, sugar, and orange juice and bring to a boil. Reduce the heat and simmer the beets until tender, about 45 minutes. They should pierce easily with a knife but still have some firmness. Let the beets cool in their pickling liquid, then strain. Set aside or refrigerate until use.

## TO MAKE THE CROUTONS
Preheat the oven to 350°. Melt the butter in a small sauté pan over low heat. Cut the bread into ½-inch cubes and toss the cubes with the melted butter and a pinch of salt. Spread the cubes on a baking sheet in a single layer and bake until crispy, about 10 minutes. The color of pumpernickel makes it hard to tell if they are toasted fully. I recommend tasting one to see if it is crisp.

## TO MAKE THE HORSERADISH DRESSING
Whisk together all the ingredients. Refrigerate until ready to use.

## TO MAKE THE VINAIGRETTE
Whisk together the citrus juice and mustard, then slowly whisk in the oil and emulsify. Set aside.

## TO ASSEMBLE
With a ladle or spoon, spread a few tablespoons of the horseradish dressing in a circle that covers three-quarters of each plate. In a large bowl, gently toss the beets, croutons, arugula, and Havarti with the vinaigrette. Season the salad with a pinch of salt and arrange it on the plate, leaving some of the horseradish dressing exposed.

**FOR THE PICKLED BEETS**
2 large beets, peeled, quartered, and sliced into 1-inch wedges
½ cup white wine vinegar
1 ½ teaspoons kosher salt
2 tablespoons sugar
¼ cup fresh orange juice

**FOR THE CROUTONS**
2 tablespoons unsalted butter
3 slices pumpernickel bread, crusts removed
Pinch of kosher salt

**FOR THE HORSERADISH DRESSING**
½ cup sour cream
¼ cup Duke's mayonnaise
1 tablespoon horseradish
¼ teaspoon Worcestershire sauce

**FOR THE VINAIGRETTE**
1 tablespoon fresh lemon juice
2 teaspoons fresh orange juice
1 teaspoon Dijon mustard
¼ cup neutral oil, such as grapeseed or canola

8 ounces baby arugula
4 ounces dill Havarti, cut into ½-inch cubes
Kosher salt

# Butternut Squash Salad with Cranberries, Goat Cheese, Toasted Pecans, and Brown Butter Vinaigrette

**FOR THE VINAIGRETTE**

8 tablespoons (1 stick)
    unsalted butter
1 medium shallot, sliced
⅓ cup sherry vinegar
2 tablespoons Dijon mustard
1 teaspoon kosher salt
1 tablespoon sugar
1 cup neutral oil, such as
    grapeseed or canola

**FOR THE TOASTED PECANS**

½ cup pecans
1 tablespoon vegetable oil
1 teaspoon honey
¼ teaspoon kosher salt
Dash Tabasco sauce

**FOR THE SALAD**

1 cup crumbled goat cheese
1 cup dried cranberries
1 cup Pickled Butternut
    Squash Ribbons (page 22)
6–8 ounces mixed greens
½ teaspoon kosher salt
½ teaspoon black pepper

Nutty brown butter becomes the perfect backdrop for a vinaigrette that dresses this autumn salad filled with toasted pecans, cranberries, pickled butternut squash, and creamy goat cheese.

**SERVES 4**

**TO MAKE THE VINAIGRETTE**

Place the butter and shallots in a medium pan over high heat. Cook the shallots until the butter begins to brown, about 7 minutes. The butter will bubble and foam gently and will give off a nutty aroma. Make sure it does not burn. Once browned, remove the butter from the heat and transfer it to a blender. Use a rubber spatula to scrape in any brown bits that may have stuck to the bottom of the pan. Add the vinegar, mustard, salt, and sugar, and blend well. With the blender running, slowly add the oil and emulsify. Set aside.

**TO TOAST THE PECANS**

Preheat the oven to 350°. Mix all the ingredients in a bowl. Spread the nuts in a single layer on a small sheet pan. Bake for 10 minutes, or until the pecans start to brown.

**TO ASSEMBLE**

In a large bowl, toss together the goat cheese, pecans, cranberries, and butternut squash ribbons. Add the mixed greens, ⅓ cup of the vinaigrette, and the salt and pepper; toss gently. Distribute the salad evenly on 4 plates and serve. Extra dressing can be stored in the refrigerator for 1 week.

# Watermelon Salad with Feta and Minted Lime Vinaigrette

1 European cucumber

1 ½ teaspoons kosher salt, divided

1 small watermelon

Juice of 3 limes

¼ cup rice vinegar

1 tablespoon honey

¾ cup mint leaves, divided

½ cup neutral oil, such as grapeseed or canola

8 ounces feta, cut into cubes

I look forward to watermelon season. I can eat an entire melon in just one sitting. I like to spit the seeds into the yard but get annoyed when they stick to my feet. In the Carolinas, we are spoiled with Bradford watermelons, an heirloom variety that has a sweetness and depth of flavor that I find satisfying and refreshing.

SERVES 6–8

Peel the cucumber, then cut it lengthwise and remove the seeds. Cut each half lengthwise again, then chop it into 1-inch cubes. Toss the cucumbers with 1 teaspoon of the salt. Let the cucumbers sit for 20 minutes to extract their moisture. Meanwhile, cut enough watermelon into 1-inch cubes to yield approximately 3 cups. Set aside.

Combine the lime juice, vinegar, honey, ½ cup of the mint leaves, and the remaining salt in a blender and mix on high speed. With the blender running, slowly stream in the oil to bind the dressing.

Drain the excess liquid from the cucumbers. Tear the remaining mint leaves and combine them with the cucumbers, watermelon cubes, and feta. Toss this mixture with just enough dressing to coat, then cover and refrigerate at least 1 hour.

Just before serving, remove the salad from the refrigerator and toss again. Adjust seasoning and add more dressing, if desired.

# Vegetables & Sides

When I moved to Charlotte, protein was the king of the plate. Most dishes were served with mashed potatoes and a vegetable of the day, or VOD, as I liked to call it. The VOD was usually a medley of zucchini, yellow squash, carrots, and red onions. I never understood this combination. I wanted to create composed dishes where the sides were on the plate for a reason. I wanted to convey that the quality of the vegetables and various starches mattered just as much as the protein. After my first trip to the Matthews Community Farmers' Market, I knew this would be possible.

In this chapter you will see the simple ways we treat vegetables when they arrive at their peak— sweet spring peas folded into a rich risotto, fresh field peas straight from the market, and a whole head of cauliflower transformed with butter and herbs. Other dishes, like the ricotta-stuffed Delicata squash and skillet-roasted beets with tahini and mint, are meal-worthy all by themselves.

# New South Collards

3 tablespoons vegetable oil

2 ounces thick-cut bacon

1 large bunch collards, rinsed
    and ribs removed

1 medium Vidalia onion,
    cut into ¼-inch dice

2 garlic cloves, peeled and
    sliced

½ cup apple cider vinegar

2 cups chicken stock

½ teaspoon red chili flakes

1 tablespoon kosher salt

2 tablespoons sugar

Collards are part of my southern food education. I didn't grow up eating them. For the longest time I heard the term "potlikker" and assumed that meant the greens were so good, you wanted to lick the pot. I'm embarrassed to admit that I only recently found out that potlikker refers to the flavorful cooking liquid—or liquor—at the bottom of the collards pot.

What I know for sure is that collards benefit from a low and slow cook on the stovetop and that bacon, onion, chili flakes, and a little vinegar help even this New Englander pass for southern at the dinner table.

SERVES 6

In a large Dutch oven, heat the oil over medium-high heat, then add the bacon and cook it until crispy. Meanwhile, stack the collard leaves in batches and roughly cut them into bite-size pieces. Set aside.

Add the onions and garlic to the pot and sweat until translucent, stirring occasionally, about 3 minutes. Next, add the collards and vinegar and stir. Cook for 1 minute, then add the chicken stock, 2 cups water, chili flakes, salt, and sugar. Partially cover and cook for 2 hours, checking every 20 minutes to make sure there is still liquid in the pot. If it looks dry, add more stock. The collards are done when they are glossy and tender.

# Skillet-Roasted Beets with Tahini and Mint

The natural sweetness of beets comes alive when the earthy flesh caramelizes against the searing heat of a cast-iron skillet. This is beets at their best. Following the global purview we take at Good Food on Montford, we gave this dish a Middle Eastern touch by pairing it with plenty of fresh mint and a tahini dressing made simply with lemon juice, garlic, and olive oil.

**SERVES 2**

### TO ROAST THE BEETS

Place the beets into a pot and cover completely with water. Throw in a few generous pinches of salt and bring to a boil. Continue to boil for 1 minute, then reduce the heat to low, cover, and simmer. Cook for 45–60 minutes, or until the beets can be pierced with a fork without resistance. Times will differ depending on the size of the beets. Drain. Once the beets are cool enough to handle, peel them with paper towels, then cut them in half.

Heat a skillet with the olive oil over medium-high heat and preheat the oven to 375°. When the oil is shimmering, add the beets, cut side-down, and cook for 1 minute. Season lightly with salt and pepper. Add the butter and cook for 5 minutes more, tossing the beets on occasion. Place the beets into the oven to keep warm, then make the tahini.

### TO MAKE THE TAHINI

Combine the garlic, lemon juice, salt, and sugar in a blender and mix on high speed. Add the tahini to a bowl, then whisk in the blended mixture. Add water to loosen up the consistency. Slowly drizzle in the olive oil, whisking constantly, until the mixture is smooth and glossy. If the consistency is still too thick, add more water until you reach the consistency of a creamy Caesar dressing.

### TO ASSEMBLE

Remove the beets from the oven. Spoon the tahini dressing on a rimmed serving plate, then add the roasted beets. Drizzle with more tahini dressing, then sprinkle with the fresh mint and serve.

**FOR THE BEETS**

1½ pounds baby beets, tops removed

2 tablespoons extra-virgin olive oil

Kosher salt and black pepper

1 tablespoon unsalted butter

**FOR THE TAHINI**

6 garlic cloves

¼ cup fresh lemon juice

1 teaspoon kosher salt

1 teaspoon sugar

½ cup tahini

¼ cup water, plus more for thinning

¼ cup extra-virgin olive oil

2 sprigs fresh mint, rolled and thinly sliced

# Field Pea Salad with Red Wine Vinaigrette

**FOR THE FIELD PEAS**
Kosher salt
2 pounds fresh field peas
1 medium carrot, peeled
½ medium yellow onion
1 celery rib
2 fresh bay leaves
1 small red onion, cut into
    ¼-inch dice
1 medium red bell pepper,
    cut into ¼-inch dice
1 jalapeño, seeded and cut
    into ¼-inch dice
1 pint cherry tomatoes,
    quartered

**FOR THE VINAIGRETTE**
⅓ cup red wine vinegar
2 tablespoons Dijon mustard
1 tablespoon sugar
1 cup extra-virgin olive oil
¼ cup finely chopped fresh
    parsley
¼ cup finely chopped basil
    leaves
1 tablespoon finely chopped
    fresh oregano
1 teaspoon finely chopped
    fresh thyme
Kosher salt and black pepper

Field peas were not a thing in Rhode Island. After a few years in the South, however, I grew to love them. When they're in season, you'll find them in every corner of the market, packed tightly into bags and piled into large coolers. That's when it's time to make a good field pea salad, with fresh, creamy peas and crunchy vegetables tossed together in an herb vinaigrette.

The best thing about this salad is that it gets better with time. It calls for fresh peas, but if you use dried ones, just soak them in water overnight and increase the cooking time from 15 to 60 minutes.

SERVES 8–10

TO MAKE THE FIELD PEAS
Fill a medium pot with 1 gallon water and add a generous pinch of salt. Add the field peas, carrots, onions, celery, and bay leaves and boil for 2 minutes. Reduce the heat and simmer for 15 minutes, or until the peas are tender. Drain the peas and remove the aromatics. Chill the peas in the refrigerator.

TO MAKE THE VINAIGRETTE
Whisk together the vinegar, mustard, and sugar. Slowly whisk in the olive oil and emulsify. Stir in the fresh herbs, and season with salt and pepper.

TO ASSEMBLE
Combine the chilled peas with the onions, red bell peppers, jalapeños, and tomatoes. Toss with the vinaigrette. Serve the salad immediately, or let it rest in the refrigerator for 24 hours for better flavor. It will keep for 4 days.

# Bounty of the South:
# An Exploration of Charlotte Farmers' Markets

One things that makes Charlotte stand out is its abundance of area farmers' markets. Even better is the roster of familiar faces you'll encounter on a Saturday morning, many of them Charlotte's best chefs and dedicated farmers—salt-of-the-earth people who have become friends over the years.

When I got here in 2000, things were vastly different. I remember getting my first produce order for Barrington's from one of the big-name food distributors. Inside the boxes were bruised zucchinis, mealy tomatoes, mushy chives, and a host of vegetables that came from somewhere else. I knew they wouldn't do. I asked around and discovered that fellow chefs flew in good ingredients. Back then, it was hip to overnight specialty products from places like Hawaii or California, but it was expensive. This didn't make sense to me, someone who had grown up with access to fresh ingredients.

To say I was discouraged when I got here would be an understatement. But a few chefs in the city shared a similar philosophy. Guys like Gene Briggs and Tim Groody, two chefs who made me feel welcome in a new city, showed me where to source ingredients locally.

I was introduced to the Matthews Community Farmers' Market, a small, growers-only market, in a charming southeastern suburb of Charlotte. The market was established in 1991 by its community—local farmers, the town council, the local hardware store, a nonprofit organization, and the chamber of commerce. What I found there was a breath of fresh air on Saturday mornings, a place where I could meet and connect with the local food community, capitalize on of-the-moment ingredients, and learn how to eat seasonally in the South. Soon after I started attending, the market asked me to do cooking demos for the Saturday morning crowd. That was in 2003, and I'm still doing demos.

In southwest Charlotte lies the Charlotte Regional Farmers Market, also known as the Yorkmont Farmers Market because of its location off Yorkmont Road. This is Charlotte's largest area market, full of local and regional producers, plants, and crafts. As more and more chefs have turned to using local produce, Saturday mornings at the regional market have become a place for chefs to convene before diving back into the kitchen for a hellish Saturday night service. Many of the morning's finds appear as specials on Charlotte restaurant menus that same night.

Another, more contemporary market to peruse is the Atherton Farmers Market in South End. The routine for many Charlotte chefs is to hit a few markets in the morning, usually Matthews or the regional market, and then end up at Atherton, where the bustle continues inside Atherton Mill. To see the support that chefs and consumers have shown to local growers and producers over the years, and to see that support grow into the vibrant community it is today, has been one of the most satisfying telltales of Charlotte's transformation into a bona fide food city.

# Roasted Mushrooms

**2 pounds assorted mushrooms (such as oysters, shiitakes, and creminis)**

**¼ cup extra-virgin olive oil**

**1 tablespoon kosher salt**

**1 tablespoon unsalted butter**

**¼ cup peeled and thinly sliced garlic**

**2 tablespoons chopped fresh rosemary**

**1 tablespoon chopped fresh thyme**

**2 tablespoons chopped fresh oregano**

**1 teaspoon black pepper**

At Good Food on Montford, we serve roasted mushrooms as a stand-alone dish on our small plates menu, but it marries with all kinds of flavors, particularly those from the Mediterranean. For instance, they go nicely with our Pork Saltimbocca on page 183. We treat them simply, sautéed in butter and olive oil with garlic and a fistful of fresh herbs. The result is a versatile recipe that works nicely as a side dish but also qualifies to occupy the center of plate.

## SERVES 6

Trim any mushrooms that need to be stemmed, then tear or cut them into roughly 2-inch pieces.

Heat the olive oil in a large, nonstick sauté pan over medium heat. Add the mushrooms and salt. Cook, stirring occasionally for 5 minutes, or until the mushrooms start to release their liquid. Continue cooking until the mushrooms take on a deep, concentrated color, another 6–10 minutes.

Push the mushrooms to the far side of the pan to make room for the remaining ingredients. Add the butter and garlic and cook until the garlic is lightly browned. Add the herbs and black pepper to the garlic, stirring for a few seconds to release their oils. Stir everything together, incorporating the mushrooms. Serve immediately.

# Sweet Pea Risotto with Pea Butter

As the chef of a small restaurant in Boston's historic South End, I was instructed by the owner to have a daily risotto special. I quickly learned how to be one with the rice. Risotto, when cooked properly, has a neutral flavor, wonderful texture, and delicate creaminess. I am always on the lookout for seasonal ingredients to pair with risotto. In this recipe, I tried to capture spring by incorporating whole English peas and a sweet pea butter into the risotto.

In the more traditional method, risotto is cooked by ladling in liquid, a little at a time, to hydrate the rice slowly. Here, we parcook the rice (that means we partially cook it) and then finish it the traditional way—just in half the time.

You will often see risotto made with Arborio rice, but I recommend Carnaroli, another medium-grain variety with a higher starch content that's a little firmer (so that it holds its texture). And it's slightly more forgiving if you stir a little too long. Look for it at specialty grocers, Italian markets, or online.

**FOR THE PEA BUTTER**

1 cup diced white onion (from about ½ large onion)

1 cup (2 sticks) unsalted butter, divided

1 tablespoon kosher salt

1 teaspoon chopped fresh thyme

1 pound fresh English peas (or thawed frozen peas)

---

**SERVES 8**

................................................................

## TO MAKE THE PEA BUTTER

In a small saucepan over medium heat, sweat the onions in 2 tablespoons of the butter and the salt. Add the thyme, cover, and cook for about 5 minutes. Add the peas and toss together. Increase the heat to medium high and add 2 tablespoons water, then cover again and cook for 3 minutes. Remove the pan from the heat. Place the cooked peas and the remaining butter in a blender and purée until smooth. Strain the pea butter using the back of a ladle through a fine-mesh strainer and refrigerate until use.

## FOR THE RISOTTO

2 cups diced bacon (from about 10 slices)

2 tablespoons extra-virgin olive oil

2 cups minced white onion (from about 2 medium onions)

2 tablespoons unsalted butter

2 ½ cups Carnaroli rice

¼ cup white wine

3 cups chicken stock

1 (8-ounce) bag frozen peas, thawed

Shaved Parmesan

Lemon-infused olive oil (or good-quality olive oil)

## TO MAKE THE RISOTTO

Cook the bacon and olive oil together in a sauté pan over high heat for 5–7 minutes. Reserve the bacon and 2 tablespoons of the bacon fat.

In a separate pot, cook the onions in the reserved bacon fat with the butter over medium-high heat until the onions are translucent, about 4 minutes. Add the Carnaroli rice and cook 2 minutes more, stirring constantly. Add the wine and reduce for 1 minute, continuing to stir. Add the chicken stock and bring the mixture to a boil. Continue to stir constantly until all of the liquid has been absorbed, about 6–8 minutes.

Remove the risotto from the heat, scrape down the sides, and let it rest for 15 minutes. Give it a good stir about halfway through to keep the top from drying out and to eliminate any clumps.

Return the risotto to the stove. Add 1 cup hot water and cook over medium-high heat, stirring constantly, until the liquid has been absorbed. Continue to add hot water, about ½ cup at a time, and stir until the risotto is al dente, about 10–12 minutes. Add the peas and pea butter; stir together until the butter is melted. Garnish with shaved Parmesan, crispy bacon, and a drizzle of lemon-infused olive oil.

# Orange-Honey Glazed Carrots

In New England, I was ambivalent about carrots. They never did much to inspire me. But when I moved south, I discovered carrots that were delicate and incredibly sweet. To amplify the natural sweetness of local carrots, I add orange juice and honey. We serve them with Braised Short Ribs with Pommes Anna (page 186), but they also make an excellent seasonal side dish.

3 bunches baby carrots,
    trimmed and peeled
2 tablespoons unsalted butter
2 tablespoons honey
2 teaspoons kosher salt
1 teaspoon grated orange zest
½ cup fresh orange juice
½ teaspoon black pepper

**SERVES 6**

Place all the ingredients into a sauté pan and bring to a boil over high heat, stirring occasionally to coat the carrots evenly. Reduce the heat to low and simmer, covered, for 5 minutes.

Remove the lid and increase the heat to medium. Cook the carrots, stirring occasionally, until the liquid has reduced enough to cling to the carrots, about 10 minutes. If the carrots are still too crunchy at this point, add 1–2 tablespoons water and reduce the liquid again. If the carrots cook too quickly, remove them from the pan and continue to reduce the liquid until it forms a glaze, then briefly toss the carrots in the glaze. Transfer them to a plate and serve immediately.

# Ricotta-Stuffed Delicata Squash with Roasted Pepitas

Delicata squash, as its name suggests, is a winter squash prized for its tender and edible skin. The flesh is nutty and sweet, and it deepens with a proper roasting in the oven. At Stagioni, we serve it as a hearty small plate topped with crispy quinoa. In this recipe, we use roasted pumpkin seeds.

If you cannot find Delicata squash, substitute any winter squash, such as acorn or kabocha. Just remember, the skin will be tougher on these other varieties and the roasting times will vary.

**SERVES 8**

Preheat the oven to 325°. Toss the pepitas with the olive oil and spread them on a baking sheet in a single layer. Roast them for 10–15 minutes, turning occasionally with a spatula, until they are lightly browned. Remove the pan from the oven and toss the pepitas with a pinch of salt. Set aside.

Increase the oven temperature to 400°. Cut the squash lengthwise and scoop out the seeds and pulp. Coat the insides of the squash with 2 tablespoons of the salsa verde. Place the squash halves on a roasting pan lined with parchment, skin-side up. Drizzle them with olive oil and roast for 20–25 minutes, or until they are slightly softened. Remove the squash from the oven and cool to room temperature.

In a stand mixer fitted with a paddle attachment, whip together the ricotta, 1 cup of the mozzarella, the mascarpone, and the remaining salsa verde. Taste and adjust seasoning, then chill the cheese mixture in the refrigerator for 30 minutes (to make it easier to work with).

Increase the oven temperature to 450°. Fill the squash with the chilled cheese filling and top with the remaining mozzarella. Roast for 10–15 minutes, or until the cheese has melted and browned. Top with the dressed arugula and roasted pepitas. Drizzle with extra hot sauce if desired. Serve immediately.

½ cup pepitas

½ teaspoon extra-virgin olive oil, plus more for drizzling

Kosher salt

4 medium Delicata squash

3 tablespoons Salsa Verde (page 9), divided

1 ½ cups whole-milk ricotta or fresh Ricotta (page 33)

1 ½ cups shredded smoked mozzarella, divided

½ cup mascarpone

1 cup baby arugula, tossed lightly with Lemon Vinaigrette (page 17)

# Whole Roasted Cauliflower with Salsa Verde

**1 head cauliflower**

**1 cup (2 sticks) unsalted
butter, plus more for
troubleshooting**

**2 sprigs each fresh rosemary,
oregano, and thyme,
bundled together**

**1 fresh bay leaf**

**Kosher salt**

**1 cup Salsa Verde (page 9)**

Basting an entire head of cauliflower in butter is a feat of endurance. Though the epitome of simplicity, this recipe requires steadfast patience and a strong wrist. At a dinner party, this dish makes for theater of the best kind.

The cauliflower cooks slowly in this recipe, developing a crispy, golden exterior as you baste it with butter. Its subtle sweetness plays nicely with nutty browned butter, while an herbaceous salsa verde balances the richness with a bright acidotic contrast.

---

SERVES 4

Trim the leaves from the cauliflower head, leaving the naked stem intact. Wrap the stem with aluminum foil. Set a deep sauté pan on the stovetop and use a heat-resistant object (such as another pan) to prop the pan toward you at an angle. You want the butter to pool in the bottom curve of the pan. Alternatively, you can use a wok, which allows the butter to pool more easily. A wok ring will make it even easier to prop the cauliflower head as instructed below. Find a large, wide metal spoon to use as a basting spoon.

Melt the butter over medium heat and add the herbs. Place the cauliflower into the pan, propping it up on its stem. Using your basting spoon, scoop the butter from the curve of the pan and baste the cauliflower continuously and consistently for 30 minutes. Find a rhythm.

To slow down cooking and protect the butter from browning too much or too quickly, add more butter to the pan. It should be bubbling and browning, but it should never burn. If the butter burns, switch pans, melt new butter, and keep basting.

After 30 minutes, the cauliflower should be golden in color and cooked through. Use a cake tester to pierce the cauliflower. If it meets some resistance, keep basting, 5–10 minutes more.

To serve family style, serve the entire cauliflower head with a sprinkling of salt and a drizzle of salsa verde, plus more on the side. To serve individually, slice the cauliflower into thick-cut "steaks" and top with salsa verde.

# Fish & Shellfish

New England spoiled me for seafood. In my youth, the routine was to go down to Skip's Dock and shop for fresh fish. I could watch the boats motor in and find fishermen cleaning their latest flounder haul. There were lobster tanks where one could pick out a fresh lobster and a small fish market with cod, tuna, swordfish, and striped bass. Plain and simple, our seafood choices hinged on what was fresh and available.

As a working chef in Boston, seafood was at my fingertips, or at least a quick phone call away. When I moved, it was confusing to discover that most fish was either flown in (which was expensive) or "refreshed" (a term for previously frozen). It took some time, but Charlotte has finally come around to the notion of fresh seafood. Fish that was previously trucked in from Atlanta is now processed in a new facility in our city. Also, there are now fisherman like Tim Griner (see sidebar, page 139) who introduced me to triggerfish and grunt, in addition to the fresh-caught grouper and North Carolina shrimp he brought in weekly from the coast.

In this chapter, you will find an equal blend of dishes that tap into my northern sensibilities, such as Pan-Roasted Cod with New England Clam Chowder, Bacon, and Fingerling Potatoes (page 161) and Swordfish with Summer Succotash (page 140), alongside dishes that evoke the South like Cornmeal-Dusted Catfish with Black-Eyed Peas, Collards, and Red Pepper Broth (page 157) and Bacon-Wrapped Trout with Sweet Potato and Apple Hash (page 146). All make use of fresh seafood and celebrate my time both above and below the Mason-Dixon Line.

# Striped Bass with Wilted Napa Cabbage, Smoked Bacon, and Chardonnay Cream

**FOR THE CABBAGE BRAISE**

4 ounces slab bacon, cut into lardons (¼ × 1-inch long)

1 small head napa cabbage

12 Garlic Confit cloves (page 15) or plain garlic cloves

¼ teaspoon crushed chili flakes

½ cup white wine

½ cup clam juice

1 cup heavy cream

1 tablespoon fresh lemon juice

½ teaspoon kosher salt

Growing up in New England, I had friends with boats. During the summer, we would venture to Narragansett Bay with our fishing rods and troll for striped bass. If we got lucky enough to catch one, we would head in, clean it on the dock, and cook it for dinner. I was pleasantly surprised when I found out that they run off the North Carolina coast, too.

In this midwinter dish, we serve striped bass with cabbage that's practically melted in a flavorful braise of white wine, roasted garlic, cream, and smoked bacon. The crisp skin of the bass provides a nice contrast to the soft textures of the braise.

Striped bass is easy to find at good-quality grocery stores, but this recipe will also work with halibut, black sea bass, and cod.

SERVES 4

TO MAKE THE CABBAGE BRAISE

Place the bacon in a sauté pan over high heat and render the lardons until they are crispy. While the bacon cooks, core the cabbage and slice it into ½-inch-wide ribbons. Add the garlic and chili flakes to the pan, then add the wine, scraping up any browned bits. Reduce the contents by half, then decrease the heat to medium, add the clam juice and cream, and simmer for 3 minutes. Add the cabbage, lemon juice, and salt and return to a simmer, stirring occasionally, about 4–5 minutes. Look for the cabbage to be wilted but still have some texture. Taste and adjust seasoning with more salt, lemon juice, or chili flakes if needed. Keep warm.

## TO MAKE THE STRIPED BASS

Pat the fish dry with a paper towel. Score the skins with a sharp knife in a crosshatch pattern, being careful to cut through the skin but not the flesh. Season the flesh sides with salt and white pepper. Heat a heavy-bottomed sauté pan with vegetable oil over high heat. When the oil is shimmering, add the striped bass, skin-side down. Use a weight, such as a grill press or heavy dish, to prevent the fillets from curling.

After about 4 minutes, carefully check with a spatula to see if the skin has released from the pan. If the skin releases easily, flip the fillets and cook another 4 minutes. If the skin sticks to the pan, leave the fillets alone for another minute and try again. When cooked through, the flesh will be firm and opaque. The skin should be crispy and brown. If there is still some pink, cook for another minute or so.

## TO SERVE

Serve the warm striped bass atop the stewed cabbage and bacon.

**FOR THE STRIPED BASS**

4 (6-ounce) fillets wild striped bass

Kosher salt and ground white pepper

3 tablespoons vegetable oil

# Seared Scallops with Pesto Pasta, Tomato Confit, and Lemon Cream Sauce

This dish is personal to me. It was the first composed dish I made for my mother on enrolling in culinary school. I wanted to make a plate that captured summer and showed off what I had learned. In our seafood class, we had recently practiced searing a scallop to develop a golden-brown outer crust and a tender, sweet center. With this in mind I formulated a plan. I grabbed a box of angel hair pasta from the pantry and ventured into the garden to find the rest of the ingredients. My mom was impressed with the result. I think it was then that she realized I had found my passion.

I recommend purchasing dry-pack scallops because they sear the best. "Wet" scallops are treated with a water solution and a preservative called tripolyphosphate. However, this method of preservation causes wet scallops to retain water, which alters the flavor and jeopardizes the perfect sear.

**SPECIAL EQUIPMENT:** butcher's twine

**SERVES 5**

## TO MAKE THE TOMATO CONFIT
Combine the olive oil and garlic in a saucepan over medium-high heat. Heat until the garlic gets a touch of color, about 2 minutes. Carefully add the tomatoes (they might spit due to their high water content) and cook them until they blister, about 4 minutes. Tie the herbs together with the twine and add them to the pot, along with the chili flakes, black pepper, and salt. Turn off the heat, stir the mixture together, and let it rest. Discard the herbs. Set aside.

## TO MAKE THE PASTA
Bring a pot of water seasoned with 1 tablespoon of the salt to a rolling boil. Meanwhile, heat a nonstick pan with the olive oil over high heat. Once the oil is shimmering, add the corn and season with the remaining salt and the pepper. Cook for 2 minutes, or long enough to add a touch of color, then set aside.

Cook the pasta according to the package instructions. Drain the pasta, rinse it under cold water, and toss it with olive oil to prevent sticking. Hold at room temperature.

**FOR THE TOMATO CONFIT**
1 cup extra-virgin olive oil
10 garlic cloves, peeled
2 cups cherry or golden tomatoes
6 sprigs fresh thyme
6 sprigs fresh parsley
1 fresh bay leaf
½ teaspoon crushed chili flakes
½ teaspoon black pepper
1 teaspoon kosher salt

**FOR THE PASTA**
1 tablespoon plus ½ teaspoon kosher salt, divided
2 tablespoons extra-virgin olive oil, plus more for coating the cooked pasta
2 cups fresh corn kernels
½ teaspoon black pepper
1 pound angel hair pasta
6 Roma tomatoes, seeded and diced

## FOR THE SCALLOPS

1 ½ pounds U-10 dry-pack
    scallops (about 3 scallops
    per person)

Kosher salt and black pepper

Neutral oil, such as grapeseed
    or canola

## FOR THE LEMON CREAM SAUCE

4 tablespoons (½ stick)
    unsalted butter, divided

1 medium shallot, sliced thin

1 teaspoon chopped fresh
    thyme

¼ teaspoon kosher salt

¼ teaspoon ground white
    pepper

¼ cup white wine

2 tablespoons fresh lemon
    juice

½ cup heavy cream

1 recipe Basil Pesto (page 17)

## TO MAKE THE SCALLOPS

Pat the scallops dry with a paper towel and season them with salt and pepper. Heat a nonstick pan over medium-high heat. Add enough oil to coat the bottom of the pan, then add the scallops in a single layer (working in batches if necessary) and sear them until they are golden, 2–4 minutes. Flip them gently and sear for 2 minutes more. Transfer the scallops to a plate lined with paper towels. Remove the excess oil from the pan and return it to the stovetop.

## TO MAKE THE LEMON CREAM SAUCE

Add 1 tablespoon of the butter to the pan, along with the shallots, thyme, salt, and white pepper. Cook over medium-low heat until the shallots have softened, then add the wine and lemon juice and bring to a boil. Reduce the contents by half, then whisk in the cream. Return the sauce to a boil, then whisk in the remaining butter.

## TO ASSEMBLE

Using your hands, toss ¼ cup of the pesto with the pasta, then add the tomatoes and corn and toss again. Add more pesto, if desired. Place into a large pasta bowl or 4 individual bowls, then spoon the lemon cream sauce around the perimeter. Place the scallops on top of the pasta (or 3 scallops per person, if plating individually), and spoon the tomato confit over the top.

# Tim Griner, Charlotte Fish Company

As a New England native, I find seafood integral to life. By that I mean fresh seafood, just off the boats. It wasn't unusual to watch the fishermen deliver their haul to the local dock and do our shopping as they unloaded their catch. Clamming was a pastime for us kids, too, as was grabbing mussels from the breakwater. Inside the Boston restaurants where I worked, we had similar access. Fresh fish was just a phone call away.

All this is to say that things were vastly different when I got to Charlotte, and it's why I'm thankful to have Tim Griner, our "fish guy," as one of our primary producers. Before meeting Tim, I often struggled to find the high-quality seafood I wanted. Too much of what was available was being shipped from all over the world, and that just didn't make sense to me because we have great fishing grounds just three hours away.

Tim owns the Charlotte Fish Company, a small, sustainable seafood business that promises fresh fish, as his company motto goes, "from our dock to your dinner table." Though that sounds like an easy proposition, the seafood business is substantially more complicated. A civil engineer by trade, Tim ventured into the fishing industry in the wake of the 2008 housing crisis. Before that, he had worked for a commercial construction development company that began to decline in 2006 and came to a screeching halt by 2008.

As he remembers it, "I'd still go to the office and we'd sit around twiddling our thumbs and think about what we were going to do all day. I finally said, 'I'm going fishing.'" This was nothing new for Tim, who had fished all his life. He had even done some commercial fishing with his college roommate in Wilmington.

Fishing started out as a hobby, for friends and family, with Tim delivering fish to loved ones and eating it himself because he couldn't find it fresher elsewhere. By 2009, he started getting calls. People were asking him to sell them fish, something he couldn't do without going professional. From that point, Tim unpacked the dizzying pile of regulations, permits, and licensing riddles of the commercial fishing realm to fulfill the promise of fresh fish without the middleman.

If he was going to sell fish, Tim said, he wanted it never to touch another's hand. To do that, he had to gain control of the entire supply chain, an arduous process that took a year and half to attain. In 2010, he walked into Barrington's. He had a pickup full of coolers packed with ice and fresh whole fish of the caliber I had seen only back in New England. Tim brings in lots of grouper and snapper from the Carolina coast, but also black bass, triggerfish, and bluefish, among others. We began buying from him instantly and look forward to seeing his truck pull up, the energetic ball-capped fisherman eager to show off his catch.

As I see it, we help each other. I'm able to support his business across three restaurants, and Tim brings us the freshest product around. It's a partnership that I couldn't do without.

# Swordfish with Summer Succotash

**FOR THE SWORDFISH**

3 tablespoons extra-virgin
    olive oil

4 (1-inch-thick) swordfish
    steaks

Kosher salt and black pepper

**FOR THE SUCCOTASH**

3 tablespoons extra-virgin
    olive oil

4 ears of corn, kernels cut
    from cob

1 small yellow onion, diced

3 cups fresh (or frozen) lima
    beans

½ cup cherry tomatoes,
    quartered

½ cup white wine

1 teaspoon fresh lemon juice

½ cup clam juice

1 cup heavy cream

2 teaspoons kosher salt, plus
    more for seasoning

½ teaspoon ground white
    pepper

¼ cup Basil Pesto (page 17),
    or more as desired

Black pepper

This is my go-to dish in the summertime, when I gather all that's good about the season from the local farmers' market. I use swordfish because it's always been my favorite, but this recipe works well with other white, meaty fish, including wahoo and cobia.

**SPECIAL EQUIPMENT:** high-speed blender

**SERVES 4**

### TO MAKE THE SWORDFISH

Preheat the oven to 400°. Heat the olive oil in a large, ovenproof pan over medium-high heat. Season the swordfish with salt and pepper on both sides and add the steaks to the pan. Sear them until a golden crust develops on the bottom, about 3–4 minutes. Flip the steaks, then finish them in the oven, about 10 minutes more. When ready, the fish should be just barely cooked through. Meanwhile, cook the succotash.

### TO MAKE THE SUCCOTASH

Get a pan screaming hot, then add the olive oil. Add the corn and toss the kernels for 2 minutes, until they have a little color. Add the onions and cook for 1 minute, then add the lima beans and cook for 1 minute more, continually tossing. Add the tomatoes, cook for 1 minute, then add the wine, lemon juice, and clam juice. Let the wine cook off, about 3–5 minutes, then add the cream, salt, and pepper, and simmer for 4 minutes. The mixture will reduce and thicken slightly. Once it reduces, turn off the heat and stir in the pesto. Add more pesto, if desired.

### TO ASSEMBLE

For each serving, spoon some succotash on a plate or into a wide, shallow bowl. Top with a swordfish steak and garnish with extra basil.

# Grouper with Creamy Grits and Tomato Vinaigrette

**FOR THE GRITS**

1½ cups grits (preferably
    Anson Mills Antebellum
    Coarse Yellow Grits)

2 cups whole milk

3 tablespoons unsalted butter

1 medium yellow onion, cut
    into ½-inch dice

2 teaspoons kosher salt

½ teaspoon ground white
    pepper

**FOR THE FISH**

Vegetable oil

6 (6-ounce) grouper fillets,
    skinned

Kosher salt and ground
    white pepper

Our fish guy, Tim Griner (see sidebar, page 139), is known for his fresh grouper. His model is simple: catch fish off the North Carolina coast and deliver it directly to the customer within a day. We have a similar model: purchase only the fish we'll serve in a day's time. This dish allows fresh fish to shine, paired with creamy grits and an herb-enriched vinaigrette.

**SERVES 6**

TO MAKE THE GRITS

In a mixing bowl, cover the grits with 3 cups of cold water. Skim any hulls that float to the top with a fine-mesh strainer. Drain the grits and set aside. Bring the milk and 4 cups of water to a simmer over high heat. Once simmering, remove from the heat.

Meanwhile, add the butter to a heavy-bottomed saucepan. Melt the butter over medium heat, then add the onions and sweat them until they are translucent. Add the grits and stir them with a wooden spoon until they are coated with the butter. (This helps prevent clumping.) Pour the hot milk mixture over the grits and stir constantly until they return to a simmer, then reduce the heat to low and stir occasionally for 40 minutes. The grits should be tender and creamy with a slight bite. Season with salt and pepper. Keep the grits warm until assembly time.

TO MAKE THE FISH

Coat the bottom of a large skillet with oil and place over high heat. Test the pan to see if it is hot enough by placing the corner of the fish in the oil. If it sizzles, it's ready. Carefully lower the fish into the pan, and gently drop the fillet away from you. This will help prevent painful oil splashes. Work in batches to avoid overcrowding.

Cook the fillets over high heat for about 3 minutes. When the bottom edges begin to turn brown, use a spatula to gently lift the fish. If ready, it should release from the pan easily. If it doesn't, cook for 1 minute more and check again. Once it releases, reduce the heat to medium and cook for another 5 minutes, or until the bottom has browned ⅛ inch up the sides. Flip the fillets and cook for 2 minutes more, then turn off the heat and keep the fish in the hot pan for another 3–4 minutes. The fish should be barely cooked through but opaque and white. If there is any pink, cook the fillets on medium heat for another 1–2 minutes, then transfer the fish to a plate.

## TO MAKE THE VINAIGRETTE

Whisk all the ingredients except for the tomatoes together in a small bowl. Gently toss the tomatoes in the vinaigrette, then season with salt and pepper to taste.

## TO ASSEMBLE

Ladle the grits into a shallow bowl. Add the fish, then spoon approximately 2 tablespoons of the vinaigrette over it and serve immediately.

**FOR THE VINAIGRETTE**

**1 medium shallot, minced**
**1 garlic clove, minced**
**2 tablespoons extra-virgin olive oil**
**2 tablespoons sherry vinegar**
**2 tablespoons chopped fresh basil**
**2 tablespoons chopped fresh parsley**
**½ teaspoon sugar**
**½ teaspoon chopped fresh oregano**
**¼ teaspoon chopped fresh thyme**
**2 large, ripe tomatoes, cut into 1-inch dice**
**Kosher salt and black pepper**

# Batter-Dipped Cod with Coleslaw, Ramp Tartar Sauce, and Malt Vinegar Reduction

**FOR THE MALT VINEGAR REDUCTION**

2 cups malt vinegar

1 cup sugar

**FOR THE COLESLAW**

2 medium carrots, peeled and
    cut into 2-inch segments

½ head green cabbage

1 medium red bell pepper,
    julienned (cut into
    ⅛ × 2-inch batons)

½ teaspoon kosher salt

1 teaspoon sugar

2 tablespoons rice vinegar

½ cup Duke's mayonnaise

¼ teaspoon celery seeds

¼ teaspoon ground white
    pepper

A New England fish fry often features golden fried pieces of batter-dipped cod. In this recipe, my New England sensibilities collide with one of my favorite Appalachian food discoveries: ramps. I pickle them (page 24) to use throughout the year in recipes like this tartar sauce, which pairs nicely with the airily crisp beer batter. A creamy slaw accented with celery seeds and rice vinegar rounds out the dish. This is my version of fish and chips, and I love to eat it with a side of french fries (page 109).

*Note:* If you don't have access to ramps, you can substitute scallions. In the South, many cooks prefer using Duke's mayonnaise, which has a richer, creamier texture and contains no sugar. If it's not available locally, purchase it online or just use another mayonnaise. If you can't find cod, you can substitute another mild white fish, such as grouper, mahi, or black sea bass, in its place.

**SPECIAL EQUIPMENT:** mandoline, cooking thermometer

**SERVES 6–8**

**TO MAKE THE MALT VINEGAR REDUCTION**
In a small saucepan, bring the vinegar and sugar to a boil over high heat; reduce the heat to medium low and simmer until the mixture thickens enough to coat the back of a spoon, about 25–30 minutes. (If the reduction starts to boil over, decrease the heat slightly.) Allow the sauce to cool. As the reduction cools to room temperature, it should reach the consistency of corn syrup. Set aside.

**TO MAKE THE COLESLAW**
Using the julienne blade on a mandoline, shave the carrot segments lengthwise (minding your fingers). Remove the julienne blade. Cut the cabbage in quarters and use the mandoline or a knife to cut it into thin ribbons.

In a large mixing bowl, toss the carrots, cabbage, and bell peppers with the salt and sugar. Allow the mixture to sit for 30 minutes to extract moisture. Drain the vegetables in a colander, gently squeezing them to remove additional liquid. Return the vegetables to the bowl and add the vinegar, mayonnaise, celery seeds, and white pepper. Toss well. Cover and refrigerate until use.

## TO MAKE THE TARTAR SAUCE

Finely chop the ramps, capers, parsley, and chives together. In a medium bowl, fold them with the lemon zest, lemon juice, Tabasco sauce, and mayonnaise. Cover and refrigerate until use.

## TO MAKE THE COD

In a medium bowl, whisk together the flour, cornstarch, baking powder, and salt. Whisk in the beer until it is fully incorporated. The batter should thinly coat the fillets. Any excess should drip off slowly.

Fill an 8-quart pot almost halfway with vegetable oil and heat to 350°. Make sure there is ample room left at the top to prevent oil from splashing out. Line a sheet pan with paper towels. Take one portion of cod and dip it into the beer batter. Allow excess batter to drop off, then gently submerge the fish into the hot oil. Fry until golden and cooked through, about 5 minutes. Using tongs, transfer the fish to the sheet pan. Repeat the process with the remaining portions.

To serve, sprinkle the cod with coarse sea salt. Top with coleslaw and a drizzle of the malt vinegar reduction. Serve with tartar sauce on the side.

**FOR THE TARTAR SAUCE**
¼ cup Ramp Pickles (page 24)
1 tablespoon capers
1 teaspoon chopped fresh
    parsley
1 teaspoon chopped fresh
    chives
Zest of 1 lemon
½ teaspoon fresh lemon juice
Dash Tabasco sauce
1 cup Duke's mayonnaise

**FOR THE COD**
1 cup flour
½ cup cornstarch
1 tablespoon baking powder
½ teaspoon kosher salt
1 (12-ounce) bottle of light
    beer (minus 1 long sip)
1 gallon vegetable oil
1 ½–2 pounds cod, cut into
    2–2 ½-ounce portions
Coarse sea salt

# Bacon-Wrapped Trout with Sweet Potato and Apple Hash

**6 (8-ounce) boneless trout,
cleaned and skinned**

**18 slices thin-cut bacon**

**FOR THE HASH**

**1 tablespoon fresh sage
(about 6 leaves)**

**½ teaspoon fresh thyme**

**4 tablespoons neutral oil,
such as grapeseed or
canola, divided**

**2 large sweet potatoes,
cut into ½-inch dice**

**1 large yellow onion, cut into
¼-inch dice**

**2 large green apples, peeled,
cut into 1-inch dice**

**1 tablespoon unsalted butter**

**½ teaspoon kosher salt**

**¼ teaspoon black pepper**

High-quality trout is readily available to us, thanks to local purveyors like Sunburst Trout Farms, a family farm located in the mountains of western North Carolina. In this recipe, fresh trout fillets are wrapped with bacon and pan seared for a crisp exterior. We serve the fish with a sweet potato and apple hash that works especially well in the cooler months. If trout is difficult to find, you can substitute catfish, black bass, cod, or another mild white fish.

---

SERVES 6

.............................................................................................................................

Stack the 2 halves of each trout together, with the former skin sides facing out.

Lay 3 slices of bacon vertically on a work surface, overlapping them like shingles; repeat to make 5 more sets. Center a whole trout, positioned horizontally, on a set of the 3 bacon slices, leaving a 1-inch space at the bottom. Fold the inch of bacon over the side of the trout, then roll it away from you until the trout is completely wrapped. Repeat with the remaining trout. Place the fish on a sheet tray, cover with plastic wrap, and refrigerate until ready to cook.

TO MAKE THE HASH

Finely chop the sage and thyme together; set aside. Heat a cast-iron skillet over high heat. Add 2 tablespoons of the oil, then the sweet potatoes. Cook for 5 minutes, tossing to get color on all sides. Add the onions and cook for 2 minutes, then add the apples and cook 2 minutes more. Add the butter to the pan and toss together. Add the herbs and toss again. The sweet potatoes should be tender. If not, place the skillet in a 350° oven for 10 minutes to finish them. Season with salt and pepper.

## TO MAKE THE BEURRE BLANC

In a small saucepan, combine all the ingredients except the butter and salt and bring the sauce to a rapid boil. Reduce the liquid completely, about 10 minutes, stirring only to avoid burning. Reduce the heat to low and whisk in the cold butter, a few cubes at a time. Once the butter is fully incorporated, remove the sauce from the heat, add the salt, and strain it to remove any solids. Keep warm until the trout is ready.

## TO COOK THE TROUT

Heat the remaining oil over medium-high heat. Season the fillets lightly with salt and pepper. Working in batches (or using multiple pans at once to speed things up), cook the trout until the bacon is browned and crispy on one side, about 6 minutes. Flip the fillets and cook until the bacon is browned on the other side.

To serve, place the trout atop the sweet potato hash and drizzle with the warm beurre blanc.

**FOR THE BEURRE BLANC**

½ cup white wine
½ cup apple cider
¼ cup apple cider vinegar
¼ cup heavy cream
¼ cup chicken stock
4 fresh sage leaves
6 sprigs fresh thyme
1 large shallot
1 teaspoon whole black peppercorns
1 teaspoon ground coriander
8 tablespoons (1 stick) cold unsalted butter, cubed
½ teaspoon kosher salt

# Blackened Mahi with Tomato Gazpacho, Avocado Salsa, and Crab Cakes

This dish is inspired by walks through the farmers' market at the height of summertime, when tomatoes, peppers, and cucumbers are practically spilling from the market stands. The hot and humid days of July and August demand a cooling gazpacho, and they also mark the time when mahi and crab are readily available from the North Carolina coast.

I like to play with hot and cold elements in the same dish. Here, a fresh avocado salsa and the gazpacho are kept cool, while the blackened mahi and crab cake are served warm.

While not necessary, I recommend making the crab cakes a day in advance because they'll hold together better.

**SERVES 4**

### TO MAKE THE CRAB CAKES

In a small bowl, mix together the celery, onions, bell peppers, jalapeños, mustard, and mayonnaise. Add the eggs and thoroughly incorporate them, then add the Old Bay Seasoning, Tabasco, lemon juice, and salt; mix thoroughly. Add the panko and crab meat and mix again. Use a small ice cream scoop to portion the crab cakes. Form each cake into a 1-inch-thick disc, then arrange them on a sheet pan and cover it with plastic wrap. Refrigerate overnight.

**FOR THE CRAB CAKES**

2 celery ribs, cut into ¼-inch dice

¼ medium red onion, cut into ¼-inch dice

½ large red bell pepper, seeded, ribs removed, and cut into ¼-inch dice

½ jalapeño, seeded and cut into ¼-inch dice

½ cup whole-grain mustard

½ cup Duke's mayonnaise

2 large eggs

1 tablespoon Old Bay Seasoning

Dash Tabasco sauce

1 tablespoon fresh lemon juice

½ teaspoon kosher salt

2 cups panko

1 pound jumbo lump crab meat, shells removed

Unsalted butter, for cooking

**FOR THE GAZPACHO**

2 slices white bread, crusts
    removed and cubed
½ cup extra-virgin olive oil
1 small red onion, roughly
    chopped
2 large red bell peppers,
    seeded and roughly
    chopped
3 European cucumbers,
    peeled and roughly
    chopped
½ jalapeño, seeded
6 Roma tomatoes, ends
    removed and roughly
    chopped
5 garlic cloves
1 orange, zested and juiced
2 limes, zested and juiced
1 lemon, zested and juiced
½ cup loosely packed cilantro
    leaves (from about 5 stems)
1 tablespoon Old Bay
    Seasoning
Dash Tabasco sauce
3 cups tomato juice
1 tablespoon kosher salt

**FOR THE AVOCADO SALSA**

2 avocados, cut into
    ½-inch dice
1 tablespoon red pepper,
    cut into ¼-inch dice
1 tablespoon red onion,
    cut into ¼-inch dice
1 garlic clove, crushed
Juice of 1 lime
Dash Tabasco sauce
½ teaspoon kosher salt
¼ teaspoon black pepper

**FOR THE BLACKENING SPICE**

¼ cup paprika
2 tablespoons chili powder
½ teaspoon cayenne pepper
1 teaspoon granulated garlic
1 teaspoon dried oregano
1 teaspoon dried thyme

TO MAKE THE GAZPACHO

In a small bowl, soak the bread cubes in the olive oil, pressing them down gently. Allow the oil to saturate the bread for a few minutes.

Meanwhile, blend the remaining ingredients for 1–2 minutes on medium speed until you have a slightly chunky texture. Add the bread cubes and oil to the blender and pulse several times on low speed, for 2–3 seconds each time. Pulsing keeps the oil from emulsifying, which protects the soup's vivid color.

Strain the gazpacho through a large-holed strainer to remove the tomato skins and anything that did not break down. Refrigerate until use.

TO MAKE THE AVOCADO SALSA

Mash half an avocado with the back of a fork until smooth. Add the other half of the avocado, along with the remaining ingredients; gently mix to incorporate. Season with salt and pepper; set aside.

TO MAKE THE BLACKENING SPICE

Combine all the ingredients in a small bowl. Set aside.

## TO ASSEMBLE

Preheat the oven to 350°.

In a large sauté pan set over medium heat, melt enough butter to cover the bottom by 1/8 inch. After the foam subsides, add the crab cakes, working in batches to avoid overcrowding. Fry until the cakes are golden brown and warmed through, about 3 minutes on each side. Drain the crab cakes on a plate lined with paper towels. Transfer them to a sheet pan and keep warm in the oven while you cook the fish.

Sprinkle the tops of the fillets with salt and pepper. Dredge that same side in the blackening spice, coating well.

Heat the oil in a large sauté pan over high heat. When the oil shimmers, carefully place the fish, spice-side down, into the pan. (If necessary, work in batches.) Immediately reduce the heat to medium to prevent scorching. Cook until the bottom third of the fillets turn opaque, about 4–5 minutes. Flip the fish and continue to cook until the fillets are completely firm (another 4–5 minutes, depending on thickness).

To serve, ladle enough gazpacho into a wide bowl to cover it with 1/4 inch of soup. Arrange 2 crab cakes in the middle of the bowl, creating a base to hold up the fish. Add the fish, then top the fillet with a generous spoonful of avocado salsa. Drizzle with extra-virgin olive oil to finish.

**FOR THE MAHI**

**4 (6-ounce) mahi fillets, skinned**

**Kosher salt and black pepper**

**3 tablespoons vegetable oil**

# Tilefish Schnitzel with Poached Egg and Shaved Fennel

1 pound tilefish, cleaned,
  skinned, and filleted
1 large fennel bulb, including
  fronds
¼ cup neutral oil, such as
  grapeseed or canola
Squeeze of fresh lemon juice
Kosher salt and black pepper

**FOR THE VINAIGRETTE**
1 medium shallot, chopped
¼ cup Dijon mustard
2 tablespoons apple cider
  vinegar
2 tablespoons white wine
  vinegar
1 tablespoon honey
1 large egg yolk
1 teaspoon Garlic Confit
  (page 15) or finely
  minced garlic
1 teaspoon fresh thyme
½ cup neutral oil, such as
  grapeseed or canola
¼ cup whole-grain mustard

When fresh tilefish shows up from the Carolina coast, we get excited. Tilefish has a delicate, sweet flavor and cooks up white and flaky.

In this recipe, a traditional German schnitzel gets the Good Food on Montford treatment with a twist that swaps veal for fish. We pound it thin, bread it, and crisp it in the frying pan. To round out the dish, we add a poached egg for extra richness, along with a mustard vinaigrette and fresh fennel for brightness and acidity. If you cannot find tilefish, you can substitute grouper or use chicken or veal for a more traditional schnitzel.

*Note:* Fresh farm eggs are the best eggs for this recipe. Try to find some at your local farmers' market.

**SPECIAL EQUIPMENT:** mandoline, meat mallet

**SERVES 4**

Slice the tilefish into 4 equal portions, about 4 ounces each. Place the fillets between 2 pieces of plastic wrap and use the smooth side of a meat mallet to pound them gently to ¼ inch thick. Remove the fillets from the plastic wrap and set aside.

Trim the stalks from the top of the fennel bulb; remove and discard any wilted outer layers. Cut a few of the delicate fronds from the stalks and chop enough to yield ½ cup. Place the fronds in a small mixing bowl and set aside. Using a mandoline, shave the fennel bulb paper thin. Add the shaved fennel to the mixing bowl and cover with water and ice. Set aside.

TO MAKE THE VINAIGRETTE
Combine the shallots, Dijon mustard, both vinegars, honey, egg yolk, garlic, and thyme in a blender and purée on high speed until smooth. With the blender running, slowly add the oil and emulsify. Transfer the vinaigrette to a small bowl and stir in the whole-grain mustard. Set aside.

## TO BREAD AND COOK THE SCHNITZEL

Preheat the oven to 225°. Place the flour into a shallow bowl. Whisk the eggs with salt and place them in a second bowl. Put the panko into a third bowl or on a plate.

Season the fish with salt and pepper. Dredge a fish fillet in the flour and gently shake off any excess before dipping it into the egg wash. Allow the excess to drip off, then gently press all sides into the bread crumbs until the fillet is fully coated. Repeat this process with the remaining portions.

Coat a large pan with the oil over medium-high heat. Test to see if the oil is at the proper temperature by dipping a corner of one fish portion into the oil. If the oil gently bubbles, add the fish to the pan. Cook the fillets until they are golden brown, about 2 minutes. Flip the fish and cook for 2 minutes more, or until the breading on that side is also golden brown. Transfer the fish to a baking sheet lined with paper towels to drain, then keep it warm in the oven.

## TO MAKE THE POACHED EGGS

Fill a 2-quart pot with water; add the vinegar and salt. Bring the water to a gentle simmer over medium-low heat. Crack the eggs into separate containers. Gently stir the water in a circular motion to create a whirlpool. Quickly ease 1 egg at a time into the center. Poach the eggs for 3 minutes, or until the whites are opaque and set. Gently remove the eggs with a slotted spoon and place them on a warm plate.

## TO ASSEMBLE

Drain the fennel and fronds. Pat the fennel dry to remove excess moisture, then toss it lightly with the lemon juice and a pinch of salt. Place 1 piece of schnitzel on a plate and spoon about 2 tablespoons of the vinaigrette around the edges. Top the schnitzel with a poached egg, then garnish the plate with the fennel. Serve immediately.

**FOR THE BREADING**

1 cup all-purpose flour

6 large eggs

1 teaspoon kosher salt

2 cups panko

**FOR THE POACHED EGGS**

2 tablespoons distilled white vinegar

1 tablespoon kosher salt

4 large eggs

# Halibut with Crab-Stuffed Zucchini Blossoms

Zucchini blossoms are a summertime delicacy, commonly found in Latin and Italian cuisines. At Stagioni, we stuff them with a crab and mascarpone filling, dip them in an effervescent Prosecco batter, and fry them. They make a worthy companion to a perfectly seared piece of halibut, basted in butter until it is golden brown.

Zucchini blossoms can be tough to find at a standard grocery store. Look for *flor de calabaza* in Latin groceries or international markets or check your local farmers' market.

**SPECIAL EQUIPMENT:** stand mixer with paddle attachment, piping bag, tweezer, thermometer

**SERVES 4**

**FOR THE HALIBUT**

**4 (6-ounce) halibut fillets**

**Kosher salt**

**2 tablespoons extra-virgin olive oil**

**1 tablespoon unsalted butter**

**3 sprigs fresh thyme**

**Juice of ½ lemon**

## TO MAKE THE HALIBUT

Preheat the oven to 400°. Generously season the halibut fillets with salt on both sides. Heat an ovenproof sauté pan with the olive oil over high heat. When the oil is shimmering, add the fillets, flesh-side down, and cook them for 1 minute. Reduce the heat to medium high and cook for 1 minute more. Turn off the heat and place the fish into the preheated oven for 2 minutes. Flip the fillets and return them to the oven for 3 minutes more. Remove the halibut from the oven and cover it loosely with foil; it will be finished on the stovetop later.

1 tablespoon unsalted butter

1 cup zucchini, seeded and cut
   into ⅛-inch dice

1 cup yellow squash, seeded
   and cut into ⅛-inch dice

1 medium red bell pepper,
   seeded and cut into ⅛-
   inch dice

1 cup mascarpone

½ cup plus 1 tablespoon
   cream cheese (5 ounces),
   softened

Zest and juice of 1 lemon

1 tablespoon kosher salt,
   plus more to taste, divided

1 tablespoon chopped fresh
   chives

1 tablespoon chopped fresh
   parsley

½ pound lump crab, drained

8 zucchini blossoms

Neutral oil, such as grapeseed
   or canola

1 cup all-purpose flour

1 cup tapioca flour (or corn
   starch)

1 tablespoon baking powder

2 teaspoons kosher salt

1½ cups Prosecco

1½ cups soda water

## TO MAKE THE ZUCCHINI BLOSSOMS

Heat the butter in a pan over high heat. Add the zucchini, squash, and bell peppers with a pinch of salt and sauté them until softened, about 4 minutes. Remove from the heat and let cool.

In the bowl of a stand mixer fitted with the paddle attachment, combine the mascarpone, cream cheese, lemon zest and juice, salt, chives, and parsley. Add the cooled vegetables and paddle together on medium speed. Remove the bowl from the stand mixer and fold in the crab with a spatula. Place the filling into a piping bag and set aside.

Trim the stems of the zucchini blossoms, leaving ½ inch intact. Using a tweezer, remove the pistil from the center of each blossom. Place the piping tip toward the back of a blossom and fill it three-quarters full, then close with a gentle twist. Repeat the process until all the blossoms are filled.

Fill a large pot halfway with oil and heat to 350°. Meanwhile, whisk together both flours, baking powder, and salt. Combine the Prosecco and soda water in a separate bowl, then add the liquid to the dry ingredients and whisk again, breaking up any lumps.

Line a plate with paper towels. Hold each blossom by the stem end to dredge in the batter. Slowly place the tip of a blossom into the hot oil, moving it back and forth a few times before lowering completely. Working in batches, fry the blossoms for 4 minutes, or until they are golden brown. Using a slotted spoon, gently remove the blossoms and transfer them to the plate. Remove excess fry bits from oil between batches. Set aside.

## TO FINISH THE HALIBUT

Melt the butter in a sauté pan over high heat, then add the thyme and lemon, followed by the halibut. Use the butter to baste the fillets for 2 minutes, tilting the pan toward you and repeatedly scooping the butter on the fish with a spoon. The halibut is done when it has a golden crust and an internal temperature of 145°.

## TO ASSEMBLE

Place 2 blossoms on each plate and add a halibut fillet. Serve immediately.

# Cornmeal-Dusted Catfish with Black-Eyed Peas, Collards, and Red Pepper Broth

When I first opened Barrington's, customers complained that there were no traditional southern dishes on the menu. I addressed this by settling on three standards: catfish, collards, and black-eyed peas. The combination far exceeded my expectations and ushered in my appreciation for local ingredients.

You'll have plenty of black-eyed peas and mayonnaise left over. Try making Field Pea Salad with Red Wine Vinaigrette (page 120) by combining them with finely diced celery, onions, and carrots, along with some olive oil, red wine vinegar, and hot sauce.

*Note*: The collards take a while to cook down, so start them first and work on the rest while they cook. If you make the collards in advance, you can reheat them right before cooking the catfish.

### SERVES 6

Place the catfish fillets in a storage container and completely cover them with buttermilk. Refrigerate for 60–90 minutes. Prepare the collards according to the instructions on page 118.

#### TO MAKE THE BLACK-EYED PEAS
Drain the peas from their soaking liquid. Add oil to a heavy-bottomed pot and sweat the celery, carrots, and onions over medium-high heat until they start to soften. Add the peas, bay leaves, and chicken stock and bring to a boil. Reduce the heat and simmer for 45 minutes, or until the peas are tender but still holding their shape. While they cook, make the red pepper broth and spicy mayo.

#### TO MAKE THE BROTH
Combine the onions, peppers, and wine in a pot over medium heat. Cover and cook 15 minutes. Add the clam juice and 1 cup water, and simmer uncovered for 20–25 minutes. Transfer the broth to a blender, add Tabasco and salt, and blend on high speed. Pass through a fine-mesh sieve for a smooth texture. Set aside.

6 (6-ounce) catfish fillets

3 cups whole-milk buttermilk

1 recipe New South Collards (page 118)

Neutral oil, such as grapeseed or canola

**FOR THE BLACK-EYED PEAS**

20 ounces dried black-eyed peas, soaked overnight

Neutral oil, such as grapeseed or canola

2 celery ribs, cut into ¼-inch dice

1 medium carrot, cut into ¼-inch dice

1 small yellow onion, cut into ¼-inch dice

4 fresh bay leaves

4 cups chicken stock

1 teaspoon kosher salt

1 teaspoon black pepper

**FOR THE BROTH**

1 medium yellow onion, roughly chopped

2 red bell peppers, seeded, roughly chopped

1 cup white wine

1 cup clam juice

2 dashes Tabasco sauce

½ teaspoon kosher salt

**FOR THE SPICY MAYO**

½ cup Duke's mayonnaise

1 teaspoon fresh lime juice

Dash Tabasco sauce

½ teaspoon chili powder

½ teaspoon paprika

**FOR THE CATFISH DREDGE**

1 cup all-purpose flour

½ cup medium-grind
    cornmeal

½ teaspoon paprika

1 teaspoon chili powder

Extra-virgin olive oil, for
    drizzling

## TO MAKE THE SPICY MAYO

Whisk together all the ingredients and refrigerate until use.

## TO FINISH THE BLACK-EYED PEAS

Remove the bay leaves from the peas, then strain and reserve their liquid. Combine ¼ cup of this liquid with ½ cup of the peas and mash them together with a fork or potato masher. Stir the mash back into the peas. Season with salt and pepper.

## TO DREDGE AND COOK THE CATFISH

Remove the catfish from the buttermilk and season the fillets with salt and pepper. Combine the flour, cornmeal, paprika, and chili powder in a medium bowl. Dredge each fillet in the mixture and set aside.

Heat a large skillet with ½ inch oil until shimmering. Add the fillets, one at a time, being careful not to splash hot oil. Cook for 3 minutes, or until the edges are golden brown, then flip the fish and cook for 2 minutes more. Transfer the catfish to a plate lined with paper towels to drain.

## TO ASSEMBLE

For each serving, add red pepper broth to a wide bowl and drizzle it with olive oil. Add a scoop of black-eyed peas, topped with warmed collard greens followed by a catfish fillet. Finish with a dollop of spicy mayo.

# Pan-Roasted Cod with New England Clam Chowder, Bacon, and Fingerling Potatoes

Ok, I admit it. Even after seventeen years of living in the South and coming to love its culture, I still miss New England. I miss the summers on the shores of Matunuck, Rhode Island. I miss the excursions to Skip's Dock, where we would pick out fresh cod and purchase candy necklaces to eat on the way home. I miss the annual Labor Day clambake at Willow Dell Beach Club, a big bash that was a bittersweet close to the season. If Cornmeal-Dusted Catfish with Black-Eyed Peas, Collards, and Red Pepper Broth (page 157) is my ode to the South, this cod with clam chowder is my homage to the North.

**SPECIAL EQUIPMENT:** cheesecloth, butcher's twine

**SERVES 4**

Prepare an ice bath. Rinse the clams in a container of cold water 2 times to remove excess sand. For the third and final rinse, add cold water to the container, then gently pull the clams out of the water to allow any additional sand to settle to the bottom of the container. Transfer the clams to the ice bath and set aside.

## TO MAKE THE POTATOES

Place the baby potatoes in a pot with the salt and enough water to cover. Bundle the peppercorns, coriander, bay leaves, and thyme in the cheesecloth and tie with twine; add the bundle to the pot. Cook on medium-low heat, barely simmering, for 30–40 minutes, or until the potatoes are tender and can be easily pierced. Drain the potatoes and set aside.

Render the bacon in a saucepan over medium heat until crispy. Add the celery, carrots, and onions and sweat them for 5–6 minutes. The vegetables will be tender but should not develop any color. Add the baby potatoes to this mixture and set aside.

2 pounds cherrystone clams (also called littleneck clams)

**FOR THE POTATOES**
1 pound baby potatoes, quartered into bite-size rounds
2 teaspoons kosher salt
1 tablespoon black peppercorns
1 tablespoon coriander seeds
3 fresh bay leaves
1 small bunch thyme
4 ounces thick-cut bacon, cut into ½-inch dice
1 celery rib, cut into ½-inch dice
1 medium carrot, cut into ½-inch dice
½ medium yellow onion, cut into ½-inch dice

## FOR THE CHOWDER

1 medium yellow onion, sliced

2 large russet potatoes, peeled and roughly sliced into rounds

2 cups white wine, divided

2 cups clam juice, divided

5 fresh bay leaves

1 celery rib, cut in half

1 small yellow onion

1 medium carrot, peeled and halved

¼ teaspoon crushed chili flakes

1 cup heavy cream

1 teaspoon fresh lemon juice

1 teaspoon kosher salt

Dash Tabasco sauce

## FOR THE COD

Neutral oil, such as grapeseed or canola

4 (6-ounce) cod fillets

### TO MAKE THE CHOWDER

Place the sliced onions and potatoes in a medium pot with 1 cup of the white wine and cover. Simmer over medium heat for 5 minutes. Add 2 cups water and 1 cup of the clam juice and continue to simmer, uncovered, for another 20 minutes, or until the potatoes are very tender. This is the chowder base.

Meanwhile, in a medium stockpot, combine the clams, bay leaves, celery, onions, carrots, and chili flakes with the remaining clam juice and wine. Set over high heat, covered, and steam for 10 minutes, until all the clams open (discard any unopened clams). Remove the clams from their shells, keeping 8 in the shell for serving. Mix the clams that you removed from the shells with the potato-bacon mixture and set aside.

When the potatoes in the chowder base are soft, add the heavy cream, lemon juice, salt, and Tabasco. Transfer the mixture to a blender and blend on high speed until smooth. Return the purée to the pot and keep warm.

### TO MAKE THE COD

Generously coat a large pan with oil over high heat. Once the oil is shimmering, add the fillets and sear them for 3–4 minutes, or until the bottom sides turn golden brown. Cod is an extremely flaky fish, so flip the fillets gently, cook them for 2 minutes more, and then turn off the heat.

### TO ASSEMBLE

For each serving, ladle ¾–1 cup of chowder into a wide bowl. Spoon the potato, clam, and bacon mixture over the top. Add a cod fillet and top with 2 in-shell clams per serving. Serve immediately.

# Meat

Since opening Barrington's, my belief in high-quality ingredients has driven my purchasing decisions. I like to use local meat when it makes sense and have forged relationships with local purveyors, like Isaac Oliver at Harmony Ridge Farms (see sidebar, page 185). This is one of many farms that's afforded me the opportunity to showcase locally raised ingredients, and having two other restaurants has allowed me to purchase large cuts of meat. I enjoy butchering whole animals and utilizing every part to create specific cuts of meat. As a chef who works and trains other chefs I appreciate the ample teaching moments meat provides during prep and on the line. To a young cook, working with meat is one of the most intimidating tasks, and one of the most rewarding. Mastering the hot line and turning out consistent temperatures is, after all, the hallmark of a proficient cook.

In this chapter, you will find a array of techniques and flavors, including a workhorse recipe for fennel sausage and a perfectly seared rib-eye steak with bull's-eye toast. Other recipes, like the slow-braised short ribs or pork saltimbocca, can, I hope, serve as essentials to a solid understanding of technique. Included, too, are recipes for a special occasion meal, such as the rabbit pot pie and the pecan-crusted lamb chops. Each one offers insight into the care and consideration that goes into preparing an excellent dish at any level.

# Calabrian Pepper–Glazed Pork Belly

Preparing pork belly is a process, but the results are well worth the time. Here, pork belly is cured, cooked, and tossed with a Calabrian chili pepper glaze that is sweet and tart, with a spicy punch. Use the leftover glaze to brush over grilled chicken, make spicy wings, or upgrade your favorite barbecue sauce. For an impressive small plate, pair this pork belly with a serving of creamy grits (page 142). Or try Pork Belly Pizza with Charred Eggplant and Smoked Mozzarella (page 240).

Give yourself two days for the pork belly. It needs twenty-four hours to cure and spends several hours in the oven the next day. Use gloves when handling pink salt (it is dangerous otherwise) and for the peppers. Calabrian chilis (look for them at specialty grocers or online) have varying heat levels. Give them a taste before proceeding with recipe and adjust the measurement to meet your preferred level of heat.

**SPECIAL EQUIPMENT:** splatter screen

**SERVES 12**

### TO CURE THE PORK BELLY

In a food processor, blend the brown sugar, salt, curing salt, thyme, and Aleppo pepper together. Pour the cure on a baking sheet, spreading it out into a layer slightly wider than the pork belly. Add the belly to the pan, skin-side up, packing any excess salt around the edges. Avoid getting the cure on the pork skin. Refrigerate the pork belly, uncovered, for 24 hours. The next day, use a damp towel to remove the cure thoroughly, and then pat the pork dry with a dry towel.

Preheat the oven to 250°.

Add 1 cup of the pork lard to a deep roasting pan. Place the pork belly into the pan, skin-side down. Cover it completely with the remaining pork lard. Cover the dish tightly with parchment paper and then aluminum foil. Seal tightly. Set the pan on a baking sheet to avoid splashing hot lard on the oven floor. Place the pork belly in the oven for 3–4 hours. To check for doneness, use a cake tester to pierce the flesh. When the tester meets with no resistance, the meat is done. If there is resistance, continue to cook until there is none.

**FOR THE PORK BELLY**

¾ cup packed light brown
   sugar
¾ cup kosher salt
1 teaspoon #1 pink curing salt
   (can be found at a specialty
   grocery or online)
6 sprigs fresh thyme
2 tablespoons Aleppo pepper
   (or red pepper flakes)
3 pounds side pork belly,
   skin on
6–8 cups pork lard (or Crisco),
   melted and divided
1 tablespoon vegetable oil

FOR THE GLAZE

2 cups sugar

2 ¼ cups white balsamic
  vinegar

½ cup Calabrian chili peppers
  in oil, stemmed and seeded

1 cup roasted red peppers

2 tablespoons sriracha

Remove the pan from the oven, cool the pork belly to room temperature, and then carefully remove it from the oil and place it on a sheet pan lined with parchment paper. Place another sheet pan on top and weigh it down with something heavy (at least 5 pounds). Cool the pork belly completely in the refrigerator under the weighted press. This will allow for even cooking and a good sear.

## TO MAKE THE GLAZE

While the pork belly cools, combine 1 cup water with the sugar in a stainless steel pot; stir together gently. Bring to a boil (do not stir once the heat is on) and cook the liquid until the sugar is dissolved and begins to turn amber in color, about 15 minutes. Carefully add the vinegar (it will bubble up) and stir with a wooden spoon. Add the peppers and hot sauce, and reduce the mixture by one-third, about 5 minutes. Remove the glaze from the heat and transfer it to a blender. Purée on high speed, then strain and reserve the glaze. Once the pork belly has cooled completely, trim the fatty edges and slice the meat into uniform 1½-inch cubes (about 3 ounces each).

## TO SEAR THE PORK BELLY

Preheat the oven to 450°. Heat an ovenproof pan on the stovetop over medium-high heat. Add the vegetable oil. Once the oil is hot, add the pork belly cubes, skin-side down. Use a screen to cover the belly because it will pop. Cook for 2 minutes, or until the bottoms develop color and start to look crisp. Place in the oven for 10 minutes to finish cooking.

Using a fish spatula, gently release the pork belly cubes from the pan and flip them. It is important to keep the skin intact, so gently wiggle the pan to help release the pork from the pan. Ladle some of the reserved glaze over the pork belly and return the meat to the oven for 4 minutes.

Repeat this glazing process twice more. The pork belly will take on a lacquered, amber appearance. Serve hot.

# Fennel Sausage

Making your own sausage is worthwhile and rewarding; it yields something that tastes better than a store-bought version. We use this recipe across the restaurants: in Garganelli with Italian Sausage at Good Food on Montford (page 211) and on Pepperoni and Sausage Pizza (page 239) at Stagioni. It's sweet and garlicky, with a hint of spice that builds throughout the meal.

*Note*: When grinding meat, it's important to keep your ingredients and equipment cold. If you do not have a meat grinder or a grinder attachment, ask your local butcher to grind the meat for you. Ask if it can be ground twice, once coarsely and again more finely.

**SPECIAL EQUIPMENT**: stand mixer with grinder attachment or a meat grinder with large and small die, mini food processor or spice grinder

2 ½ pounds pork butt, cleaned of all glands, veins, and sinew
2 tablespoons fennel seeds
½ tablespoon crushed chili flakes
2 teaspoons black pepper
2 tablespoons kosher salt
5 tablespoons sugar
¼ cup roughly chopped yellow onion
¼ cup peeled garlic cloves
¼ cup white wine

**MAKES 2½ POUNDS**

Prechill the grinder components, mixing bowls, and paddle attachment in the freezer.

Roughly chop the pork butt into 2-inch pieces (small enough to fit into the grinder's opening). Spread the pieces on a sheet tray and place them in the freezer to chill for 20 minutes. You want the pork to firm up but not freeze solid.

In a mini food processor or spice grinder, grind together the fennel seeds, chili flakes, and black pepper. Transfer the spice mixture to a small bowl and combine it with the salt and sugar.

Purée the onions, garlic, and wine in the mini food processor, scraping down the sides. Transfer the purée to a separate bowl. (You want to keep the wet and dry ingredients separate to prevent clumping.) While you grind the meat, refrigerate this mixture and the spices.

Remove the pork butt from the freezer and grind it using the large die. Spread the ground meat on a baking sheet and return it to the freezer for 20 more minutes. While the meat chills, clean and dry the grinder; return it to the freezer to rechill. After 20 minutes, reassemble the grinder with the small die and grind the pork again. Return the pork to the baking sheet and chill in the freezer for another 5 minutes.

Using a spatula, fold the spices and onion mixture together in the bowl of a stand mixer. Attach the paddle to the stand mixer. Add the pork to the mixing bowl and whip on high speed for 45–60 seconds, or until it sticks to the side of the bowl. Cover and chill until use. The sausage will keep in the refrigerator for 3 days or in the freezer for 1 month.

# Pecan-Crusted Lamb with Chipotle BBQ Sauce, Sweet Potatoes, and Green Beans

I remember being impressed by the sheer volume of sweet potatoes on display when I first visited a Charlotte farmers' market. I really didn't know what to do with them, but they were plentiful. Over the years I have learned to embrace North Carolina's state vegetable and have even incorporated it into the logo at Barrington's. In this recipe you will find sweet potatoes three ways—puréed, roasted, and made into crispy chips—served with pecan-crusted lamb chops and perfectly cooked green beans. This recipe calls for a frenched rack of lamb. Ask your butcher to prepare it for you.

**SPECIAL EQUIPMENT:** food processor, mandoline

**SERVES 2**

## TO MARINATE THE LAMB
Place the shallots, garlic, pecans, wine, and mustard into a food processor. With the food processor running, slowly drizzle in the oil until it is incorporated. You are looking for a coarse texture. Rub the marinade on the lamb. Cover and refrigerate for at least 1 hour and up to 24 hours.

## TO ROAST THE SWEET POTATOES
Preheat the oven to 350°. Place 2 of the sweet potatoes in a casserole dish filled with 1 inch of water. Seal the dish tightly with foil and bake for 1 hour, or until the sweet potatoes are easily pierced with a fork. Cool to room temperature, then carefully peel the skins. Cut the sweet potatoes into 6 (½-inch) rounds and set aside. Reserve the leftover scraps for the purée.

## TO COOK THE GREEN BEANS
Prepare an ice bath. Bring a saucepan filled with water and a generous pinch of salt to a rolling boil and add the green beans. Boil for 4 minutes, then immediately transfer the beans to the ice bath. You should be able to bite through the green bean with the slightest resistance, but it should still have structure. Drain and set aside.

1 rack of lamb, about 1 ¾ pounds (approximately 8 chops), frenched

**FOR THE MARINADE**
1 small shallot, roughly chopped
2 garlic cloves, peeled
½ cup pecan pieces
¼ cup dry red wine
2 teaspoons Dijon mustard
¼ cup canola oil, plus more for cooking

**FOR THE SIDE DISHES**
2 ½ large sweet potatoes, divided
Kosher salt
3 ounces green beans, ends trimmed
1 cup heavy cream
1 tablespoon unsalted butter
Black pepper
Chipotle BBQ Sauce (page 31)

### TO MAKE THE POTATO CHIPS AND PURÉE

Peel the remaining half of the sweet potato. Using a mandoline, shave it into wafer thin rounds. Rinse the rounds thoroughly with water to remove the starch (for even cooking). Fill a small pot one-third of the way with oil and heat to 300°. (Cooking at a low temperature will preserve the color and allow the sweet potatoes to cook evenly.)

Meanwhile, place the reserved sweet potato scraps in a saucepan with the cream. Bring to a boil, then reduce the heat and simmer for 5 minutes. Transfer the mixture to a blender and purée until silky smooth. Set aside.

Add the rounds to the heated oil and fry them until they are cooked through. Remove the chips with a slotted spoon or skimmer and place them on a plate lined with paper towels to drain. Sprinkle with salt.

Increase the oil temperature to 350° and fry the sliced rounds for 3–4 minutes, or until browned. Transfer the chips to a plate lined with paper towels to drain. Sprinkle with salt. Keep warm.

### TO COOK THE LAMB

Add 2 tablespoons oil to a large sauté pan over high heat. Once the oil shimmers, add the lamb rack and sear, about 3 minutes. Place the lamb into the 350° oven to finish, about 10–15 minutes for medium rare, or use a meat thermometer to cook the lamb to your desired temperature. Let the lamb rest for 5 minutes, and reheat the chipotle BBQ sauce.

### TO ASSEMBLE

In a saucepan over high heat, melt the butter and add the green beans, along with some salt and pepper. Cook until just heated through, 2–3 minutes.

Spread a dollop of sweet potato purée on a plate. Add 3 roasted sweet potato rounds, then add the green beans. Slice the lamb rack into quarters. Place 2 quarters on each plate, drizzle with chipotle BBQ sauce, and garnish with sweet potato chips. Serve immediately.

# Rabbit Pot Pie with Black Pepper Crust

Wintertime weather summons comfort food. At Barrington's, it's the season when rabbit pot pie returns to the menu, usually in January. Of course, calls from customers asking for the dish start the first week of December. We braise rabbit until tender, add it to a classic béchamel sauce with vegetables, then top it with a flaky black pepper piecrust. Our rabbits come from farmer Dan Kypena of Middle Ground Farm, who raises them in Monroe, a small town forty miles southeast of Charlotte.

**SPECIAL EQUIPMENT:** 4 (10-ounce) ramekins

**SERVES 4**

## TO MAKE THE PIECRUST

In a food processor, pulse together the flour, salt, and pepper. Add the butter and pulse until it resembles coarse meal. Add the ice water and pulse a few more times until it is incorporated. Dump the dough mixture on a work surface and form it into a disc. Wrap the dough in plastic and refrigerate for 1 hour.

## TO MAKE THE RABBIT

Preheat the oven to 350°.

Butcher the rabbit by first removing the front and back legs. Rest the rabbit on its rib cage and run a knife along the spine to remove and reserve the loins. Do this on both sides. Keeping the knife close to the body, slice toward the ribs to remove the belly. Roast the carcass in the preheated oven while you prepare the braise.

Coat a large cast-iron skillet with a slick of oil and place it over high heat. Season the rabbit meat with salt and pepper, then brown it on one side. Keep an eye on the belly and loin, which cook fast. Flip the meat and brown the other side. This should take about 7–8 minutes per side. Remove the meat from the pan and place it into a large roasting pan. Set aside.

Add the celery, carrots, and onions to the empty skillet, along with the thyme, rosemary, and bay leaves. Move the skillet off the heat and add the wine, then return it to the stovetop and reduce the wine over high heat for 3 minutes. Add the chicken stock and simmer. Pour the

**FOR THE PIECRUST**

½ pound all-purpose flour
    plus more for dusting
1 teaspoon kosher salt
1 teaspoon black pepper
8 tablespoons (1 stick) cold
    unsalted butter, cubed
3 tablespoons ice water

**FOR THE RABBIT**

1 whole rabbit
Neutral oil, such as grapeseed
    or canola
Kosher salt and black pepper
2 celery ribs, chopped
1 large carrot, peeled and
    chopped
1 small yellow onion, chopped
1 bunch thyme
1 sprig fresh rosemary
2 fresh bay leaves
1 cup white wine
5 cups chicken stock

contents over the rabbit to cover. Remove the carcass from the oven and add it to the roasting pan. Cover the pan tightly with foil and return it to oven for 1½–2 hours, or when the meat easily separates from the bone.

## TO MAKE THE FILLING

In a separate pan, add the oil, celery, onions, and carrots. Cook until the vegetables have softened, about 3–5 minutes. Remove from the heat and set aside. This is the mirepoix.

When the rabbit is done, pull the meat out of the pan and set it on a baking sheet to cool to room temperature. Strain the liquid into a separate pot with 1 cup of the milk. Bring the liquid to a simmer.

Make a roux: Melt the butter in a sauté pan and sprinkle in the flour, whisking constantly to break up any lumps, until it becomes a smooth paste. Add the roux, a little at time, to the milk mixture and whisk until it is fully incorporated. Once the sauce thickens, add the salt. Let the sauce bubble for 10 minutes, to cook the rest of the flour out, stirring frequently. Remove from the heat. Pull the rabbit meat from the leg bones and add all of it to the sauce, along with the mirepoix.

Whisk together the egg and remaining milk to make an egg wash.

## TO ASSEMBLE

On a floured work surface, roll out the chilled dough to ⅛ inch thick. Place a ramekin over the dough and cut a circle 1 inch wider than the ramekin. Repeat this 3 times for a total of 4 crusts.

Fill the ramekins with pot pie filling, then place the cut rounds on top of the prepared ramekins, crimping or pressing tightly around edges. Cut a few decorative vents in the top, brush tops with the egg wash, place the ramekins on a sheet pan, and bake for 20–25 minutes, or until the crusts are golden brown and bubbling. Serve immediately.

**FOR THE FILLING**

1 tablespoon neutral oil, such as grapeseed or canola

2 celery ribs, cut into ½-inch dice

1 medium yellow onion, cut into ½-inch dice

3 medium carrots, cut into ½-inch dice

1 cup plus 2 tablespoons whole milk, divided

8 tablespoons (1 stick) unsalted butter

½ cup all-purpose flour

1 teaspoon kosher salt

1 large egg

# Roasted Pork Chop with Fig-Port Sauce and Gruyère and Prosciutto Panini

The Barrington's kitchen staff is obsessed with grilled cheese sandwiches. Sometimes we have contests to see who can make the best one for staff meal. We decided to take it a step further and add it to a main course. Here, we cook a thick-cut pork chop and pair it with a fancy grilled cheese filled with Gruyère and prosciutto. It's finished with a glossy, sweet sauce made of figs, port wine, and crispy pieces of prosciutto.

---

SERVES 6

................................................................

### TO COOK THE PORK CHOPS

Preheat the oven to 350°. Generously season the pork chops with salt and pepper on both sides. Heat a large skillet with the oil until shimmering. Add the chops to the pan, working in batches if necessary, and sear for 4 minutes, or until a nice crust develops. Flip the chops and sear for 4 minutes more. Set the chops on a sheet pan and finish them in the oven, about 8–10 minutes. The pork should have a warm, pink center for medium. Let the chops rest before slicing them.

### TO MAKE THE SAUCE

Cut the prosciutto slices into thin ribbons and add them to the same skillet over medium-high heat; toss until crispy. Add the shallots and sage and toss until the shallots are browned. Add the port and reduce the sauce until it is syrupy, 3 minutes, then add the veal stock and reduce the sauce again until it coats the back of a spoon, 7–10 minutes. Add a pinch of salt and pepper, and swirl in the butter. Add the figs and toss once more. Set aside.

**FOR THE PORK CHOPS**

6 (8–10-ounce) bone-in pork chops

Kosher salt and black pepper

3 tablespoons vegetable oil

**FOR THE SAUCE**

12 thin slices prosciutto

6 large shallots, sliced

12 fresh sage leaves

½ cup port

1 cup veal stock (or beef stock)

2 tablespoons unsalted butter

1 pint fresh figs, quartered

**FOR THE GRILLED CHEESE**

**6 slices crusty country bread (we recommend pain paisan)**

**6 thin slices prosciutto**

**6 ounces Gruyère**

**6 tablespoons unsalted butter, divided**

## TO MAKE THE GRILLED CHEESE

Cut each slice of bread in half. Place 1 ounce of Gruyère and 1 slice of prosciutto on one half and cover with the other half. Repeat with the remaining bread, cheese, and prosciutto. In a sauté pan, melt 2–3 tablespoons of the butter. Add several sandwiches at a time, pressing down with a sandwich press or the back of a spatula to aid browning. Cook for 3 minutes until the bread is golden brown on bottom, then flip the sandwiches and cook for 3 minutes more. Repeat the process until all the sandwiches are heated, adding butter as needed, 2 tablespoons at a time.

## TO ASSEMBLE

Slice the crusts off each panini, cut them in half diagonally, and stack them on the plate. Slice the pork chop and add it to the plate. Spoon the fig-port sauce over the top and serve.

# Rib-Eye Steak with Bull's-Eye Toast

Egg in a basket. Toad in the hole. Whatever you call it, this version of steak and eggs doubles as a hearty breakfast or a simple dinner. Either way, it satisfies comfort-food cravings with a little restaurant flair.

*Note*: Fresh farm eggs are the best eggs for this recipe. Try to find some at your local farmers' market.

**SPECIAL EQUIPMENT:** 2½-inch biscuit cutter

**SERVES 4**

Preheat the oven to 400°. Heat a large cast-iron skillet over high heat. Add 1 tablespoon of the oil to coat the pan. Season the rib-eye steaks generously with salt and cracked black pepper. Press the pepper into the steaks before cooking to create a nice crust.

Sear the steaks in the skillet until a nice brown crust forms on the bottom, about 3–4 minutes. Turn the steak over and add the remaining oil to the pan. Sear for 3–4 more minutes, then reduce the heat to medium. Melt 2 tablespoons of the butter in the pan, then add the herbs and garlic.

Using a spoon, baste the steak with the butter for 1 minute. Place the garlic and herbs on top of the steak to keep them from burning, and baste for 1 minute more. By this time, the steak should be almost medium rare (use a meat thermometer to check for your desired doneness). When done, transfer the steaks to a cutting board and let them rest.

Meanwhile, cut the crusts from the brioche slices. Use a biscuit cutter to cut a circle in the center of each slice. Melt 1½ tablespoons of the butter in a nonstick pan over medium-high heat; swirl to cover the bottom of the pan. Add 2 slices of brioche and toast them for 1 minute, then flip the slices. Carefully crack an egg into the center of each slice and season with salt. Place the pan in the oven to finish, about 3–4 minutes. Repeat with the remaining slices of brioche.

Slice the steak and serve it alongside the bull's-eye toast with your favorite hot sauce (or Fermented Hot Sauce, page 16).

2 tablespoons vegetable oil, divided
4 (10–12-ounce portions) eye of rib eye
Kosher salt
Cracked black pepper
5 tablespoons unsalted butter, divided
2 sprigs fresh rosemary
2 sprigs fresh sage
2 garlic cloves, peeled
4 (1-inch) slices Brioche (page 246) or store-bought brioche
4 large eggs

# Veal Piccata with Creamy Polenta

**FOR THE PICCATA**
**AND SAUCE**

1 ½ pounds veal loin, trimmed
and cleaned

¼ cup plus 2 tablespoons
extra-virgin olive oil,
divided

½ cup yellow onion, cut into
¼-inch dice

1 cup white wine

4 cups white veal (or chicken)
stock

Kosher salt and black pepper

2 cups all-purpose flour

1 tablespoon fresh lemon juice

1 tablespoon capers

8 tablespoons (1 stick)
unsalted butter, cubed

**FOR THE POLENTA**

1 fresh bay leaf

1 quart stock (vegetable,
chicken, or water)

1 tablespoon kosher salt

3 cups polenta

½ cup heavy cream

½ cup mascarpone

3 tablespoons unsalted butter

Lemon, butter, capers, and white wine create the classic flavors of a piccata that, in this case, involve tender cutlets of veal. We serve this with a polenta fortified with cream and mascarpone.

We recommend a veal loin for this recipe, but veal scaloppini or cutlets purchased straight from the butcher's case will work, too. The recipe calls for white veal stock, which is veal stock without tomatoes; we want a neutral color. Chicken stock is a fine substitute.

**SPECIAL EQUIPMENT:** meat mallet

**SERVES 4**

### TO PREPARE THE VEAL

Make sure the veal loin is cleaned of all fat and sinew. Cut the veal into 4 equal portions, about 5 ounces each. Butterfly each portion, slicing each in half to create 2 cutlets. Place the slices between 2 pieces of plastic wrap, and pound them with the smooth side of a mallet into paper-thin cutlets. Set aside.

### TO BEGIN THE PICCATA SAUCE

Heat a pan over medium heat and add 2 tablespoons of the olive oil and the onions. Cook until the onions are translucent, about 6 minutes. Add the wine, bring to a boil, and reduce the contents by three-fourths, 6–10 minutes. Add the stock and reduce by three-fourths again, 6–10 minutes more. Set aside.

### TO MAKE THE POLENTA

Place the bay leaf, stock, and salt in a pot and bring the liquid to a rolling boil. Turn off the heat and whisk in the polenta, then return the mixture to a boil over medium-high heat, whisking constantly until the polenta thickens and bubbles. Reduce the heat to low and simmer the polenta, stirring frequently, for about 1 hour, or according to the package instructions. Add the heavy cream and whisk to incorporate. Turn off the heat and fold in the mascarpone and butter. Add more salt, if needed. Set aside.

## TO COOK THE VEAL

Season the veal cutlets with salt and pepper on both sides. Place the flour in a shallow container and dredge each cutlet lightly, tapping off any excess. Line a plate with paper towels. In a sauté pan over high heat, add the remaining olive oil and heat until it shimmers. Reduce the heat to medium high and add the veal cutlets. Brown the veal for 1 minute on each side; transfer it to the plate.

## TO FINISH THE PICCATA AND SERVE

Pour off the excess oil and return the pan to the stove, then add the reserved piccata sauce to the pan and deglaze for 1 minute. Return the veal to the pan with the sauce for 1 minute, then remove from the heat. Immediately add the lemon juice, capers, and butter, swirling the pan constantly to bind the sauce. The sauce is finished when all the butter has melted. Add more lemon juice at this point, if desired. Serve the veal atop creamy polenta, spooning extra sauce on top.

# Pork Saltimbocca

Saltimbocca is a simple classic, and sometimes I like to remind my guests why a classic became a classic in the first place. Thin cutlets of pork tenderloin are topped with provolone, prosciutto, and fresh sage, then finished with a buttery marsala sauce. We like to serve it with creamy polenta (page 180), but herb-roasted potatoes or asparagus would also be good companions.

*Note*: This is probably not an ideal dish for those with sensitivities to salt.

**SPECIAL EQUIPMENT**: meat mallet

**SERVES 6**

2 pounds pork tenderloin
Kosher salt and black pepper
1 bundle fresh sage (about 24 leaves), divided
12 slices provolone
12 pieces prosciutto, thinly sliced
Extra-virgin olive oil
½ cup Marsala
1 cup chicken stock
1 tablespoon unsalted butter

Preheat the oven to 250°. Trim the tenderloin of all fat and silver skin and slice it into 6 equal portions.

Place one portion of the tenderloin, cut-side up, on a piece of plastic wrap. Cover it with another sheet of plastic wrap. Gently pound the pork with the smooth side of a meat mallet to ¼ inch thick. Remove the plastic wrap and lightly salt and pepper the pork. (Keep in mind that the prosciutto will add a good amount of salt.) Repeat the process with the remaining portions.

To assemble, place 3 leaves of sage on top of each tenderloin, then cover the sage with 2 slices of provolone and 1 slice of prosciutto. Repeat the process with the remaining portions.

Heat a nonstick pan over medium-high heat, coating the bottom with olive oil. When the oil starts to shimmer, add the assembled saltimbocca, prosciutto-side down. Cook in batches to avoid overcrowding.

When the pork begins to turn white around the edges (about 3 minutes), flip the saltimbocca and cook for 1 minute more. Transfer the pork to an oven-safe plate and hold in the warm oven. Keep the pan handy for the sauce.

Drain the grease from the pan in which the pork was cooked. Add 6–7 sage leaves and toast them slightly. Remove the pan from the stovetop and add the Marsala. This will prevent a dangerous flare-up while you pour. Return the pan to the stovetop. (The Marsala will flame. Be careful.) When the Marsala reduces by half, add the chicken stock and reduce the sauce until it coats the back of a spoon. Swirl in the butter until it has melted, then remove the pan from the heat. Spoon the Marsala sauce over the entire dish and serve.

# Isaac Oliver, Harmony Ridge Farms

Meeting the next generation of young producers is one of the perks of my job. A chef can never have too many local producers, and when we find a relationship that works, we hold on to it. Our farmers become part of our restaurant family.

Larry Schreiber, our executive chef at Good Food on Montford, was the first to contact Isaac Oliver, the farmer and co-owner of Harmony Ridge. Isaac began working with both Good Food and Stagioni, delivering fresh produce, eggs, and pork. He learned about Barrington's and decided to pay me a visit one afternoon on his delivery route.

As Isaac remembers it: "I stopped in at Barrington's to meet Bruce, and told him that we serviced 'Stag-ee-oni' to which Bruce quickly corrected me (Stagioni is actually pronounced 'staj-ee-oni')." It was an amusing first encounter, but the beginning of a fruitful partnership.

Harmony Ridge supplies fresh eggs, seasonal produce, and sides of pork to our restaurants. The most exciting item is the pork that Isaac delivers. Because we have three restaurants to service, we can purchase half-sides of the animal to butcher in-house and divide among them. This means that we get to use the entire animal and dig into more primal techniques, which is fun for us.

Harmony Ridge is in Tobaccoville, North Carolina, a small town near Winston-Salem, about an hour northeast of Charlotte. Isaac started the farm with his father, Kevin Oliver, in 2009. As he tells it, his father had reached retirement and was eager to put his energies into something new.

Having grown up on a small farm in Ohio that maintained a side butchery business, the senior Oliver was interested in livestock farming.

The two men started small, with twelve acres of purchased land, and began growing vegetables on one acre of it. The first few years of operation were dedicated to a community-supported agriculture (CSA) program, where customers would purchase a share of vegetables for the season.

By the third year, Isaac and his father discovered restaurant opportunities, first in Winston-Salem, then in Charlotte. They started with eggs, and then started raising ducks, a unique offering for a local producer. Soon, the two expanded to include pigs and cattle. Harmony Ridge Farms now occupies three separate properties, including a fifty-acre property for livestock, and serves customers in Winston-Salem, Greensboro, and Charlotte. All the produce from Harmony Ridge is grown organically. The pigs are raised on pasture, as are the ducks, a rarity for commercial operations.

Harmony Ridge now employs four full-time individuals in addition to Isaac and his father, Kevin. They serve underprivileged families through a nonprofit partnership with the Wake Forest Baptist School of Medicine: Farm Fresh Healthy Living allows low-income families to receive a CSA with produce from Harmony Ridge and other area farms. In turn, that farmer-to-farmer relationship allows Harmony Ridge to bring goods from other farms to their restaurant customers, a win-win for their customers and peers.

As the city of Charlotte grows, culinarily and otherwise, so does the demand for people who are serving their communities authentically. Harmony Ridge is one of our newest relationships, one that we hope will long continue.

# Braised Short Ribs with Pommes Anna and Glazed Carrots

**FOR THE SHORT RIBS**

6 bone-in short ribs

Kosher salt and black pepper

¼ cup extra-virgin olive oil

1 large yellow onion, sliced

2 celery ribs, sliced into
    1-inch pieces

2 medium carrots, peeled and
    sliced into 1-inch pieces

2 garlic cloves, sliced

4 cups dry red wine

2 cups chicken stock

2 cups veal or beef stock

2 cups crushed tomatoes

4 sprigs each fresh thyme
    and oregano

2 sprigs fresh rosemary

2 fresh bay leaves

I first learned how to braise short ribs by watching my mother do it. On one of my first attempts, I thought I'd save some time and throw all the liquids into the pot at once. I learned the hard way that failing to take the proper steps means sacrificing flavor. With this recipe it is all about the journey.

At Barrington's we serve the short ribs with pommes Anna, thinly sliced potatoes bathed in butter and herbs, stacked decoratively, and roasted golden. It's one of my favorite ways to eat potatoes. We add a side of glazed carrots (page 127) to complete the meal.

**SPECIAL EQUIPMENT:** pastry brush, nonstick standard muffin pan, mandoline

SERVES 6

## TO MAKE THE SHORT RIBS

Preheat the oven to 375°. Season each short rib generously with salt and pepper. Coat a Dutch oven with oil and place over high heat. When the oil is shimmering, add the short ribs to the pan and cook for about 2–3 minutes per side, or until the meat is deeply browned. Cook in batches, if necessary, to avoid overcrowding. Transfer the short ribs to a plate; set aside.

Add the vegetables and cook, stirring occasionally, for 5–7 minutes, or until they are browned. Add the wine and scrape the browned bits from the bottom of the pot. Reduce the wine by half, then return the short ribs to the pot. Add both stocks and the tomatoes, barely covering the meat. Add the herbs and bring to a simmer. Cover the pot and place it in the oven for 3 hours.

While the short ribs cook, make the pommes Anna. Check periodically during the cooking process and add more stock if the dish begins to look dried out. Halfway through the cooking time, turn the ribs. Remove the lid during the last 20 minutes of cooking. The meat should be tender but not falling apart.

## TO MAKE THE POMMES ANNA

Melt the butter in a small saucepan over medium heat. Brush a muffin tin with melted butter, pouring an extra ½ teaspoon into the bottom of each cup. Add the thyme, parsley, rosemary, and garlic to the remaining butter in the saucepan. Stir over medium-low heat for 2 minutes, then remove from the stovetop.

Peel the potatoes. Use a mandoline to slice them into very thin rounds, about ⅛ inch thick. Place the slices in a large bowl and pour the herbed butter over them. Season with salt and pepper, and toss to coat well.

Divide the potato slices among the muffin tins, layering and overlapping slices in a circular pattern. Lightly press the center of each to compact them. Bake for 20 minutes, then use a small, offset spatula to flip the discs. Bake for 15 minutes more, or until the edges start to crisp and brown. Carefully remove the potatoes from the muffin tins.

## TO ASSEMBLE

Remove the short ribs and strain the vegetables from the braising liquid. Skim the fat from the top of the liquid. Return the strained liquid back to the pot and reduce it by half over high heat. Use this reduction to sauce the ribs. Serve with pommes Anna and glazed carrots.

**FOR THE POMMES ANNA**

**8 tablespoons (1 stick) unsalted butter**

**½ teaspoon chopped fresh thyme**

**1 teaspoon chopped fresh parsley**

**1 teaspoon chopped fresh rosemary**

**1 garlic clove, minced**

**1 ½ pounds small Yukon Gold potatoes**

**2 teaspoons kosher salt**

**Black pepper**

**1 recipe Orange-Honey Glazed Carrots**

# Birds

One of the first recipes to appear on the menu at Barrington's is one that is simple yet timeless: pan-roasted chicken with mashed potatoes and wilted greens. I've tried to take it off the menu, but my customers won't let me.

I distinctly remember helping my mother make roast chicken. We would smear herbed butter on the skin and stuff the cavity with sliced lemons, sage, and onions. It felt like an eternity staring into the oven, waiting for the skin to turn crisp and golden brown. I remember, too, my first southern fried chicken experience at Price's Chicken Coop shortly after I moved to Charlotte. I believe the hype, by the way.

I love all types of poultry. Whether it is chicken, duck, quail, or squab, I enjoy highlighting the attributes of each. In this chapter, you'll find that special chicken recipe from Barrington's, brought to North Carolina as an homage to the Boston restaurant that taught it to me, in addition to a hunter's dish that we serve at Stagioni. My mother taught me that one. There is a recipe for roasted duck breast with tips for attaining the crispiest skin and a unique recipe for lemongrass chicken sausage that we pair with lettuce wraps and pickled vegetables at Good Food on Montford. I hope the recipes in this chapter inspire a new dish or favored technique for your household.

# A Word on Chicken

If you are a discerning diner, there are many considerations to think about when purchasing chicken. How was it raised? Is it packed with artificial additives? My first inclination, not surprisingly, is to think about how it tastes. Of course, an animal that is raised in good conditions and fed properly, without chemicals and added hormones, is bound to taste better. But it can be tricky as a consumer, wading in the murky waters of deceptive marketing lingo, to determine what's best. I've compiled a short list of tips to consider when shopping for chicken, including what to look for in a supermarket bird.

**FARMERS' MARKETS ARE IDEAL:** The first place to look for excellent chicken and eggs is your local farmers' market. These are the folks you can talk to and who are open to questions. Most of the time, too, you'll be speaking to the people who raised the birds themselves. If knowing your source is paramount, why not go directly to it?

**USE THE WHOLE ANIMAL:** Often the most economical decision (especially if you purchase at the farmers' market) is to use the whole bird. A whole chicken can provide multiple meals in one package, and its carcass offers the opportunity to make great stock for soups and sauces. We waste nothing inside the restaurants and encourage the same mind-set at home. (See below for how to quarter a whole chicken.)

**NAVIGATE THE LABELS:** A lot of misinformation in the supermarkets can make navigating the aisles a challenge. If you don't know what to look for, it's easy to be confused by marketing language that suggests a healthy or farm-raised environment for chickens. Culprits include terms like "all natural" and "cage free" paired with idyllic farm imagery. Instead, look for certifications like Animal Welfare Approved and Certified Humane. These denote that the company has been subjected to a rigorous third-party inspection. The stamp of approval says that this company meets a stricter set of standards than its conventional counterparts.

**MEAT DOES NOT HAVE TO BE THE MAIN COURSE:** The trend in the culinary world is leaning more and more toward vegetable-centric plates, with meat proteins as a smaller, secondary item. The demand for meat in our society has far exceeded the natural supply. To keep up, factory farms and large corporate operations go to unsustainable extremes, placing strains on the environment, animal welfare standards, and our health. Historically, meat was not present at every meal. It was seasonal and for special occasions. By getting creative in the kitchen without meat, you're participating in economically smart cooking and relieving some of the burden on our food system.

## How to Quarter a Whole Chicken

1. Place the chicken breast-side up with the legs closest to you.
2. Find the natural break in the joint between the wing and the tip of the wing. Cut through this natural break, and reserve the wing tips for stock.
3. On the chicken breast, you will see a white line of fat running through the center. This line is your guide to knowing where to cut. Using a chef's knife, cut down the center of this line through the breastbone, but not all the way through the bottom half of the chicken.
4. Once you make this cut, open the chicken as you would a book. You will see the spine. Cut down the left side of the spine and then the right side to remove the entire spine. Reserve it for the stock.
5. Slice the hindquarters off by running the knife along the bottom of the breastbone. Then remove the breasts.
6. Remove the wings and reserve them for the stock.
7. You should now have 2 breasts and 2 leg-and-thigh combos.
8. If desired, separate the legs from the thighs: Bend the leg at a 90° angle and use a boning knife to slice at the joint where the drumette meets the wingette (flat). Twist the wing backward to dislocate the joint. Slice any additional connective flesh. Use a chef's knife to cut the joint between the flat and wing tip. Discard the tip.
9. If you are not ready to use the carcass to make stock, place it in a storage bag and freeze it for later.

# Pan-Seared Chicken with Wilted Spinach and Mashed Potatoes

**FOR THE MASHED POTATOES**

3 medium russet potatoes

4 garlic cloves, peeled

2 teaspoons kosher salt, divided

1 cup heavy cream

8 tablespoons (1 stick) unsalted butter, softened

¼ teaspoon ground white pepper

This dish is special to me. I first prepared it at Metropolis Café in Boston. The meat is amazingly moist, the skin golden and crisp. The mashed potatoes and spinach—when combined with the pan reduction sauce with roasted garlic—elevate the dish to another level entirely. When I opened Barrington's, I was compelled to put my own stamp on the requisite chicken entrée. For two weeks I grappled with whether to serve chicken at all before finally coming to the obvious conclusion that I needed to share this simple yet elegant dish with my new home city. At the restaurant, we serve half a chicken that we bone out. You may find it easier to use an airline chicken breast (boneless chicken breasts with the drumette attached).

**SPECIAL EQUIPMENT:** potato ricer

**SERVES 4**

TO MAKE THE MASHED POTATOES

Preheat the oven to 400°. Peel and slice the potatoes into ¼-inch rounds. Place the potatoes in a medium saucepan and cover them with cold water. Add the garlic and 1 teaspoon of the salt and gently simmer over medium heat for 20 minutes, or until the potatoes become fork tender. Drain the potatoes, spread them on a baking sheet, and dry them in the heated oven for 2 minutes.

Meanwhile, pour the heavy cream into a small saucepan over high heat; remove the pan from the heat when the cream starts to bubble. Run the potatoes through a potato ricer, then gently fold the warm cream into the potatoes with a rubber spatula. When the cream is fully incorporated, add the butter, remaining salt, and white pepper. Gently mix again, then reserve in a warm place (about 80°). Keep the oven at 400° for the chicken.

## TO MAKE THE SPINACH

Place the garlic and olive oil in a large sauté pan over high heat. When the garlic starts to brown, add the spinach and stir it with tongs or a large spoon until the spinach wilts. Season with salt and pepper, then transfer the spinach to a colander and squeeze out any excess liquid. Reserve in a warm place.

## TO MAKE THE CHICKEN

Pat the chicken dry with a paper towel. Season the flesh side with salt and pepper. Add the oil to a medium sauté pan over high heat. When the oil is shimmering, add the chicken, skin-side down. Cook over high heat for about 3 minutes, or until the skin starts to brown. Transfer the chicken to the oven to continue cooking, about 14 minutes. With a pair of tongs, check for doneness by gently separating the meat where the wing bone meets the breast. If there is any pink, cook for 2 minutes longer and check again. When done, transfer the chicken to a plate, skin-side up, and reserve. The skin should be a crispy golden brown.

## TO MAKE THE PAN SAUCE

Return the pan you used for the chicken to the stovetop over high heat. Add the chicken stock and reduce it by half, then add the butter and whisk until the sauce has thickened enough to coat the back of a spoon. Add the garlic, salt, and pepper. Remove from the heat.

## TO ASSEMBLE

Place a generous mound of mashed potatoes on a dinner plate and top them with the spinach. Rest the chicken, at an angle, skin-side up, over the potatoes and spinach. Spoon the pan sauce over the chicken and serve immediately.

**FOR THE SPINACH**

2 garlic cloves, shaved thin
2 tablespoons extra-virgin olive oil
10 ounces baby spinach
Kosher salt and black pepper

**FOR THE CHICKEN**

4 (10–12 ounce) airline chicken breasts
Kosher salt and black pepper
3 tablespoons vegetable oil

**FOR THE PAN SAUCE**

1 cup chicken stock
3 tablespoons unsalted butter
8 Garlic Confit cloves (page 15)
¼ teaspoon kosher salt
¼ teaspoon black pepper

# Fried Chicken Plate with Collard Greens and Warm Potato Salad

1 (5-pound) pack skin-on
  chicken thighs, deboned
  (about 10 total)

**FOR THE CHICKEN BRINE
AND BUTTERMILK SOAK**
½ cup kosher salt
1 medium yellow onion, sliced
1 lemon, sliced
10 garlic cloves, peeled
1 tablespoon Korean chili
  flakes (or crushed chili
  flakes)
1 tablespoon coriander seeds
1 tablespoon black
  peppercorns
1 tablespoon fennel seeds
4 fresh bay leaves
½ bunch thyme
½ bunch parsley
1 quart whole-milk buttermilk

Fried chicken is a quintessential dish in parts of the South. Charlotte institutions such as Price's Chicken Coop, a cash-only spot open since 1962, often have lines of people out the door waiting to receive their grease-stained treasure boxes. For this recipe, we've taken inspiration from the southern picnic to build a plate with tangy greens, warm potato salad, and crispy fried chicken aided by a brine and a buttermilk soak.

SERVES 5

........................................................................................................

TO BRINE AND SOAK THE CHICKEN
Trim the chicken thighs of any excess fat or cartilage. Combine the salt and 2 quarts water in a large bowl; mix well to dissolve the salt. Add all the remaining ingredients, except the buttermilk, to the brine and stir, then add the chicken thighs. Cover the chicken tightly with plastic wrap and refrigerate for 24 hours.

The next day, remove the chicken thighs from the brine. Wipe off the excess spices and place the thighs in a clean container with the buttermilk. Marinate the chicken in the refrigerator for at least 2 hours. Meanwhile, prepare the collards according to the instructions on page 118. While the collards simmer, prepare the potato salad.

TO MAKE THE POTATO SALAD
Place the potatoes in a pot and cover them with water. Add a couple generous pinches of salt. Bring the potatoes to a boil and cook for 5 minutes. Turn off the heat and allow the potatoes to rest in the pot until they are al dente. They should remain slightly firm, but this step keeps the potatoes from falling apart. Drain the potatoes and spread them on a sheet pan; cool them, uncovered, in the refrigerator until use.

In a grill pan over medium-high heat, grill the onions until they are soft and charred. Alternatively, you can roast them in the oven on high heat (450°). Roughly chop the onions and set them aside until use.

Preheat the oven to 450°. Combine the garlic, thyme, vinegar, both mustards, honey, and oil in a blender and mix on high speed to make the dressing. Set aside.

Coat the bottom of a skillet with oil and set it over medium-high heat. Add the cooled potatoes, cut-side down, to the pan. Work in batches if necessary. Season with salt and pepper, and cook until the potatoes brown slightly. Finish the potatoes in the oven for 5 minutes. Transfer the potatoes to a bowl, add the charred onions, and toss with the dressing. Garnish with lots of parsley and chives. Set aside until serving.

## TO FRY THE CHICKEN

Fill a large pot halfway with oil and heat to 350°. Meanwhile, combine both flours and cornstarch to create a dredge. Remove the chicken from the buttermilk, letting the excess drip off. Dredge the chicken in the flour mixture and set aside.

Working in batches, add the chicken to the hot oil and fry for 8–10 minutes, or until the outside is crisp and golden and the internal temperature reaches 165°–185°. (You can err on the high side with chicken thighs without them drying out.) Use tongs to remove the chicken from the pot, and set the pieces on a plate lined with paper towels. Sprinkle with salt while hot.

## TO ASSEMBLE

Serve 2 pieces of fried chicken per person with a scoop of warm potato salad and a helping of collard greens.

**FOR THE POTATO SALAD**
1 pound small creamer potatoes, halved
Kosher salt
½ medium Vidalia onion, cut into thick rings
Scant tablespoon Garlic Confit (page 15) or finely minced garlic
Pinch fresh thyme leaves
¼ cup apple cider vinegar
1 tablespoon whole-grain mustard
1 tablespoon Dijon mustard
2 tablespoons honey
¼ cup extra-virgin olive oil
½ bunch parsley, finely chopped
1 small bunch chives, finely chopped

**FOR FRYING THE CHICKEN**
Peanut oil (or substitute canola or vegetable oil)
2 cups cake flour
1½ cups all-purpose flour
1 cup cornstarch
1 recipe New South Collards (page 118)

# Chicken Cacciatore

The Italian term *cacciatore* translates as "hunter's style" and signals a rustic dish. Though we've updated the preparation at Stagioni, it mimics a recipe my mother used religiously. Back then, my job was to brown the chicken before the braise. This was one of my earliest culinary duties—so early, in fact, that I had to stand on a wooden stool to reach the stove.

Our version comes with chicken made two ways—roasted and braised—with vegetables and a rich tomato sauce. For deeper flavor, we brine the chicken breasts one day ahead. Because the sauce gets better with time, we recommend cooking the dish early in the day so that the flavors can develop.

---

**SERVES 4**

................................................................

### TO MAKE THE BRINE
In a medium saucepan, combine all the ingredients for the brine over medium-high heat and stir until the salt fully dissolves. Remove the pan from the heat and cool completely. In the meantime, follow the instructions for butchering the chicken (below), separating the breasts from the thighs and drumsticks. Place the chicken breasts in a storage bag and pour the cooled brine over them. Refrigerate for 8–24 hours. Place the legs and thighs in a separate storage bag; refrigerate until use.

### TO MAKE THE CACCIATORE
Preheat the oven to 450°. In a large braising pan at least 2 inches deep, heat 2 tablespoons of the olive oil over high heat. Season the chicken legs and thighs generously with salt and pepper. Once the oil begins to shimmer, add the chicken legs and thighs (skin-side down for the thighs). Sear for 3 minutes on each side, or until a nice, golden color and crisp appearance develops. Remove the chicken from the pan and set aside.

**FOR THE BRINE**

½ cup kosher salt

8 cups water

2 garlic cloves, crushed

4 sprigs each thyme, sage, oregano, and rosemary

4 fresh bay leaves

**FOR THE CACCIATORE**

2 (2 ½-pound) whole chickens

5 tablespoons extra-virgin olive oil, divided

Kosher salt and black pepper

5 garlic cloves, peeled and sliced

4 large carrots, peeled and cut on the bias

1 large yellow onion, cut into ½-inch dice

2 red large bell peppers, seeded and chopped

⅔ cup white wine

4 cups Pomì crushed tomatoes

4 ¼ cups chicken stock

2 fresh bay leaves

1 tablespoon unsalted butter

1 recipe Salsa Verde (page 9)

Add the garlic to the same pan and cook until golden brown. Add the carrots, onions, and bell peppers. Season with salt and pepper and sauté 2 minutes. You want the vegetables to be slightly softened but still maintain a nice texture. Add the wine and reduce it almost completely, about 2–4 minutes more. Add the tomatoes, stock, and bay leaves. Stir together. Return the chicken thighs and drumsticks to the pan. Braise the thighs and drumsticks in the oven for 30 minutes, then return the pan to the stovetop over very low heat while you prepare the chicken breasts.

Remove the chicken breasts from the brine and pat them dry. Heat an ovenproof pan over high heat with the remaining olive oil. Season the breasts lightly with salt and pepper, keeping in mind that the brine has already imparted a fair amount of salt. Place the breasts into the hot pan, skin-side down, and sear for 3 minutes. Place the pan in the oven for 15 minutes.

While the chicken breasts cook, finish the sauce by adding the butter to the braising pan. Turn off the heat and adjust the seasoning. Plate the chicken cacciatore on a large platter. Remove the breasts from the oven, add them to the platter, and top with the Salsa Verde.

# Crispy Quail with Truffle Potato Purée and Foie Gras Reduction

This is the type of meticulous dish that I wholly classify as a restaurant recipe. A dish like this is why I hope people come to my restaurants: to eat something that they wouldn't make at home. I dreamed this one up for Barrington's years ago. It marries the richness of foie gras with crispy quail and a time-intensive reduction infused with even more foie gras. A silky potato purée laced with truffle oil makes this dish a truly a knockout. To make this at home is a feat—but a tasty one.

**SPECIAL EQUIPMENT:** potato ricer

**SERVES 4**

### TO PREPARE THE QUAIL

In a bowl, coat each quail with oil. In a separate bowl, combine the rosemary, parsley, oregano, thyme, and garlic. Rub about 1 teaspoon of the herb mixture on each quail. Tuck the quail legs into the body cavity and refrigerate the quail.

### TO MAKE THE FOIE GRAS REDUCTION

Coat the bottom of a medium saucepan with the oil and get it scorching hot. Add the reserved quail bones and onions and brown for 1 minute. Reduce the heat to medium high and continue to brown, about 5 minutes more. (This extracts flavor from the bones and ensures a deeply flavored foundation for the sauce.) Add the wine and reduce it almost completely, about 5 minutes. Add the chicken and beef stocks and return the liquid to a boil, then simmer and reduce for 45 minutes, or until the sauce coats the back of a spoon. Meanwhile, make the potato purée.

### TO MAKE THE POTATO PURÉE

Preheat the oven to 350°. Place the potatoes and 1 teaspoon of the salt into a large pot and cover with water. Simmer over medium-high heat for 30 minutes, or until the potatoes are soft. Drain the potatoes well, then place them on a sheet pan and into the oven for 3 minutes to remove excess moisture.

**FOR THE QUAIL**

8 quail, deboned, bones reserved

1 tablespoon neutral oil, such as grapeseed or canola, plus more for cooking

1 tablespoon chopped fresh rosemary

1 tablespoon chopped fresh parsley

1 tablespoon chopped fresh oregano

1 teaspoon chopped fresh thyme

2 garlic cloves, grated fine

**FOR THE FOIE GRAS REDUCTION**

3 tablespoons neutral oil, such as grapeseed or canola

1 small yellow onion, chopped

1 cup white wine

4 cups chicken stock

2 cups beef stock

Kosher salt

½ ounce foie gras

1 tablespoon unsalted butter

**FOR THE POTATO PURÉE**

2 medium russet potatoes, peeled and sliced into rounds

2 teaspoons kosher salt, divided

8 tablespoons (1 stick) unsalted butter

¾ cup heavy cream

¼ teaspoon ground white pepper

2 teaspoons truffle oil

In a medium saucepan, melt the butter and cream together over medium-high heat, then reduce the heat and allow the cream to bubble gently. Keep warm.

Rice the potatoes. Immediately fold in the cream and butter, working quickly to avoid creating a gluey texture. The potatoes should be loose enough to not hold shape. If they need thinning, add more cream, 1 tablespoon at a time. Season with the remaining salt, white pepper, and truffle oil. Keep the purée warm on a very low setting until use, adding a little cream and butter if it starts to dry out.

## TO FINISH THE SAUCE
Once the sauce has thickened, pass it through a fine-mesh strainer, discarding the bones. Pour the sauce into a blender and add a pinch of salt, foie gras, and butter. Blend at high speed until silky smooth. Set aside.

## TO COOK THE QUAIL
Preheat the oven to 350°. Coat a sauté pan with oil over high heat. Once it begins to smoke, add the quail, breast-side down, and brown for 3 minutes. Flip the quail and brown the other side, about 1 minute more. Finish the quail in the oven, about 5 minutes. In the meantime, prepare the toast. When the quail is done, allow it to rest while you make the foie gras.

## TO MAKE THE TOAST AND SEARED FOIE GRAS
Melt the butter in a skillet and toast the bread until golden and crisped. Slice the toast in half and set aside.

Set a dry pan over high heat. Using a knife, cut crosshatches into one side of each foie gras portion. Season generously with salt and pepper. Add the fois gras to the scorching-hot pan and sear for 2 minutes per side, or until it turns a deep brown.

## TO ASSEMBLE
Place a large spoonful of potato purée on a plate. Spread a small amount of purée on the toast halves and set them on the plate. (This will act as a glue to help the quail stay in place.) Place 2 quail on top of the toast, add the foie gras, and drizzle with the reduction. Serve immediately.

**FOR THE TOAST AND SEARED FOIE GRAS**
**2 tablespoons unsalted butter**
**2 slices crusty white bread**
**4 (1-ounce) portions of foie gras**

# Roasted Duck Breast with Farrotto and Cherry Demiglace

**4 duck breasts, skin on**

**FOR THE DEMIGLACE**
**2 quarts duck stock
   (or chicken stock)**
**1 cup cherry jam**
**¼ cup red wine vinegar**
**8 tablespoons (1 stick)
   unsalted butter**

**FOR THE FARRO**
**1 cup medium yellow onion,
   chopped**
**9 tablespoons unsalted butter,
   divided**
**4 quarts whey (or low-sodium
   vegetable stock)**
**2 cups farro piccolo**
**¼ cup white wine**
**1 tablespoon kosher salt**
**1 teaspoon black pepper**
**½ cup freshly grated
   Parmesan**

In this recipe, we'll walk you through some techniques for achieving crispy duck skin. The most important part of this process involves extracting as much fat as possible from the skin. Preparation begins a day in advance, so plan accordingly. The duck is served with a rich demiglace and grains of farro, cooked risotto-style.

Find farro piccolo at ansonmills.com. You can substitute pearled farro, although the cooking process will take significantly longer and will likely need more stock. Use low-sodium stock if you are using a store-bought variety.

SERVES 4

Score the skin of each duck breast. Place the breasts on a plate and refrigerate, uncovered, for 24 hours.

### TO MAKE THE DEMIGLACE
Heat the stock to a rapid simmer and reduce by 90 percent. Stir in the cherry jam, followed by the vinegar; continue to simmer and reduce, watching the sauce carefully. When the bubbles start to get big, remove the sauce from the heat and whisk in the butter until it has fully melted and the sauce thickens. Reserve and keep warm.

### TO MAKE THE FARRO
In a large pot, combine the onions and 8 tablespoons of the butter over low heat. Place the whey or stock into a separate pot and simmer over medium-high heat. Once the onions soften, add the farro to the pot. Deglaze the pan with the wine, then reduce the heat to medium low. Begin ladling the stock into the pot, a little at a time, barely covering the grains. Stir frequently until the liquid cooks out, as you would with risotto, then ladle in more stock.

Continue this process, stirring constantly, until all the stock has been used and the farro is al dente. This should take about 20 minutes. (If the farro is not cooked through, add more stock.) Season with salt and pepper, then add the remaining butter and the Parmesan. Keep warm until ready to serve.

## TO COOK THE DUCK

Preheat the oven to 450°. Place the duck breasts in a cold cast-iron skillet, skin-side down. Set the pan over low heat and season the duck with salt. Find a weight, such as a heatproof dish or a sandwich press, to place atop the duck breasts while they cook. The weight helps the fat render out of the skin.

As the duck renders, use a spoon to transfer the fat to a container to store it for another use. Continue this process of spooning out the fat for 10–15 minutes, or until the skin gets crispy. Flip the duck breasts, then finish in them the oven for 4 minutes. Remove the duck and let it rest, uncovered (covering it will ruin the crispy skin), for 5 minutes before slicing.

## TO ASSEMBLE

Spoon the farro on a plate and top it with slices of duck breast. Finish with the demiglace and serve immediately.

# Lemongrass Chicken Meatball Wraps
# with Napa Slaw and Peanut Sauce

## FOR THE MEATBALLS

2 pounds boneless chicken
    thighs, skin on

1 jalapeño, seeded

1/3 cup lemongrass, peeled to
    tender stems

1/3 cup scallions, white parts
    only

2 garlic cloves, peeled

1 (2-inch) nub of ginger, peeled

3 tablespoons fish sauce

2 teaspoons palm sugar

3 tablespoons yellow curry
    paste (such as Mae Ploy)

1/2 bunch cilantro leaves
    with stems, plus 1/4 cup
    chopped cilantro leaves

1/2 bunch Thai basil leaves,
    chopped

2 teaspoons powdered milk

Nonstick spray

## FOR THE SLAW

1 head savoy cabbage, cored,
    quartered, and thinly sliced

5 celery ribs, peeled and cut
    on the bias

2 large carrots, peeled
    and julienned (cut into
    1/8 × 2-inch pieces)

1 European cucumber, seeded
    and julienned (cut into
    1/8 × 2-inch pieces)

These lettuce wraps are a tasty way to feed a crowd. We developed this recipe at Good Food on Montford, melding classic Southeast Asian flavors—lemongrass, ginger, and fish sauce— to make chicken meatballs similar to traditional Vietnamese *nem nuong*. We serve these with an Asian inspired slaw and an addictive, sweet-and-spicy peanut sauce.

We grind our own meat for the meatballs so that we can fully utilize the entire chicken. You can grind the sausage a day ahead and cook it when you're ready to serve. If this feels like too much work, you can purchase ground chicken instead. A good Asian grocery or other market with a sizable international section would be a helpful resource for this recipe.

SPECIAL EQUIPMENT: stand mixer with grinder attachment and small die (if grinding your own meat), 3/4-ounce scoop

SERVES 8–12

### TO MAKE THE MEATBALLS

Dice the chicken thighs and set them on a baking sheet. To aid the grinding process, place the chicken, grinder attachments, and mixing bowl in the freezer for 20 minutes.

In a blender, purée the jalapeños, lemongrass, scallions, garlic, ginger, fish sauce, palm sugar, curry paste, and 1/2 bunch cilantro with stems. Pour the lemongrass mixture into a container, refrigerate, and reserve while you grind the sausage.

Remove the chicken, grinder parts, and bowl from the freezer. Assemble the grinder with the small die and grind the chicken into the bowl of a stand mixer. Add the reserved lemongrass mixture. Using the paddle attachment, whip on medium-high speed for 30 seconds, then add the chopped cilantro leaves, Thai basil, and powdered milk. Whip on medium-high speed again for about 30 seconds more, or until the mixture sticks to the side of the bowl. Set aside or cover and refrigerate until use.

## TO MAKE THE SLAW

Combine all the vegetables in a large bowl. In a blender, combine the lime juice, ginger, mirin, scallions, soy sauce, vinegar, palm sugar, and sambal oelek to make the dressing. Pour over the slaw and toss well. Cover and refrigerate 1 hour to allow the flavors to meld together. Toss again before serving.

## TO MAKE THE SAUCE

Whisk the peanut butter with 1 tablespoon water to loosen it up to the consistency of hollandaise. Add the remaining ingredients and whisk until blended. Adjust seasoning to taste—more sriracha if you like it spicy, more hoisin for a sweeter version.

## TO COOK THE MEATBALLS

Spray nonstick spray on a baking sheet. Remove the chicken from the refrigerator. Scoop out a small portion (about ¾ ounce) and roll into a meatball. Place it on the baking sheet and press down lightly to form a patty. Repeat the process until all the meat is used.

Heat a grill or grill pan over high heat. Spray the tops of the patties with nonstick spray and place them on a hot grill. Cook for 5 minutes. Flip the patties and cook them for 4 minutes more, or until they are cooked through.

## TO ASSEMBLE

This dish can be assembled individually or served family style. To assemble individually, place a dollop of slaw into the center of a lettuce leaf. Top with 1 or 2 meatball patties, followed by the peanut sauce. Garnish with chopped peanuts, Thai basil, and cilantro.

To serve family style, arrange the chicken meatballs in the center of a platter and arrange the lettuce leaves decoratively on the perimeter. Place the slaw, peanut sauce, and garnishes in separate bowls and position them next to the meatball platter.

1 large red bell pepper,
  julienned (cut into
  ⅛ × 2-inch pieces)
2 jalapeños, seeded and
  julienned (cut into
  ⅛ × 2-inch pieces)
½ cup fresh lime juice
  (from about 3 limes)
1 (2-inch) nub of ginger, peeled
½ cup mirin
1 bunch scallions, whites only
½ cup soy sauce
½ cup rice vinegar
1 tablespoon palm sugar
1 teaspoon sambal oelek

**FOR THE SAUCE**
1 cup creamy peanut butter
½ teaspoon curry powder
1 tablespoon hoisin
1 tablespoon sriracha
Pinch kosher salt

Leafy lettuce, such as Bibb
½ bunch cilantro leaves,
  for garnish
½ bunch Thai basil leaves,
  for garnish
Chopped salted peanuts,
  for garnish (optional)

# Duck Confit

¼ cup kosher salt

1 teaspoon Aleppo pepper
or black pepper

4 garlic cloves, crushed

1 medium shallot, peeled
and sliced

6 sprigs fresh thyme
(stems discarded)

4 whole duck legs

4 cups duck fat or lard

Back in the days without refrigeration, cooking and preserving meats in their fat was a practical way to extend their shelf life. This French technique, called *confit*, has stood the test of time even though refrigeration eliminated the need for it—mostly because the result is supremely delicious, tender, and flavorful.

A classic preparation using the confit technique is duck cooked low and slow in its own fat until it surrenders itself from the bone. Duck confit is rich and decadent. I like to eat it on a cold winter night with stewed white beans and roasted carrots. It is also great atop salads or folded into soups. At our restaurants we use it in a variety of dishes including our Duck Confit Pizza with Butternut Squash and Gorgonzola (page 236), which we serve at Stagioni. The duck fat in which the legs are stored can also be used to fry potatoes or to roast vegetables. Find duck fat online at dartagnan.com or at specialty markets.

### SERVES 4

Combine the salt, pepper, garlic, shallots, and thyme. Rub the mixture evenly all over the duck legs. Place duck legs skin-side down on a wire rack, then place the rack over a sheet pan. Place another sheet pan over the legs and add a weight on top, such as a soup can or heavy plate. Refrigerate for 12–24 hours.

Preheat the oven to 225°F. Melt the duck fat on the stovetop. Use a wet rag to thoroughly wipe the cure from the duck legs, then pat them dry with a paper towel.

In a high-sided baking dish or an ovenproof pan, arrange the duck legs skin-side up in a single, snug layer. Carefully pour the melted fat over top to completely cover. Secure the pan tightly with foil and place in the oven. Cook for 2–3 hours, or until the duck is tender and can be easily pulled from the bone. Cool the duck, then store it by submerging the duck in its own fat. It will keep this way for 2 weeks.

# Pasta & Pizza

When I walked through the doors of the Villa, a historic Tuscan Revival–style house in Charlotte (see sidebar, page 226), I knew that I'd found the spot that could be a backdrop for the kind of wood-fired pizzas and pastas I'd enjoyed during my youth. Soon we transformed the space into Stagioni, my third restaurant.

Rhode Island is known for its large population of Italian Americans, people who have shaped the community and culture since the nineteenth century. In my hometown of Barrington, Rhode Island, that translated to mom and pop joints that served pizza and Italian American classics. I clearly remember invites to Sunday suppers where heaping portions of fresh cavatelli were the norm. I got another taste of Italian American influence in Boston, where its vibrant North End neighborhood (Boston's Little Italy) is one of its most famous cultural draws.

Italian food brings a certain nostalgia for New England, and I wanted to bring that sense of rich comfort to Charlotte. This chapter is largely influenced by what we do at Stagioni, including a host of creative pizzas and fresh handmade pastas, but it also contains some of the best dishes from my other restaurants, such as Barrington's famous gnocchi and Good Food's garganelli with Italian sausage.

# Parmesan Gnocchi with Ragout of Braised Veal and Porcini Mushrooms

You would think that this dish is one we serve at Stagioni, my Italian restaurant, but it's actually been at Barrington's since the beginning. I learned to make gnocchi while working in Boston, where the Italian influence is prevalent. This is the first dish I came up with that made it on a restaurant menu. I love how the earthiness of the porcini works with tender veal and airy potato dumplings.

Staying organized will help you navigate this recipe. Cut all the meat and vegetables for the stock in advance. You can make the gnocchi a day ahead and freeze it. If you do not care for veal or have a hard time finding it, beef stew meat is a good substitute.

**SPECIAL EQUIPMENT:** cheesecloth, potato ricer, stand mixer with paddle attachment

---

**SERVES 6–8**

TO PREPARE THE POTATOES FOR THE GNOCCHI

Preheat the oven to 350°. Place the potatoes in a large roasting dish and fill one-third of the way with water. Cover the pan tightly with foil and roast the potatoes for 90 minutes, or until a knife inserted into the potato meets no resistance. Peel and rice the potatoes, then spread them on a baking sheet and let cool to room temperature.

TO MAKE THE RAGOUT

Cut the veal into 1-inch cubes. Place the cubes on a baking sheet lined with kitchen towels and pat them dry. Season with salt and pepper. Coat a Dutch oven with olive oil over high heat. When the oil is shimmering, add the veal and brown for 12–15 minutes, giving it a stir every 2 minutes.

While the veal browns, pour 2 cups of hot water over the porcini mushrooms to rehydrate them. Steep the mushrooms for 5 minutes, then remove them, reserving the liquid. Set aside.

Once the veal is completely browned, add the vegetables, salt, and pepper, and sweat the vegetables for 2 minutes, or until translucent. Add both wines and reduce by two-thirds, about 6 minutes. Add the tomatoes, mushrooms, and veal stock. Strain the reserved porcini liquid

**FOR THE GNOCCHI**

4 large russet potatoes

3 cups all-purpose flour, plus more for rolling

1 cup plus 2 tablespoons finely grated Parmesan, divided, plus more for serving

1 tablespoon kosher salt

1 teaspoon ground white pepper

3 large eggs

Nonstick spray

2 tablespoons unsalted butter, divided

Extra-virgin olive oil

**FOR THE RAGOUT**

2 pounds veal stew meat, cleaned and trimmed

3 tablespoons olive oil

1 cup dried porcini mushrooms

2 medium carrots, cut into ⅛-inch dice

1 large yellow onion, cut into ¼-inch dice

4 stalks celery, cut into ⅛-inch dice

1 tablespoon kosher salt

1 teaspoon black pepper

1 cup red wine

1 cup white wine

2 cups chopped fresh tomatoes with juice

2 cups veal stock (can substitute beef or chicken stock)

4 fresh bay leaves

≫ ≫ ≫

into the pot with a cheesecloth to avoid adding any sediment. Add the bay leaves and simmer over medium-low heat for 1½–2 hours, or until the veal is tender. Keep warm until ready to use. Meanwhile, make the gnocchi.

### TO MAKE THE GNOCCHI

In a stand mixer fitted with a paddle attachment, add the cooled potatoes, flour, 1 cup of the Parmesan, the salt, and the white pepper. Mix on medium-low speed until the dough is homogenous. Add the eggs, one at a time, and fully incorporate them into the dough.

Remove the dough from the bowl (it should have the same consistency as playdough) and press it together to form a solid log. Slice off a small piece and test it in a pot of boiling water; it should float to the surface and not fall apart. If it does fall apart, add ½ cup flour to the dough and reshape.

Spray a baking sheet with nonstick spray and dust with flour. Slice the log of dough into 1-inch-thick rounds. On a floured work surface, roll the rounds into a thin rope about ½ inch diameter. Cut the rope into ½ × ½-inch pieces to make the gnocchi. Sprinkle them with flour and place them on the baking sheet in a single layer. Repeat this process until all the gnocchi is cut. (At this point, you can freeze the gnocchi on the baking sheet if not using right away; once frozen, transfer the gnocchi to a storage bag and return to the freezer until ready to use.)

Bring a pot of salted water to a rolling boil. Drop the gnocchi into the pot. Cook until they float to the surface, about 5 minutes, then remove them with a skimmer and transfer to a baking sheet. Drizzle with olive oil.

### TO ASSEMBLE

Melt 1 tablespoon of the butter in a nonstick sauté pan over medium-high heat until it starts to brown. Working in batches, add the gnocchi and toss them until lightly browned, about 3 minutes. Stir the remaining butter and Parmesan into the veal braise. Ladle the stew into a large serving bowl and gently spoon the gnocchi on top. Serve with more Parmesan and crusty bread.

# Garganelli with Italian Sausage

Staff meal has always been an important part of restaurant culture. Every day, someone in the kitchen is responsible for producing a meal for the entire staff. At 4:30 p.m., we sit down, relax for a moment and enjoy food together. When I first opened Barrington's, staff meal was always on my prep list. I made this garganelli to use up ingredients I had in the kitchen. It became very popular; everyone always had seconds. Today we serve this dish at Good Food on Montford. The sauce-catching ridges of garganelli are perfect for soaking up the bright and tangy tomato sauce, and our housemade fennel sausage adds a wonderful licorice note and a little heat. Make the pasta in advance and freeze it for a perfect one-pan dish at the end of a busy day.

*Note*: If you're using store-bought sausage, remove the casing and break it into crumbles while cooking. Add a little crushed chili flakes to the sauce when you add your seasoning.

**SPECIAL EQUIPMENT:** pasta maker or stand mixer with pasta attachment, garganelli comb and stripper (or gnocchi board and pencil), ruler

**SERVES 4**

### TO MAKE THE PASTA

Place all the ingredients for the pasta into a food processor and process until the mixture resembles a coarse meal. Transfer the mixture to a bowl and press it together, gathering up the crumbs and forming a ball. Continue to work the dough on a floured work surface, pressing and folding it in on itself until the dough is smooth and firm. Wrap the dough in plastic and refrigerate for at least 1 hour.

Remove the chilled dough from the refrigerator and let it rest for 10 minutes. Cut the dough into 4 equal portions. Lightly flour a work surface and roll one portion into a rectangle a little less than the width of the pasta maker (or attachment). Lightly flour the top of the dough and pass it through the pasta maker on its widest setting. Flour the dough again, tapping off excess flour, and pass it through a second time. Move the pasta maker to the next setting down, dust the pasta sheet with flour, and pass it through again. Continue this process, dusting the dough with flour each time and moving to the next setting after every 2 passes, until the pasta sheet is $\frac{1}{16}$ inch thick.

**FOR THE PASTA**

**1 pound all-purpose flour,**
   **plus more for dusting**
**2 large eggs**
**8 large egg yolks**
**1 tablespoon whole milk**
**1 tablespoon extra-virgin**
   **olive oil**
**Semolina flour, for dusting**

## FOR THE SAUCE

- 2 tablespoons extra-virgin olive oil
- ½ pound fennel sausage (page 167) or store-bought sweet Italian sausage
- 2 tablespoons sliced garlic
- 1½ teaspoons chopped fresh thyme
- 1 teaspoon kosher salt
- ½ teaspoon black pepper
- 1 cup white wine
- 1 tablespoon fresh lemon juice
- 4 cups crushed tomatoes
- 8 tablespoons (1 stick) unsalted butter
- ½ cup finely grated Parmesan, plus more for serving

Use a ruler to cut the pasta into 1½ × 1½-inch squares. Line a baking sheet with parchment paper and dust it with semolina flour; set aside.

Place the garganelli comb or gnocchi board with the lines vertically facing your body. Place a square of cut pasta on the board with a corner of the square facing you, so that it looks like a diamond. Place a gnocchi stripper (dowel) or pencil on the top third of the pasta square. Fold the top corner over the dowel and roll it toward you until the pasta is tubular in shape. (Use consistent pressure to impress the ridges into the pasta and seal properly.) When the pasta is completely sealed, gently remove it and place it on the prepared baking sheet. Repeat the process for the remaining pasta squares. Use the garganelli within 1 hour of preparation, or freeze them in a single layer, then place them in a storage bag until use. Bring a large pot of salted water to a boil.

### TO MAKE THE SAUCE

Meanwhile, heat the olive oil over high heat in a large saucepot and brown the sausage. Add the garlic and lightly brown. Pour off extra fat, then add the thyme, salt, and pepper; cook for 30 seconds. Add the wine and reduce slightly, then add the lemon juice, tomatoes, butter, and Parmesan; bring to a boil. Lower the heat to medium and simmer until the sauce has thickened slightly, about 5 minutes. Taste and adjust seasoning, if needed.

### TO ASSEMBLE

Add the garganelli to the boiling water and cook for 2 minutes, or until al dente. Strain the pasta and transfer it to the finished sauce. Toss and serve immediately with more Parmesan and warm crusty bread.

# Seafood Cannelloni with Lobster Sauce

## FOR THE PASTA DOUGH

1 ½ teaspoons extra-virgin olive oil

6 sprigs fresh tarragon, leaves removed

½ pound all-purpose flour, plus more for dusting

1 ½ teaspoons whole milk

4 large egg yolks

1 large egg

Semolina flour, for dusting

Dishes like this one always satisfy my New England seafood cravings. For an experienced home cook looking for a challenge, this recipe offers plenty of restaurant-level work. With fresh, tarragon-infused pasta, a flavorful seafood filling, and a silky lobster sauce, you're sure to impress a crowd—and maybe even yourself. Take liberties with the types of seafood used in the filling to enjoy what's in season.

*Note*: Make the pasta dough and lobster stock in advance. That way when you are ready to serve the cannelloni, all you need to do is assemble, stuff, and bake.

**SPECIAL EQUIPMENT**: stand mixer with pasta attachment or a pasta maker, ruler, food processor

SERVES 4

### TO MAKE THE PASTA DOUGH

Combine the olive oil and tarragon leaves in a blender and mix on high speed. Transfer the paste to a food processor and add the remaining ingredients; process until the mixture resembles couscous. Dump the contents on a clean work surface and press the dough into a solid mass. Wrap the dough in plastic and refrigerate for at least 2 hours and up to 24 hours. It is important to let this dough fully hydrate before working with it.

### TO PREPARE THE LOBSTER

Prepare an ice bath and set aside. Bring a large pot of heavily salted water to a boil and cook the lobsters for 8 minutes. Immediately plunge them into the ice bath. Once the lobsters have cooled, separate the meat from tails and claws, reserving the bodies and shells for the stock. Roughly chop the lobster tail and claw meat, picking out any shells, and chill until ready to use.

## TO MAKE THE STOCK

Remove the gills from the lobster bodies and use a butcher knife to cut the bodies into 4 equal pieces. In a large stockpot, combine the lobster shells, onions, carrots, celery, and herbs with 1 gallon water. Bring to a boil, then reduce the heat to low and simmer for 2 hours. Strain through a fine strainer and set aside.

## TO PREPARE THE REMAINING SEAFOOD

In a large saucepan, bring the wine and 1 tablespoon of the salt to a boil. Add the mussels and toss to distribute the heat. The mussels are done when the shells have opened; discard any unopened ones. Chill the mussels, then remove them from the shells and cover. Reserve in the refrigerator.

Prepare an ice bath. Combine the sugar, remaining salt, Old Bay Seasoning, and 1 quart water in a pot, and bring it to a rolling boil. Reduce the heat to medium, then add the shrimp and poach for 3–5 minutes, or until the shrimp are uniformly pink. Remove the shrimp with a slotted spoon and plunge them immediately into the ice bath. Peel the shrimp and roughly chop the meat. Cover and chill until ready to use.

## TO MAKE THE CANNELLONI FILLING

In a stand mixer fitted with a paddle attachment, mix the cheeses, herbs, lemon zest, pepper, and salt on medium speed until they are fully incorporated. Remove the bowl from the mixer and gently fold in the chilled seafood. Return the filling to the refrigerator until ready to assemble.

## TO MAKE THE TOPPING

Preheat the oven to 400°. Toss the panko, lemon zest, salsa verde, and olive oil together. Spread the bread crumbs on a parchment-lined baking sheet and bake for 5 minutes, or until crispy and lightly browned. Set aside.

**FOR THE LOBSTER STOCK**
3 (1-pound) lobsters
2 cups chopped yellow onions
1 cup chopped carrots
1 cup chopped celery
1 fresh bay leaf
½ bunch thyme

**FOR THE SEAFOOD**
½ cup white wine
3 tablespoons kosher salt, divided
2 pounds mussels, debearded
2 tablespoons sugar
1 tablespoon Old Bay Seasoning
1 pound North Carolina shrimp, shells on (16–20 count)

## FOR THE CANNELLONI FILLING

1 ½ cups mascarpone

2 cups whole-milk ricotta or fresh Ricotta (page 33)

1 cup (8 ounces) cream cheese

¼ cup chopped fresh parsley

¼ cup chopped fresh chives

1 tablespoon fresh tarragon

Zest of 4 lemons

1 teaspoon ground white pepper

Heaping tablespoon kosher salt

## FOR THE LOBSTER SAUCE

1 quart lobster stock

1 quart heavy cream

## FOR THE TOPPING

2 cups panko

Zest of 1 lemon

3 tablespoons Salsa Verde (page 9)

3 tablespoons extra-virgin olive oil

## TO MAKE THE CANNELLONI

Remove the pasta dough from the refrigerator and let it rest for 10 minutes at room temperature. Assemble the stand mixer with the pasta attachment or set up your pasta maker. Dust a work surface with all-purpose flour, then sprinkle it with semolina flour. Roll the dough into a large rectangle about ½ inch thick. Dust the top with flour and feed the dough into the pasta maker with the roller on its widest setting. Dust the dough with flour again and pass it through a second time. Keep passing the dough through the roller until it is about 1⁄16 inch thick (a setting of 2 or 3 on the stand mixer).

Line a baking sheet with parchment paper, then dust it with all-purpose flour and semolina. Bring a pot of salted water to a boil. Meanwhile, on a floured work surface use a ruler to cut the pasta sheet into 4 × 4-inch squares.

Add the cannelloni squares to the boiling water and cook for 2–3 minutes. Remove the cannelloni from the water and place them on the baking sheet; drizzle with olive oil to prevent sticking.

## TO MAKE THE LOBSTER SAUCE

In a medium saucepan, bring the lobster stock to a boil, then reduce the heat and simmer until reduced by three-fourths. Add the heavy cream and reduce again by three-fourths, or until the sauce is thick enough to coat the back of a spoon. (While the sauce reduces, assemble the cannelloni.) When it's done, adjust seasoning. Keep warm.

## TO ASSEMBLE

Preheat the oven to 325°. Place a heaping spoonful of filling on the lower side of the cannelloni square, then gently roll it up until the edges meet, pressing gently to seal and spread the filling inside evenly. Place the cannelloni seam-side down into an oven-safe baking dish. Repeat until you have filled the dish, then pour the lobster sauce on top; it should mostly cover the cannelloni. Place the baking dish on a rimmed baking sheet and bake for 15 minutes, or until the sauce is bubbling.

Garnish with crunchy panko topping and serve immediately. Then treat yourself to an adult beverage. You've earned it.

# Sweet Corn and Mascarpone Agnolotti with Butter Beans and Roasted Corn

Agnolotti is a stuffed pasta similar to ravioli, except it is just one pasta sheet (instead of two) folded over its filling and pinched into small pillows. Our summertime version is brightened by the addition of lemon zest—in the pasta dough and in the mascarpone filling. Roasted corn, fresh herbs, vegetables, and a simple white wine cream sauce keep the dish light enough for warm-weather days.

*Note*: The filling is easier to work with when chilled. The pasta also must be chilled. Be sure to account for this resting time when planning. When cooking, be gentle with the agnolotti. They are delicate and can easily burst with aggressive handling. You can make and freeze this pasta in advance. Simply flour a baking sheet and arrange the agnolotti in a single layer without overcrowding. Freeze the pasta completely on a sheet pan before cooking. The pasta can be stored in a plastic storage in the freezer for up to 1 month.

**SPECIAL EQUIPMENT**: stand mixer with whisk and pasta attachments (or a pasta maker), piping bag, food processor, pizza cutter or fluted pasta cutter, ruler

**SERVES 4–6**

### TO MAKE THE PASTA DOUGH
Combine all the ingredients for the pasta in a food processor and process until the texture resembles a coarse meal. Transfer the mixture to a bowl and press to form a ball. Work the dough, pressing down and gathering all bits. Fold the dough into itself and continue to press it together until it is smooth and homogenous. Wrap the dough in plastic and refrigerate for 1 hour, or until ready to use.

**FOR THE PASTA DOUGH**

½ pound all-purpose flour

4 large egg yolks

2 teaspoons whole milk

Zest of 1 lemon

2 teaspoons lemon-infused olive oil (or extra-virgin olive oil)

## FOR THE FILLING

2 ears corn, divided

Extra-virgin olive oil

½ cup (4 ounces) cream
    cheese, softened

1 cup mascarpone

2 tablespoons chopped
    fresh oregano

Zest of 1 lemon

2 teaspoons kosher salt

## FOR THE EGG WASH

1 large egg

½ cup water

### TO MAKE THE FILLING

Preheat the oven to 450°. Lightly brush the ears of corn with olive oil and season them with salt and pepper. Place the corn on a baking sheet lined with aluminum foil and roast for 15 minutes, rotating halfway through. Remove the baking sheet from the oven, let the corn cool to room temperature, and then slice the kernels from cob. Reserve ¾ cup kernels for the sauce and use the rest in the filling.

Add the roasted corn, cream cheese, mascarpone, oregano, lemon zest, and salt to the bowl of a stand mixer fitted with a whisk attachment. Whip on medium-high speed until the ingredients are fully combined. Transfer the filling to a piping bag or storage bag and refrigerate for 1–2 hours.

### TO MAKE THE EGG WASH

Once the filling is nearly chilled, whisk together the egg and water. Set the egg wash aside and make the pasta.

### TO MAKE THE PASTA

Affix the pasta attachment to the stand mixer (or set up your pasta maker). Liberally flour a work surface, then roll out the pasta dough into a rectangle wide enough to fit through the pasta roller, about ⅛ inch thick. Dust the dough with flour and pass it through the pasta roller at its widest setting. Dust the dough with flour again and pass it through a second time. Set the roller to the next widest setting, dust the pasta sheet, and pass it through again. Continue this process until the dough is 2–4 feet in length and about 1⁄16 inch thick.

Lay the pasta sheet flat on a floured work surface (preferably wooden). Using a ruler, cut the pasta sheet into 3½-inch-wide strips. Pipe the filling in a continuous line in the upper third of the pasta strip, leaving ½-inch space on each end. Dip your index finger into the egg wash and apply it directly beneath the filling line. Working from left to right, fold the top portion of pasta dough over the filling, tuck securely, and seal on the portion brushed with the egg wash. Press tightly and work all the way down until the strip is completely sealed.

Set the ruler at one end of the pasta strip and use the edge of your pinky fingers to press down vertically and form indentations every 2½ inches. Use a pizza cutter to trim the bottom to form a clean edge. Where your hands made indentations, cut to make individual agnolotti. Seal the agnolotti tightly, using your fingers to pinch the edges together, leaving no gap between the filling and the pasta sheet. This ensures that the filling doesn't spill out during cooking.

Bring a large pot of salted water to a gentle boil. Drizzle a baking sheet with olive oil and place it nearby. Working in batches, gently drop the agnolotti into the boiling water and cook for 4–6 minutes. Once the pasta floats, remove it and set it on the oiled baking sheet.

### TO MAKE THE SAUCE

In a sauté pan, heat 2 tablespoons of the butter over medium-high heat. Add the red peppers, butter beans, shallots, bay leaf, and salt. Sauté for 4 minutes, or until the vegetables soften. Add the wine, bring to a boil, and reduce the sauce by half. Add the cream and cook for 1 minute, then add the reserved roasted corn. Reduce the mixture by half, about 5–7 minutes. Add the reserved agnolotti to the sauce and toss gently to coat. Turn off the heat, add the lemon juice and remaining butter, and stir until melted.

### TO SERVE

For each serving, place the sauced agnolotti in a wide, shallow dish and garnish with the fresh thyme and oregano. Serve immediately, perhaps with a drizzle of Bay Oil (page 12).

**FOR THE SAUCE**

6 tablespoons unsalted butter, divided

1 red bell pepper, cut into ¼-inch dice

½ cup shelled butter beans

1 medium shallot, sliced

1 bay leaf

1 tablespoon kosher salt

¾ cup white wine

1 cup heavy cream

1 tablespoon fresh lemon juice

1 teaspoon fresh thyme, for garnish

1 tablespoon chopped fresh oregano, for garnish

# Spaghetti with Carolina Shrimp and Leeks

There is an irresistible alchemy that occurs when leeks, shallots, and garlic meet the savory richness of smoky pork and heavy cream. This dish comes together easily, each ingredient building on the next, to make a decadent meal that works well on a weeknight or for an informal dinner party. We add fresh North Carolina shrimp sautéed with butter and lemon, but the dish can stand alone.

Be sure to clean the leeks of all sediment before blanching.

**SERVES 4**

Slice the leeks into ¼-inch rings and clean them thoroughly in a bowl of warm water. Remove the leeks by scooping them from the top so that any grit falls to the bottom of the bowl. Set aside. Meanwhile, bring a pot of salted water to a boil and cook the pasta until it is al dente. Reserve 2–3 tablespoons of the pasta water. Drain and toss the pasta with olive oil to prevent sticking.

In a sauté pan over medium-high heat, add ½ tablespoon of the olive oil and the guanciale. Cook for 2–3 minutes, or until it smells toasty and deepens in color. Lower the heat to medium, add the shallots and garlic, and brown for 1 minute. Add the wine and leeks and reduce the liquid until nearly evaporated, then add the cream and reduce again by one-third. Add the pasta and the reserved pasta water. Cook for another 2 minutes, set aside, then cook the shrimp.

Season the shrimp liberally with salt and pepper. In a cold sauté pan, add the butter and remaining olive oil. Melt the butter over medium heat, then add the shrimp in an even layer. Add the lemon juice and cook for 2 minutes. Flip the shrimp and cook for 1 minute more, then turn off the heat. Remove the shrimp, then add the pasta and cream sauce to the same pan and toss them together with the residual butter and olive oil.

Portion the pasta on 4 plates, distributing the shrimp evenly. Shower with Parmesan and a few cracks of black pepper. Serve immediately.

2 medium leeks, white parts only
Kosher salt
1 (20-ounce) package spaghetti
8 ½ tablespoons extra-virgin olive oil, divided, plus more for drizzling
3 ounces guanciale (or prosciutto), julienned (cut into ⅛ × 2-inch pieces)
1 tablespoon diced shallot
1 tablespoon minced garlic
⅓ cup white wine
1 ½ cups heavy cream
1 pound North Carolina shrimp (21–25 count), shelled and deveined
Kosher salt and black pepper
8 tablespoons (1 stick) unsalted butter
Juice of ½ lemon
¼ cup finely grated Parmesan

# Sweet Potato Cavatelli with Spiced Lamb and Swiss Chard

FOR THE PASTA DOUGH

**6 medium white sweet potatoes (orange-fleshed sweet potatoes will work, too)**

**4 cups all-purpose flour, plus more for dusting**

**¼ cup whole milk**

**1 large egg**

**¼ teaspoon kosher salt**

FOR THE LAMB

**1 pound ground lamb**

**1 ½ tablespoons kosher salt**

**½ teaspoon black pepper**

**1 teaspoon hot paprika**

**½ teaspoon ground cumin**

**½ teaspoon ground coriander**

**½ teaspoon ground fennel**

**1 tablespoon minced garlic**

**Pinch cayenne pepper**

The Italian word *cavatelli* is derived from the verb *cavare*, which means to draw or hollow out. Cavatelli are rolled inward to create a hollow center, forming a pocket for capturing sauce. This can be done with a cavatelli maker, which can be purchased at specialty kitchen stores or online. For this dish, spiced lamb is prepared almost like a sausage. We pair it with Swiss chard and a simple sauce fortified with garlic, white wine, butter, and Parmesan. The sweet potatoes bring an autumnal sweetness to the pasta dough for a dish that shines in the cooler months.

This recipe makes extra lamb, which you can keep in the refrigerator for 1 week or freeze for 1 month. Use it anywhere you would use fresh ground lamb.

**SPECIAL EQUIPMENT:** cheesecloth, butcher's twine, fine-mesh strainer, potato ricer, cavatelli maker, stand mixer with paddle attachment

SERVES 8–10

TO PREPARE THE SWEET POTATOES
FOR THE PASTA DOUGH
Preheat the oven to 375°. Pierce the sweet potatoes all over and place them on a baking sheet. Roast for 1 hour. When done, cut the sweet potatoes open to release the steam and let them cool. Scoop out the flesh and place it into a square of cheesecloth. Pull the cheesecloth up from all corners, twist it into a bundle, and tie it tightly with butcher's twine. Leave extra string to hang the bundle in the refrigerator overnight. Place a small bowl beneath the sweet potatoes to catch any moisture. (This step ensures the removal of excess liquid. If you are pressed for time, you can skip it.)

TO PREPARE THE LAMB
In a stand mixer fitted with a paddle attachment, combine all the ingredients and mix until they are fully incorporated. The fat will emulsify and the lamb will lighten in color. Cover and refrigerate until use.

## TO MAKE THE PASTA

Remove the sweet potatoes from the refrigerator and pass them through a potato ricer. Use about 1 pound of the riced sweet potatoes; reserve the extra for another use. Place the sweet potatoes in the cheesecloth again, and squeeze to remove excess moisture. In a large bowl, combine the sweet potatoes, flour, milk, egg, and salt. Roll the dough into a ball, folding and pressing it on itself until it is smooth and homogenous. Wrap the dough in plastic and refrigerate for 1 hour. Line a baking sheet with parchment paper and dust with flour. Generously dust your work surface. Roll the chilled dough into a long rectangle about ¼ inch thick. Dust the dough well with flour.

Set up the cavatelli maker. Cut horizontal strips, about ½ inch wide, from the rectangle of dough. You want the strips to be as long as possible. Dust the dough with more flour, then feed it through the cavatelli maker and transfer it to the prepared baking sheet. Dust the dough again with flour. (If making a day ahead, freeze the pasta in a single layer on a baking sheet, then transfer the cavatelli immediately from the freezer into the cooking water. If preparing the same day, allow the pasta to rest on the countertop for 1 hour before cooking.)

Bring a large pot of salted water to boil. Add the cavatelli and cook until the pasta is al dente, about 4 minutes. Drain, reserving ¼ cup of the pasta water. Set aside.

## TO MAKE THE LAMB SAUCE

Heat the olive oil in a large sauté over high heat. Add the shallots, garlic, salt, and lamb, and sauté until fragrant and browned, about 5–7 minutes. Add the wine and deglaze the pan, scraping up any browned bits from the bottom of the pan. Add the chicken stock and reduce it by half over high heat. Add the cooked pasta, Swiss chard, butter, and Parmesan. Stir continuously, allowing the sauce to thicken and coat the pasta.

## TO SERVE

Transfer the pasta to a large serving bowl. Garnish with the chopped mint. Serve hot.

**FOR THE LAMB SAUCE**

2 tablespoons extra-virgin olive oil

1 teaspoon chopped shallots

1 teaspoon chopped garlic

2 teaspoons kosher salt

1 pound spiced lamb (see above)

½ cup white wine

1 cup chicken stock

2 pounds cavatelli (see above)

4 cups Swiss chard, stemmed, leaves rolled and thinly sliced

8 tablespoons (1 stick) unsalted butter, cubed

½ cup freshly grated Parmesan

Chopped mint, for garnish

# Stagioni Pizza Sauce

Along with a good dough, pizza sauce is the foundation for an excellent pie. It should be flavorful but uncomplicated. At Stagioni, we churn out thousands of pizzas every year in our wood-fired oven. Our recipe for pizza sauce has only four ingredients, but a long roast intensifies the natural sweetness of tomatoes and deepens the flavor, which we then accent with fresh oregano and red pepper flakes.

**6 pounds whole peeled tomatoes (from four 28-ounce cans, lightly drained)**
**2 tablespoons sugar**
**1 teaspoon crushed red pepper flakes**
**7 sprigs fresh oregano, divided**

**MAKES 1 ½ QUARTS**

Preheat the oven to 500°. Combine the tomatoes, sugar, red pepper flakes, and 6 sprigs of the oregano in a deep roasting pan. Roast for 90 minutes, or until the water evaporates. Stir occasionally to avoid sticking on the sides. The tomatoes should be charred and have a jam-like consistency.

Remove the pan from oven, discard the oregano stems, and carefully transfer the contents to a blender. Add the leaves from the remaining sprig of oregano and purée until smooth. Use immediately or store in a sealed container for up to 1 week.

# Stagioni Story

In Charlotte, a city known more for its spit-shined skyscrapers and unending new construction, I feel most connected to the places where you feel somehow part of the city's history. At Barrington's, it was a place recognized and loved by people who first loved Metropolitan Café (the business that was there before), and who eventually took a chance on me, a New England chef turned New Southerner. At Good Food on Montford, it was the redemptive spirit of a once shadowy strip.

At Stagioni, my third restaurant, we stepped into history. The restaurant lies inside a portion of what is formally known as the Reynolds-Gourmajenko House, an architectural marvel. Built in 1926 by renowned architect William Bottomley, the house is one of a kind—the only Tuscan Revival–style villa in Mecklenburg County and one of only four projects in North Carolina by Bottomley. The call for commission came from Charlotte native William A. Reynolds, who built his estate as an employee of the Southern Cotton Oil Company, and his unconventional wife, Blanche Reynolds. The house, guided by the whims of Blanche, was a dramatic rendition of home amid its genteel southern neighbors; there was the pitched roof, lined with tiles imported from Cuba, and a walled courtyard with a circular fountain reminiscent of those found in the piazzas of Italy, not to mention a splendor of interior decorations and original art.

When I first walked into the building some eighty years later, I blurted, "I guess we're doing Italian."

Thirteen years into my journey as a chef in the New South, I had amassed a good crew of individuals who had become more than just employees. Aware of the talent inside my kitchens and at the front of the house, I began to realize that restaurant growth was not so much for me but for those in my restaurant family who were ready to lead.

Stagioni, too, became the perfect venue to

## Andrew Dodd   EXECUTIVE CHEF, STAGIONI

Drew Dodd came to us from an executive chef post at another Charlotte restaurant and began as a line cook at Stagioni. It takes a certain kind of humility to do something like that.

A Nashville native, Drew brings a humble calm to Stagioni. Shortly after he began with us, we underwent significant changes in our kitchen staff, and Drew stepped up. His presence brought welcome stability to Stagioni at a time when we really needed it. His southern roots didn't deter him from delving into our brand of Italian cuisine and eventually making it his own. Just as quickly as Drew took over the kitchen, Stagioni settled into its true self.

revisit Italian food, an influence that stemmed from my time in Boston, where a large population of Italian Americans adds so much to the city's culture. I wanted to integrate some of those influences with my relationship to seasonal ingredients, especially those coming from the producers who'd supported me from the beginning.

By 2014, Charlotte was a new city in terms of dining culture. As we planned our opening, my peers and fellow veterans—chefs Tom Condron and Tim Groody— were on the cusp of opening their respective restaurants, chef-driven concepts guided using seasonal ingredients and years of hard work. One headline from the *Charlotte Observer* read, "Charlotte Restaurants Take a Leap with Burst of Openings." A slew of newcomers, like chefs Rocco Whalen (Fahrenheit) and Michael Shortino (Futo Buta Ramen, Lincoln's Haberdashery) started to arrive, and things were looking up for all of us. Thirteen years since moving to Charlotte, our dining culture had gathered a new momentum.

## LeeAnn Dolcetto
### MANAGER, STAGIONI

When I opened Good Food on Montford, LeeAnn Dolcetto joined on as a server and bartender. She stood out to me because she took ownership of every station she worked and quickly grasped the big picture. She immersed herself in all front-of-house aspects, quickly learning the wine list and offering up creative cocktail ideas. She is the type who stops to pick up a dropped napkin or notices when a table needs attention. And LeeAnn has never been shy about giving me her opinion on how to make my restaurants run more effectively.

In 2014, when I opened Stagioni, I needed a leader to guide our front-of-house team. LeeAnn was an obvious candidate. I told her to put her money where her mouth was and step up. LeeAnn confidently agreed. Over the years I've watched her grow as a manager. She has built a solid front-of-house staff, developed important human resource strategies, and contributed to the savvy marketing of the restaurant. Watching someone grow into their chosen role like this is one of the greatest pleasures of restaurant ownership.

# Stagioni Pizza Dough

We worked hard to perfect the pizza dough at Stagioni, because our wood-fired pizza is a keystone of the restaurant's menu. Reserve a couple days of lead time. This dough requires a poolish (a type of starter) that needs a jumpstart, and the pizza dough itself needs a twenty-four-hour rest once made.

*Note*: We recommend using a pizza peel for transferring pizzas from your work surface to the oven to prevent sticking. They can be purchased at specialty kitchen stores or online. A wooden work surface, such as a cutting board, will also work. For baking, we recommend a pizza stone. If you do not own one, use an oiled baking sheet and assemble the pizza directly on top of it.

**SPECIAL EQUIPMENT:** stand mixer with dough hook, digital scale, pizza stone, pizza peel or wooden cutting board

**MAKES 5 (8- TO 10-INCH) PIZZAS**

### TO MAKE THE POOLISH
Whisk together the cold water and yeast until combined. Add the flour and mix with a spatula until it resembles a thick batter. Cover with plastic and let it sit on the countertop for 4 hours, then refrigerate overnight.

### TO MAKE THE PIZZA DOUGH
Combine the flour, yeast, and powdered milk in the bowl of a stand mixer fitted with a dough hook. Mix for 1 minute on low speed, then add the poolish, water, olive oil, and honey. Mix for 3 minutes on medium-low speed. Add the salt, increase the speed to medium, and mix for 10 minutes more.

Spray a large bowl with nonstick spray or brush it with olive oil. Add the pizza dough to the bowl and cover with plastic. Let sit for 1 hour at room temperature, or until it doubles in size. Times will differ, depending on the temperature of your kitchen environment. Once the dough rises, measure the dough into 1-cup portions and place them in

**FOR THE POOLISH**
250 grams (1 cup plus 2 tablespoons) cold water
0.75 grams (1 teaspoon) active dry yeast
250 grams (1 ½ cups) all-purpose flour

**FOR THE PIZZA DOUGH**
500 grams (3 cups) all-purpose flour
0.50 grams (¼ teaspoon) active dry yeast
15 grams (2 tablespoons plus 1 teaspoon) powdered milk
200 grams (1 cup) water
30 grams (2 tablespoons) extra-virgin olive oil
15 grams (1 tablespoon) honey
15 grams (2 tablespoons) kosher salt
Nonstick spray
Semolina flour, for dusting

separate plastic containers (with lids) or quart-size plastic ziplock bags sprayed with nonstick spray. Let the dough rest, refrigerated, 24 hours more. After that, make some pizza! The dough will keep for 5 days.

### TO SHAPE AND BAKE THE PIZZA

Place a pizza stone into the oven and preheat to 500°. Remove the dough from the refrigerator and let it rest for 20 minutes. Fill a bowl with semolina flour and dust a wooden work surface with more semolina. While in its container, dust the pizza dough with semolina, then gently flip it over and use your hand to guide the dough ball into the bowl filled with semolina. Coat the bottom of the dough with semolina, then transfer it to your work surface.

Use your fingers to press the dough outward, forming a small circle with a raised outer edge (the crust). Drape the dough over your knuckles. Use the knuckles on both hands to work the dough into a larger circle. Once the dough is stretched to approximately 10 inches, place it on a pizza peel liberally dusted with semolina, then add your desired pizza toppings and bake immediately. If using an oiled baking sheet, assemble the pizza directly on the baking sheet, then place the sheet into the oven.

Bake the pizza on the stone or baking sheet for 8–10 minutes, or until the crust is golden. The dough can also be oiled and cooked on a hot grill.

# Mortadella Pizza with Taleggio and Braised Collard Greens

This funky pizza features crisp mortadella, pungent taleggio, and tangy collards. Assertive and aromatic, this flavorful pizza is both unique and delicious.

**SPECIAL EQUIPMENT:** pizza stone, pizza peel or wooden cutting board

**MAKES 4 (10-INCH) PIZZAS**

Place a pizza stone in the oven and preheat to 500°. Shape the pizza dough into 4 (10-inch) rounds as described on page 230. Dust a pizza peel or wooden cutting board with semolina and set 1 round on top. Ladle ½ cup sauce onto the center of the dough. Working from the center outward, spread the sauce evenly, leaving a ½-inch edge.

Evenly distribute the mozzarella over the tomato sauce, being careful to reserve ¼ cup to finish the pizza. Add an even layer of mortadella without overlapping (to ensure crisped edges). Add the taleggio and collard greens. Top with more mozzarella. Transfer the pizza to the heated pizza stone and bake for about 8–10 minutes, or until the cheese has melted and the crust is lightly golden.

Repeat the process with the remaining crusts.

1 batch Stagioni Pizza Dough (page 229) or store-bought pizza dough
1 batch Stagioni Pizza Sauce (page 225)
2 cups freshly grated mozzarella, divided
8 ounces sliced mortadella
8 ounces taleggio
1 cup New South Collards (page 118)
Semolina flour, for dusting
Kosher salt

# Brussels Sprouts Pizza with Parmesan Cream and Smoked Pancetta

**FOR THE BRUSSELS SPROUTS**

4 cups Brussels sprouts

8 tablespoons (1 stick) unsalted butter

**FOR THE PARMESAN CREAM**

2 cups heavy cream

12 garlic cloves, peeled

¼ cup finely grated Parmesan

The Brussels sprouts pizza is one of the most popular items on Stagioni's menu, and for good reason. It has an addictive blend of flavors—smoky, sweet, salty, and garlicky. To help us achieve this robust flavor profile and to add texture, we use a garnish of pickled onions and fresh Brussels sprouts. It shines against the savory backdrop of caramelized sprouts, Parmesan garlic cream, and crispy pancetta.

*Note*: Because Brussels sprout leaves break down quickly, make the garnish just before you bake the pizzas. Look for smoked sea salt and smoked oil olive at specialty spice shops or a gourmet grocery.

**SPECIAL EQUIPMENT:** pizza stone, pizza peel or wooden cutting board

**MAKES 4 (10-INCH) PIZZAS**

**TO MAKE THE BRUSSELS SPROUTS**
Remove the outer leaves of the Brussels sprouts and reserve, then quarter the Brussels sprouts. Melt the butter in a large sauté pan over medium-high heat; add the quartered Brussels sprouts and cook for 6–7 minutes, or until they soften and take on a little color. (If the sprouts soften but have no color, raise the heat briefly until they brown.) Drain excess fat and allow to cool.

**TO MAKE THE PARMESAN CREAM**
Combine the heavy cream and garlic cloves in a saucepan over medium-high heat until bubbles just begin to form along the edges. Reduce the heat to medium and cook for 25 minutes, stirring occasionally to avoid scalding. Slowly add the Parmesan, using a whisk to fully incorporate the cheese. Remove the sauce from the heat and cool slightly, whisking occasionally to avoid a milk skin. Transfer the contents to a blender and blend on high speed for 1 minute. Cool completely; set aside or refrigerate until use.

## TO MAKE THE GARNISH

Stack 4–5 of the reserved Brussels sprouts leaves together, roll them, and slice them into thin strips (this is called chiffonade). Transfer the chiffonade to a small mixing bowl. Add the pickled onions, pickling liquid, smoked olive oil, and smoked sea salt. Toss until combined; set aside.

## TO MAKE THE PIZZA

In a sauté pan over medium heat, cook the pancetta until it is brown and crispy. Drain excess fat and set aside.

Place a pizza stone in the oven and preheat to 500°. Shape the pizza dough into 4 (10-inch) rounds. Dust a pizza peel or wooden cutting board with semolina and set 1 round on top. Ladle ⅓ cup sauce on the dough center. Working from the center outward, spread the sauce evenly, leaving a ½-inch edge.

Top with ¼ cup pancetta and one-fourth of the caramelized Brussels sprouts. Sprinkle with both cheeses. Season with salt and pepper.

Transfer the pizza to the heated pizza stone and bake for 8 minutes, or until the cheese has melted and the crust is lightly golden. Top the pizza with the garnish and serve immediately.

Repeat the process with the remaining crusts to make as many pizzas as desired.

**FOR THE GARNISH**

**Reserved Brussels sprouts leaves**

**¼ cup Red Wine Pickled Onions, plus 1 tablespoon pickling liquid (page 23)**

**1 ½ tablespoons smoked olive oil (can substitute regular olive oil)**

**1 teaspoon smoked sea salt**

**FOR THE PIZZA**

**1 cup diced smoked pancetta**

**1 recipe Stagioni Pizza Dough (page 229) or store-bought pizza dough**

**Semolina flour, for dusting**

**2 cups shredded mozzarella**

**1 cup shredded smoked mozzarella**

**Kosher salt and black pepper**

# Tartufo Pizza with Mushrooms, Caramelized Onions, and Arugula

**FOR THE PICKLED MUSHROOMS**

1 cup sugar

1 cup white balsamic vinegar

1 cup water

2 fresh bay leaves

2 sprigs each fresh thyme, oregano, and rosemary

6 cups thinly sliced mushrooms (such as cremini, shiitake, oyster, and beech)

**FOR THE CARAMELIZED ONIONS**

8 medium yellow onions, sliced

2 tablespoons unsalted butter

1 tablespoon extra-virgin olive oil

This pizza features mushrooms served raw and pickled, and pairs them with deeply caramelized onions, peppery arugula, and aromatic truffle oil. The result is a marriage of sweet, sour, and earthy flavors whose sum is greater than its individual parts. Don't skip any of the ingredients in this pizza. The pickled mushrooms are best if left in the brine overnight, so plan ahead.

**SPECIAL EQUIPMENT:** pizza stone, pizza peel or wooden cutting board

MAKES 4 (10-INCH) PIZZAS

**TO PICKLE THE MUSHROOMS**
Combine the sugar, vinegar, and water in a saucepan. Bundle the bay leaves, thyme, oregano, and rosemary in cheesecloth and tie the bundle with twine. Add the herbs to the saucepan and bring the contents to a boil. Place 4 cups of the mushrooms in a heatproof container and pour the hot pickling liquid over them to cover. If needed, place a weight on top of them to keep them submerged. Bring the mushrooms to room temperature on the countertop, then refrigerate overnight.

**TO CARAMELIZE THE ONIONS**
Combine the onions, butter, and olive oil in a pan over medium-high heat and cook for 3–5 minutes, or until color develops on the onions. Turn the heat to medium low and caramelize the onions, stirring every 10–15 minutes for approximately 1 hour. Once the onions are caramelized, season them with salt and pepper and let cool completely.

## TO ASSEMBLE AND BAKE THE PIZZA

Place a pizza stone in the oven and preheat to 500°. Shape the pizza dough into 4 (10-inch) rounds as described on page 230. Dust a pizza peel or wooden cutting board with semolina and set 1 round on top.

Starting from the center, add a thin layer of caramelized onions. Add 1 cup of the mozzarella. Top with ½ cup of the remaining mushrooms and a little more cheese.

Transfer the pizza to the heated pizza stone and bake for 7–10 minutes, or until the cheese has melted and the crust is lightly golden. Add 1 cup of the arugula to each pizza, plus the pickled mushrooms and grated Parmesan. Drizzle with truffle oil. Serve hot.

Repeat the process with the remaining crusts.

**FOR THE PIZZA**

**1 batch Stagioni Pizza Dough (page 229) or store-bought pizza dough**

**4 cups freshly grated mozzarella**

**4 cups baby arugula**

**1 cup finely grated Parmesan**

**Truffle oil, for drizzling**

# Duck Confit Pizza with Butternut Squash and Gorgonzola

**FOR THE BUTTERNUT SQUASH PURÉE**

1 medium butternut squash (about 3 pounds)

3 tablespoons Salsa Verde (page 9)

1 cup heavy cream

1 teaspoon kosher salt

¼ teaspoon ground white pepper (optional)

The pizzas at Stagioni are made with the same approach as our composed dishes. Each ingredient is essential. In this pizza, we pair the richness of duck confit—tender duck legs cooked in their own fat—with sharp Gorgonzola, nutty and sweet butternut squash, and a garnish of fresh arugula dressed with lemon juice and olive oil.

Learning the classic confit technique (page 206) is a worthy endeavor but also time-consuming. If you're short on time, you can find confit duck legs at a gourmet grocery store, such as Dean and Deluca. The same goes for the pizza dough. Use our recipe or save time with a store-bought variety. The pizza dough, duck confit, and butternut purée can all be made a day in advance.

**SPECIAL EQUIPMENT:** pizza stone, pizza peel or wooden cutting board

---

**MAKES 1 (10-INCH) PIZZA**

TO MAKE THE BUTTERNUT SQUASH PURÉE
Preheat the oven to 400°. Slice off the stem and bottom ends of the squash, then slice it in half lengthwise. Peel the skin off both halves and remove the seeds. Dice the squash into ½-inch cubes, separating the cubed cuts from ones that are not square. Reserve the odd cuts for the purée. Toss the squash cubes with the salsa verde and a pinch of salt. Spread the cubes on a baking sheet lined with parchment paper and roast for 30–35 minutes, or until the squash is soft and lightly browned. Set aside.

Place the odd cuts of butternut squash into a small saucepan with the cream. Cover and cook over medium-low heat, stirring occasionally, for 20–25 minutes, or until very tender. Using a strainer, drain the cream and reserve. Transfer the squash to a blender, add the salt and white pepper (if using), and purée until smooth. Check the consistency of the purée with a spoon. It should be silky and just hold its form on the spoon. If it is too thick, add some of the reserved cream, a little at a time, until it reaches the desired consistency. Set aside or refrigerate until use. (We prefer it chilled.)

## TO MAKE THE PIZZA

Place the pizza stone in the oven and increase the oven temperature to 500°. Follow the instructions on page 230 for shaping the pizza dough. Dust a pizza peel or wooden cutting board with semolina and set the round on top. Ladle the purée on the dough center. Working from the center outward, spread the purée evenly, leaving a ½-inch edge.

Add two-thirds of the mozzarella and all of the Gorgonzola. Add the duck confit, the remaining mozzarella, and ¼ cup of the butternut squash cubes. Place the pizza on a preheated pizza stone and bake for 7–8 minutes. Meanwhile, toss the arugula with a pinch of salt, a squeeze of lemon juice, and olive oil. Top the pizza with the dressed arugula and serve immediately.

### FOR THE PIZZA

1 batch Stagioni Pizza Dough (page 229) or store-bought pizza dough

Semolina flour, for dusting

½ cup freshly grated mozzarella

¼ cup crumbled Gorgonzola

½ cup Duck Confit (page 229)

1 cup baby arugula

Pinch kosher salt

Squeeze of lemon juice

½ tablespoon extra-virgin olive oil

# Arrabbiata Pizza with Prosciutto and Local Egg

**FOR THE ARRABBIATA SAUCE**

1 (12-ounce) jar roasted red peppers in water, drained

½ teaspoon cayenne pepper

1 teaspoon crushed red pepper flakes

¼ cup extra-virgin olive oil

**FOR THE PIZZA**

1 batch Stagioni Pizza Dough (page 229) or store-bought pizza dough

Semolina flour, for dusting

2 cups freshly grated mozzarella

24 paper-thin slices prosciutto

4 large eggs

2 cups baby arugula

Shaved Parmesan, for garnish

In Italian, the word *arrabbiata* means "angry" and refers to a spicy tomato sauce made with dried red chili peppers. In this recipe from Stagioni, we use roasted red bell peppers in lieu of tomatoes to make an arrabbiata base for one of our all-time favorite pizzas. Its kick is softened by a golden egg yolk and delicate slices of salty prosciutto.

**SPECIAL EQUIPMENT:** pizza stone, pizza peel or wooden cutting board

**MAKES 4 (10-INCH) PIZZAS**

TO MAKE THE ARRABBIATA SAUCE

Combine the roasted red peppers, cayenne, and crushed red pepper flakes in a blender and purée on high speed. With the blender running, slowly add the olive oil and emulsify. Refrigerate for at least 30 minutes.

TO MAKE THE PIZZA

Place the pizza stone in the oven and preheat to 500°. Follow the instructions on page 230 for shaping the pizza dough into 4 (10-inch) crusts. Dust a pizza peel or wooden cutting board with semolina and set 1 round on top. Ladle ⅓ cup sauce on the dough center. Working from the center outward, spread the sauce evenly, leaving a ½-inch edge. Top with the mozzarella followed by the prosciutto, leaving a well in the center for the egg. Crack the egg into the center and season with salt.

Transfer the pizza to the heated pizza stone and bake for 8–10 minutes, or until the egg is cooked. (The whites should be opaque but the yolk still runny.) Top with the arugula and shaved Parmesan; serve immediately.

Repeat the process with the remaining crusts to make as many pizzas as desired.

# Pepperoni and Sausage Pizza

This is our signature pizza at Stagioni—classic, uncomplicated, and crowd pleasing. We generously dole out the pepperoni and sausage and finish it with fresh herbs. Don't skimp on the toppings for this one. Your guests will be glad you didn't.

**SPECIAL EQUIPMENT:** pizza stone, pizza peel or wooden cutting board

**MAKES 4 (10-INCH) PIZZAS**

Place a pizza stone in the oven and preheat to 500°. Shape the pizza dough into 4 (10-inch) rounds as described on page 230.

In a large skillet, crumble the sausage and brown it with the olive oil over medium-high heat until fully cooked, about 5–7 minutes. Let the sausage cool for 15 minutes, then drain the fat from the sausage and reserve.

Dust a pizza peel or wooden cutting board with semolina and set 1 dough round on top. Ladle ⅓ cup sauce on the dough center. Working from the center outward, spread the sauce evenly, leaving a ½-inch edge. Add ¼ cup of the sausage, then top with mozzarella. Add enough pepperoni to cover the pizza, about 30 slices. Bake the pizza for 7–9 minutes, until the fat has rendered from the pepperoni and the crust is lightly golden. Finish with a sprinkling of fresh herbs.

Repeat the process with the remaining crusts to make as many pizzas as desired.

2 cups fennel sausage (page 167) or store-bought ground sausage

1 tablespoon extra-virgin olive oil

Semolina flour, for dusting

1 batch Stagioni Pizza Dough (page 229)

1 batch Stagioni Pizza Sauce (page 225)

2 cups freshly grated mozzarella

Pepperoni slices, preferably ½ inch diameter (we like Olli)

1 teaspoon chopped fresh oregano

1 teaspoon chopped fresh rosemary

1 teaspoon chopped fresh parsley

# Pork Belly Pizza with Charred Eggplant and Smoked Mozzarella

1 batch Stagioni Pizza Dough
(page 229) or store-bought
pizza dough

**FOR THE EGGPLANT PURÉE**
1 eggplant
2 tablespoons Garlic Confit
(page 15) or finely minced
garlic
½ cup smoked olive oil
⅛ cup extra-virgin olive oil
1 tablespoon smoked sea salt

**FOR THE PORK BELLY**
Neutral oil, such as grapeseed
or canola
24 ounces chilled pork belly
(page 165)
8 tablespoons Calabrian
pepper glaze (page 166)

This is another example of the imaginative pizza combinations we develop at Stagioni. Instead of pizza sauce, we make a roasted eggplant purée and top it with pork belly tossed in a sweet and spicy Calabrian pepper glaze (page 165). We balance the fatty richness of pork belly with pickled Fresno peppers and a fresh parsley salad. Plan ahead for the pork belly.

**SPECIAL EQUIPMENT:** high-speed blender, thermometer, pizza stone, pizza peel or wooden cutting board

MAKES 4 (10-INCH) PIZZAS

## TO MAKE THE EGGPLANT PURÉE
Roast the eggplant in a grill pan over high heat or under a broiler set on high until charred. Use tongs to turn the eggplant to char all sides. Let the eggplant cool, then peel the charred skin and place the flesh in a blender with the garlic; purée on medium-high speed. Increase the speed and slowly add both olive oils to emulsify, then add the smoked sea salt. Continue to purée until smooth. Cool completely.

## TO COOK THE PORK BELLY
Fill a saucepot one-third of the way with oil and heat to 350°. Slice the chilled pork belly into ¼-inch strips. Fill a bowl with Calabrian pepper glaze and set it nearby. Fry the pork belly for 6 minutes or until the strips are cooked through. Using a slotted spoon, carefully transfer the pork belly to the bowl with the Calabrian pepper glaze and toss to coat. Transfer the pork to a baking sheet and cool completely.

## TO ASSEMBLE THE PIZZAS

Place a pizza stone in the oven and preheat to 500°. Shape the pizza dough into 4 (10-inch) rounds as described on page 230.

In a bowl, toss the parsley with the chopped pickles. Season with salt and drizzle with smoked olive oil. Set aside.

Dust a pizza peel or wooden cutting board with semolina and set 1 round on top. Ladle ⅓ cup of the eggplant purée on the dough center. Working from the center outward, spread the sauce evenly, leaving a ½-inch edge.

Evenly distribute one-fourth of the smoked mozzarella, followed by the pork belly. Drizzle Calabrian pepper glaze over the top and add some of the pickled Fresno peppers. Top with fresh mozzarella.

Transfer the pizza to the heated pizza stone and bake for 8–10 minutes, or until the cheese has melted and the crust is lightly golden. Garnish the pizza with the parsley salad.

Repeat the process with the remaining crusts to make as many pizzas as desired.

**FOR THE PIZZA**

**2 cups fresh parsley**

**1 cup chopped sweet pickles**

**Kosher salt**

**Smoked olive oil**

**Semolina flour, for dusting**

**2 cups freshly grated smoked mozzarella**

**Calabrian pepper glaze**

**1 cup pickled Fresno peppers (or banana peppers)**

**½ cup shredded fresh mozzarella**

# Biscuit Breakfast Pizza

**FOR THE SAUSAGE GRAVY**

½ pound breakfast sausage

1 cup chopped yellow onions

½ cup all-purpose flour

4 cups whole milk

1 ½ teaspoons kosher salt

1 tablespoon coarsely ground
 black pepper

1 fresh bay leaf

¼ cup heavy cream

**FOR THE BISCUIT DOUGH**

2 cups all-purpose flour

1 tablespoon sugar

1 tablespoon kosher salt

1 tablespoon baking powder

8 tablespoons (1 stick) cold
 unsalted butter

1 cup grated smoked
 mozzarella

1 cup whole-milk buttermilk

Nonstick spray

Stagioni's executive chef Andrew Dodd is a Nashville native with southern roots. He makes the best biscuits I've ever tasted. While the true biscuit recipe is a family secret, Andrew whips up this biscuit breakfast pizza on occasion for a family meal. Commit this gravy recipe to memory, and you'll have successfully earned a notch in expert southern cooking.

**MAKES 2 (9-INCH) BREAKFAST PIZZAS**

TO MAKE THE SAUSAGE GRAVY

Cook the sausage in a large saucepan over medium-high heat. Add the chopped onions and cook until translucent, stirring occasionally, for about 4 minutes. Decrease the heat to medium and add the flour; stir for 2 minutes. Slowly add the milk and whisk until the flour is fully incorporated. Add the salt, pepper, and bay leaf and continue to whisk for 5 minutes. Add the cream and increase the heat to medium high; continue to whisk until the mixture bubbles slightly and thickens. Remove from the heat and set aside to cool. Discard the bay leaf.

TO MAKE THE BISCUIT DOUGH

Mix together the flour, sugar, salt, and baking powder. Use a cheese grater to grate in the cold butter. Add the mozzarella. Using your hands, incorporate the butter and cheese into the flour, pressing and squeezing with your fingers to create pea-size pieces. Add the buttermilk and mix with a spatula until the dough just comes together. Transfer the dough to a generously floured work surface and knead it 3 times. Divide the dough into 2 equal-size discs.

Use a rolling pin to roll each disc to ½ inch thick. Using a 9-inch pie pan or dinner plate as a guide, cut a perfect circle from each disc. Coat a large baking sheet with nonstick spray and transfer both crusts to it, leaving ample space between them.

## TO MAKE THE PIZZA

Preheat the oven to 425°. Spread sausage gravy over both crusts, leaving a ½-inch edge. Sprinkle the pizzas with the cheese and bake for 6–8 minutes. Remove the pizzas and reduce the oven temperature to 375°. Crack an egg into the center of each pizza and return the pizzas to the oven for 10–12 minutes, or until the egg whites are opaque and the crust is a light golden brown. Garnish with chopped chives and serve.

**FOR THE PIZZA**
**¼ cup grated smoked mozzarella**
**¼ cup grated cheddar**
**¼ cup grated mozzarella**
**2 large eggs**
**Chopped fresh chives, for garnish**

# Breads &Crackers

There was a two-week stretch in my midtwenties when my life fell apart. At the time, I lived in Washington, D.C., and worked in politics. One night I came home from the job I hated, and my girlfriend announced that she was moving to California and I was not invited. Ten days later I was informed that I was no longer needed at work. Deflated, I called a friend, and he convinced me to visit Charlotte. So I did.

During my stay, my friend and I convinced each other to open a pizza place. Although the restaurant didn't make it, it was there that I leaned into my passion. One of my favorite jobs was making the dough from scratch. We would stand around the table for hours having deep conversations while we shaped the pizzas. I loved that.

Today, we don't have an extensive bread program at my restaurants, but I find that there is a baker hidden in all of us. Many of my coworkers were terrified when I first suggested working with yeast and flour. However, once they get comfortable, I find that they start coming up with menu ideas that allow them to play with their newfound skills. In this chapter you'll find examples of our experimentation, like the Rye Crackers (page 253) we pair with sauerkraut and Pastrami-Cured Salmon (page 60). Our Focaccia (page 248) graces the tables at Stagioni, and our versatile Brioche (page 246) recipe makes the perfect vessel for New England lobster rolls (page 57). I encourage you to catch the bug.

# Brioche

¾ cup whole milk

2 teaspoons active dry yeast

2 teaspoons sugar

2 ¼ cup (17 ounces) all-
purpose flour

1 ½ teaspoons kosher salt

8 tablespoons (1 stick)
unsalted butter, softened

2 large eggs, room
temperature

Nonstick spray

FOR THE EGG WASH

1 large egg

2 tablespoons whole milk

This brioche is a launching pad for many of our dishes. We use it as the soft, buttery vessel for Lobster Rolls on Brioche with Fingerling Potato Chips (page 57), and we make a sweet bread by adding cinnamon and raisins to it. At Barrington's, we even turn it into a decadent crouton for foie gras. Use it at home for a luxurious French toast or bread pudding.

SPECIAL EQUIPMENT: stand mixer with paddle and dough hook attachments, cooking thermometer, two 9 × 5-inch loaf pans

MAKES 2 (9 × 5-INCH) LOAVES OR 12 ROLLS

In a small saucepan, gently warm the milk over low heat to 100°. Sprinkle the yeast over the warm milk and dissolve, then add the sugar and stir. Remove the pan from the heat and set aside.

In a bowl, whisk together the flour and salt; set aside.

In the bowl of a stand mixer fitted with a paddle attachment, combine the milk mixture with the butter; mix on medium speed until smooth. Add the eggs, one at a time, and mix on medium-high speed until they are incorporated.

Switch to the dough hook attachment. Slowly add the flour in 3 batches, mixing on low speed. Once all the flour is added, mix on medium speed for 6–8 minutes, or until the dough looks smooth and elastic. If the dough appears too tacky, add more flour.

Remove the dough and form it into a ball on a lightly floured surface. Spray a mixing bowl with nonstick spray. Transfer the dough to the bowl and cover with plastic wrap. Place the bowl in a warm spot (80° is optimal) and allow the dough to double in size, about 1 hour.

After the first rise, punch the dough down to release most of the air bubbles.

## TO MAKE BRIOCHE LOAVES

Coat the loaf pans with nonstick spray. Cut the dough into 2 equal-size portions. Place one portion on a lightly floured surface and stretch it to form a rectangle a little longer than the pan. Tuck the ends under, turn the dough over, and pinch to close the seams. Gently roll the loaf over and place it into the pan, seam-side down. Repeat for the second loaf.

## TO MAKE BRIOCHE ROLLS

Cut the dough into 12 equal portions. Shape the portions into balls and place them on a parchment-lined baking sheet.

## TO BAKE THE BRIOCHE

Loosely cover the brioche loaves or rolls and place them in a warm spot again, allowing them to rise a second time until they come to the top of the pan, about 30–40 minutes. Meanwhile, whisk together the egg and milk to make an egg wash. Once the dough has completed its second rise, brush it with the egg wash.

Preheat the oven to 350°. Bake for 40–45 minutes, or until the brioche is puffed and golden. Let the bread cool completely before use. To store, wrap the loaves or rolls tightly in plastic. They will keep for 3 days on the countertop and 1 week in the refrigerator.

# Focaccia

**FOR THE STARTER**

330 grams (2¾ cups) all-
    purpose flour

330 grams (1½ cups) water

**FOR THE FOCACCIA**

210 grams (1 cup) water

1 cup extra-virgin olive oil,
    divided

210 grams (1¾ cups) all-
    purpose flour

210 grams (1¾ cups) bread
    flour

6 grams (1¾ teaspoons)
    active dry yeast

16 grams (1 tablespoon plus
    2 teaspoons) kosher salt

Nonstick spray

We keep a sourdough starter in the kitchen at Stagioni for this focaccia, which is complementary for every table. If you've never made a starter before, this recipe is a great reason to give it a try. Plus, it can be used for other baked items. Plan 3 days ahead and use a digital scale to follow the measurements exactly. With proper planning, this recipe is fairly easy. Quality does matter here, so use good olive oil. This recipe uses all of the starter made from this recipe. If you want a starter for future baking projects, make a second batch and continue to feed it equal parts water and flour every 3–5 days.

**SPECIAL EQUIPMENT**: digital scale, stand mixer with dough hook

---

**MAKES 1 BAKING SHEET OF FOCACCIA (12¼ × 17½ INCHES)**

........................................................................................

## TO MAKE THE STARTER

Combine the flour and water in a nonreactive container and stir together. Scrape down the sides. Cover with a dish towel or paper towel, and secure with a rubber band. Store the starter in a warm place (about 80°) for at least 10 hours and up to 24 hours, then refrigerate for 2 days. The starter is now ready to use.

## TO MAKE THE FOCACCIA

In a stand mixer fitted with a paddle attachment, add the following in order: the water, ½ cup of the olive oil, the starter, both flours, and the yeast. Mix on low speed for 5 minutes. Switch to the dough hook, add the salt, and increase the speed to medium. Mix for 10 minutes. Once the dough has come together, place it into an oiled bowl and cover the lid tightly with plastic. Place the dough in a warm area until it has doubled in size, about 4 hours.

Turn the dough on a floured work surface and fold it like an envelope. Line a baking sheet with parchment paper and grease it with the remaining olive oil. Place the dough on the baking sheet, seam-side down. Spray the top with nonstick spray and cover the dough loosely with plastic wrap, giving it room to double in size (this is the second rise).

Oil your fingers and use them to poke indentations into the dough. This is called docking the dough. At the same time, spread the dough out to the edges of the baking sheet. Drizzle the remaining olive oil over the top. Add any preferred toppings, such as herbs or olives, at this point. If you will be adding cheese, wait to add it until the focaccia has been in the oven for 15 minutes, to prevent burning.

Cover the dough loosely with plastic wrap again and let it double in size a third time. (This should take about 2 hours.)

Preheat the oven to 425°. Fill a loaf pan with water and set it on the lowest rack. This creates moisture inside the oven. Place the baking sheet on the center rack. Bake for 15 minutes, then rotate and bake for 10 minutes more, or until the focaccia is lightly browned. Transfer the sheet to a wire rack and let it cool. Remove the focaccia and drizzle it with residual oil from the bottom of the baking sheet.

Extra focaccia will keep on the countertop for 2 days and in the freezer for weeks if wrapped tightly in plastic and then placed in a storage bag.

# Self-Sufficiency:
# A Lesson Learned on the Line (and Off)

I learned an important lesson from one of my more humbling moments in the kitchen, one that has benefited me through the years. I was not too far out of culinary school, working as a line cook in Boston at L'Espalier under Chef Frank McClelland (who has maintained an impeccable French restaurant for the better part of three decades). I started out in the pantry, where I was responsible for making the cold items produced for dinner service, including salads, terrines, and cold shellfish. It was a difficult station, and I was overwhelmed. I simply was not skilled enough to keep up.

About two months in, Chef Frank asked to speak with me in his office. I thought I was about to be fired. Instead, he told me that he was taking me off the line and wanted me to be the prep person first thing in the morning. The day shift included bread baking, desserts, stocks, sauces, and general preparation to assist the hot line cooks. My confidence was shaken; I felt this as a big demotion. Still I showed up every day and did my best.

With each passing day, I picked up new skills, ones that I wouldn't have learned without such a move. After a few months, the chef started asking me to produce the amuses-bouche, which meant I was responsible for creating and executing the first bite customers enjoy when they sit down. I will never forget when Chef Frank took me aside and explained to me that he could teach most people to be line cooks but that I had a special skill. He went on to tell me that I had the gift of knowing how to balance flavors and textures in a way that elevated the ingredients. He told me not to worry, I'd be just fine.

In hindsight, the skills I learned during my time at L'Espalier were of great importance. I had gained a broad spectrum of restaurant disciplines. In fact, to this day, I don't have a dedicated pastry chef inside my restaurants. Instead, pastry and baking are two skills that I expect my cooks to learn, as I did. What has happened is the creation of a culture inside my concepts that values self-reliance within restaurant walls.

As I transition to a different chapter of my culinary career, I hope I can offer a learning kitchen, where young cooks who walk through the doors of my restaurants can gain valuable experience. By learning all parts of service, not just the coveted tasks, they can forge ahead with new skills and a deeper sense of self-sufficiency.

# Flaky Butter Crust

This dough works for practically anything; we borrowed it from Keia Mastrianni, who makes delicious pies. We use a version of this for our Rabbit Pot Pie with Black Pepper Crust (page 173). You can make this dough for savory dishes by omitting the sugar. This recipe uses a 3:2:1 ratio of flour to butter to liquid. Weighing your ingredients with a digital scale is helpful when following this method.

½ pound all-purpose flour, plus more for dusting

1 teaspoon kosher salt

2 teaspoons sugar

8 tablespoons (1 stick) cold unsalted butter, cubed

3 tablespoons ice water

1 tablespoon apple cider vinegar

**MAKES 1 (9- TO 10-INCH) PIECRUST**

In a food processor, pulse together the flour, salt, and sugar. Add the butter and pulse until the mixture resembles a coarse meal. Combine the ice water and vinegar, then add the liquid to the food processor and pulse a few more times to incorporate. Transfer the mixture to a floured work surface and form it into a disc, pressing the dough together into a solid mass. If the dough seems too dry, add more water, 1 tablespoon at a time. The dough should stick together but not be too moist. Alternatively, you can make this dough by hand. Wrap the dough in plastic and refrigerate for at least 1 hour.

# Rye Crackers

The earthy body of rye flour gives these crackers a nutty flavor, while caraway and sesame seeds add a touch of sophistication. We use these crackers for our Pastrami-Cured Salmon (page 60). You can pair them with a wide assortment of pickles, jams, meats, and cheeses.

**SPECIAL EQUIPMENT:** food processor

---

**MAKES 60 (1 × 1-INCH) CRACKERS**

In a dry pan over medium-high heat, toast the sesame and caraway seeds until they are fragrant and lightly browned. Let cool.

Sprinkle the yeast into a bowl filled with 1 cup warm water and let it bloom. Once it has dissolved, add the molasses and mix together.

Combine both flours in a food processor with the salt and pulse. Add the seeds and pulse again. Add the yeast and water mixture and pulse until the dough comes together in a solid mass. Turn the dough on a generously floured work surface. Press the dough into a disc, wrap it in plastic, and refrigerate for 1 hour.

Preheat the oven to 350°. Cut the chilled dough into 4 equal-size portions. On a floured work surface, roll each portion as thin as possible. (To save the dough for later use, wrap it tightly in plastic and refrigerate for 1 week, or freeze it in a storage bag for 1 month. To use frozen dough, thaw it, then roll it out and bake according to the instructions below.)

Cut the crackers into shapes, or keep them whole for a rustic look. Place the crackers on a baking sheet lined with parchment paper and sprinkle with salt. Bake until the crackers are fully crisp, 15–25 minutes. Remove them from the oven. If baked whole, break the cracker into large pieces once it is cool enough to handle. The crackers will keep for 1 week in an airtight container.

¼ cup toasted sesame seeds

1 ½ teaspoons caraway seeds

1 teaspoon active dry yeast

1 tablespoon blackstrap molasses

2 cups rye flour

½ cup wheat flour, plus more for dusting

¼ teaspoon kosher salt, plus more for sprinkling

# Ciabatta

500 grams (1¼ cups) sour
    starter (page 248)
425 grams (1¾ cups plus
    2 tablespoons) water
8 grams (1 tablespoon) active
    dry yeast
600 grams (4 cups) bread flour
15 grams (1 tablespoon)
    kosher salt

At Stagioni, we use this ciabatta recipe as toast to accompany our mussels and our meatballs. The dough turns out a delightfully chewy loaf that can be used for sandwiches at home. Don't be alarmed: this is an extremely wet dough. It will appear too wet at times, but it is not. Forge on. A convection oven is best for this recipe. If you have one, reduce the bake time to 15 minutes.

**SPECIAL EQUIPMENT:** stand mixer with paddle attachment

**MAKES 2 (12-INCH) LOAVES**

In this order, combine the sour starter with the water, then add the yeast, bread flour, and salt. Paddle on low speed for 90 seconds, then increase the speed to medium and paddle for 6 minutes. Grease a large mixing bowl, then add the dough to the bowl. Cover the bowl tightly with plastic wrap and let it sit in a warm space (80°) for 30 minutes. Afterward, coat your hands liberally with flour and fold the dough like an envelope. Place the dough back in the bowl, seam-side down. Cover and repeat this process every 30 minutes, 3 more times, for a total of 4 folds.

Preheat the oven to 425°. Divide the dough in half. Stretch and shape each half into a loaf, 12–14 inches long and 4 inches wide, and place the loaf on a parchment-lined baking sheet. Bake for 20 minutes, or until the loaf is golden brown. Cool to room temperature, then slice and serve. The bread, wrapped in plastic, will keep for 1 week.

# Banana Bread

This recipe is a treasured heirloom, passed down to us by my wife Katrina's Ukrainian grandmother, Katherine Hnatiw-Kuchma. A kind and considerate woman who loved to cook, Grandma Katherine was known especially for her Sunday lunch. She gave the family many rich food traditions that we are honored to preserve both in our family and in the restaurant.

**SPECIAL EQUIPMENT:** stand mixer with paddle attachment, two 9 × 5-inch loaf pans

**MAKES 2 (9 × 5-INCH) LOAVES**

5 overripe bananas
2 large eggs
⅔ cup canola oil
½ teaspoon vanilla
3 cups all-purpose flour
1½ cups sugar
2 teaspoons baking powder
2 teaspoons baking soda
1 teaspoon kosher salt

Preheat the oven to 350°. Grease the loaf pans; set aside.

Use the paddle attachment of a stand mixer to mash the bananas, leaving some small chunks intact. Add the eggs, oil, and vanilla to the bananas; mix on medium speed until they are incorporated.

Meanwhile, sift the flour, sugar, baking powder, baking soda, and salt in a separate bowl. Reduce the mixer speed to low, and slowly add the dry ingredients to the banana mixture. Continue mixing until the flour is incorporated and few or no lumps remain. Fill the pans with the batter about two-thirds full.

Bake for 40 minutes, or until a toothpick inserted into the bread center comes out clean. Allow the pans to cool before tipping the bread out. Wrap the loaves in wax paper and store at room temperature.

# Desserts

I was working in Boston at L'Espalier, green as I could be, and more or less of a train wreck on the line. After I made more mistakes than I'd like to admit to, the head chef relegated me to the daytime shift, where I prepped for service and made many of the components for the pastry team.

I was humiliated. I thought I had received a life sentence to sit on the bench for the rest of my career, and began doubting myself. Nonetheless, I did my duty pushing out a variety of mousses, ice creams, sorbets, and cakes for the night's service. Despite the ego-puncturing, I showed up and I learned. In time, dessert morphed into a memorable turning point. The temporary setback had actually expanded my skill set, and I had more creative ammo in my repertoire than before.

I grew from the experience. (More on that lesson in the sidebar on page 250.)

We don't have a dedicated pastry chef at my restaurants. Mastering the basics of dessert is part of the foundation for young cooks when they come to work for me. It's a skill they will take with them as they grow. I take heart in that.

In this chapter, you'll find a few of the sweet tastes from my childhood, such as the Lemon Bars that my grandmother made each summer and the simple and timeless Peaches with Brown Sugar, Sour Cream, and Blackberries. Then you'll find a host of classics like Pots de Crème and the airy Zeppole served at Stagioni, plus a host of delectable ice creams that can be paired with the selections in this chapter or as a stellar standalone treat.

# Dark Chocolate Brownies

I've tried to make good brownies for years. For some reason, I just can't get it right. That's why it was especially irritating when my kitchen brother, chef Larry Schreiber, nailed it on his first attempt. I have to give it to him: this brownie is moist and decadent. At the restaurant, we pair it with Biscoff Ice Cream (page 280), chocolate sauce, and unadulterated Biscoff spread for the ultimate chocolate dessert.

**SPECIAL EQUIPMENT:** stand mixer, double boiler (if you do not have a double boiler, use a saucepan with a metal bowl on top; the bowl should not touch the bottom of the saucepan)

---

MAKES 1 (9½ × 13-INCH) BAKING SHEET

Preheat the oven to 325° and grease a 9½ × 13-inch rimmed baking sheet.

Fill the bottom pan of a double boiler with 1–2 inches of water. Place the double boiler over medium-high heat and add 1 cup of the chocolate chips to the upper pan; stir until melted.

Whisk together the flour, cocoa powder, baking powder, and baking soda in a mixing bowl; set aside. In a stand mixer fitted with a paddle attachment, combine the cream cheese, butter, and sugar, and mix at medium speed for 3 minutes. Add the eggs, one at a time, until they are fully incorporated. Scrape down the sides of the bowl with a spatula and mix again. Add the dry ingredients in 2 batches, then add the melted chocolate and continue mixing until it is incorporated.

Pour the batter on the greased baking sheet, using a spatula to spread it evenly. Give the pan a few thwacks on the countertop to help settle the batter. Fill a baking dish with water and place on the lowest rack in the oven. This helps bake a moist brownie. Top the batter with the remaining chocolate chips and place the pan into the oven. Bake for 40–45 minutes, or until a toothpick inserted into the center comes out clean.

1⅓ cups dark chocolate chips, divided
¾ cup all-purpose flour
2 tablespoons cocoa powder
½ teaspoon baking powder
½ teaspoon baking soda
1 cup (8 ounces) cream cheese, softened
8 tablespoons (1 stick) unsalted butter, softened
1 cup sugar
2 large eggs, at room temperature

# Pots de Crème

1 quart cream

⅓ cup espresso or very
    strong coffee

⅔ cup roughly chopped
    dark chocolate

5 large egg yolks

½ cup sugar

Confectioners' sugar

Whipped cream (optional)

I was never a birthday cake guy, so every year on my birthday I requested my mother's pots de crème instead. This recipe has been in my family forever and has been served at Good Food on Montford since the beginning; its longevity is a testament to its timeless quality. Here, a dark chocolate custard, rich with cream and enlivened with espresso, is baked to a delicate pudding-like consistency. It's a classic that never gets old. The pots de crème need to rest overnight in the refrigerator. Make them a day ahead.

**SPECIAL EQUIPMENT:** 8 (6-ounce) ramekins, candy thermometer (optional)

**SERVES 8**

Preheat the oven to 350°. Combine the cream and espresso in a saucepan over medium heat. Bring the contents to a simmer (approximately 185°). Add the chocolate and whisk until it is fully melted. Whisk the egg yolks and sugar together in a large mixing bowl. Slowly pour the chocolate mixture over the eggs, whisking constantly. Pour the liquid back into the pot and whisk over medium-low heat until the mixture thickens enough to coat the back of a spoon, about 6 minutes. Pour the mixture into 8 (6-ounce) ramekins, and place the ramekins into a deep roasting pan or hotel pan. Pour 1 inch of water into the pan and cover the pan tightly with aluminum foil.

Carefully place the pan into the oven. Bake for 30–40 minutes, checking after 30 minutes. The custard should have a modest jiggle. It is done when it's barely set. Remove the ramekins from the oven, cool completely, and refrigerate overnight.

To serve, dust the ramekins with confectioners' sugar or top them with whipped cream.

# Peaches with Brown Sugar, Sour Cream, and Blackberries

3 freestone peaches

1 cup sour cream

6 tablespoons dark brown
  sugar

½ cup fresh blackberries

My grandmother made this dessert, and it's still one of the best things I've ever eaten. More than that, it reminds me that simplicity is best. Great ingredients don't need much. Make this dessert in the summertime, when the peaches are impossibly ripe and their juices are plentiful enough to run down your chin. This recipe maintains a sophisticated profile thanks to the balance of sweetness from the brown sugar and the tartness of the sour cream.

**SERVES 6**

Bring a large pot of water to a rolling boil. Meanwhile, prepare an ice bath. Place the peaches in the boiling water for about 20 seconds, then immediately transfer them to the ice bath. With a paring knife, peel the skin from the peaches. Carefully slice each peach in half and remove the pit.

Fill the indent of each peach half with sour cream and top with a tablespoon of brown sugar. Garnish with fresh blackberries.

# Blueberry Bundt Cake

We had a summer routine at Lawton House. We would get up early and row the boat across Round Pond and head over to Turtle Cove, a place where turtles would hang out and sun themselves. The edge of the pond in this spot was lined with wild blueberry bushes, close enough for us to pick straight from the rowboat. We collected fresh berries to make blueberry pancakes or white cake with blueberries. At Barrington's, we bake this Bundt cake in the summertime when blueberries are in season, usually late June in North Carolina. We pair it with a lemon curd and Lemon Poppy Seed Ice Cream (page 278) for a bright summer offering.

**SPECIAL EQUIPMENT:** stand mixer

---

**MAKES 12 MINI-BUNDT CAKES OR 1 LARGE BUNDT CAKE**

....................................................................................

Preheat the oven to 325°. In a stand mixer fitted with a paddle attachment, cream together the butter and sugar on medium-high speed until the mixture is pale and fluffy, about 5–7 minutes. Add the eggs, one at a time, incorporating them completely. Add the sour cream, vanilla, and lemon zest and mix until blended.

In a separate bowl, whisk together 4 cups of the flour along with the baking soda, baking powder, and salt. Add the dry mixture to the wet batter, a little at a time, mixing on medium speed. Once all the flour has been added, scrape the sides and bottom of the bowl with a spatula and fold to incorporate any dry bits.

Toss the blueberries in the remaining flour to coat. (This prevents them from sinking to the bottom of the Bundt pan.) Gently fold the blueberries into the batter. Discard excess flour.

Spray 2 (6-count) mini-Bundt pans or 1 large Bundt pan with non-stick spray. Fill them halfway with batter and bake for 50–55 minutes, rotating after 30 minutes. The cake will rise considerably while baking. It is done when a toothpick inserted into the center comes out clean. Cool the Bundt cake completely, then invert it on a rack or baking sheet to remove it from the pan.

8 tablespoons (1 stick) unsalted butter, softened
1 cup sugar
2 large eggs
1 cup sour cream
1 teaspoon vanilla
Zest of 1 lemon
5 cups all-purpose flour, divided
½ teaspoon baking soda
1 teaspoon baking powder
¼ teaspoon kosher salt
1 pint fresh blueberries
Nonstick spray

# Strawberry Goat Cheese Cobbler

FOR THE FILLING

2 quarts strawberries, hulled
    and rinsed

½ cup sugar

2 vanilla beans, scraped

½ cup red wine

¼ cup cornstarch

¾ cup cold water

½ cup crumbled goat cheese


FOR THE CRUST

1 cup cake flour

⅓ cup all-purpose flour

¼ teaspoon kosher salt

1½ teaspoons baking powder

4 tablespoons (½ stick)
    unsalted butter, frozen

⅔ cup heavy cream

2 tablespoons unsalted butter,
    melted

2 tablespoons sugar

We're lucky to have two distinct growing seasons for strawberries in the Piedmont, which means that we have access to locally grown strawberries from the beginning of spring through the fall. This play on a classic cobbler involves strawberries macerated with sugar and plenty of vanilla bean, with a touch of red wine to deepen the ripe berry flavor. Goat cheese adds just the right amount of savory to give this classic dessert a mature twist. A simple scoop of ice cream finishes this dish.

SERVES 8–10

Preheat the oven to 350° and grease a 9 × 13-inch baking dish.

TO MAKE THE FILLING

Combine the strawberries, sugar, and vanilla bean and pods, and macerate for 30 minutes. In a saucepan, bring the wine to a boil. Let the wine boil for 1 minute, then add the macerated strawberry mixture and return to a boil. Make a slurry by mixing together the cornstarch and water, then add it to the mixture, whisking constantly until it thickens. Remove the pan from the heat; discard the vanilla bean pods. Pour the filling into the prepared baking dish. Top it with the crumbled goat cheese and set aside.

TO MAKE THE CRUST

In a large mixing bowl, whisk together the flours, salt, and baking powder. Grate the frozen butter into the bowl. Use your fingers to incorporate the butter evenly until the mixture is crumbly and pea-size. Add the cream and mix just until moistened.

Transfer the contents to a floured work surface and bring the dough together into a solid mass. Roll it into a rectangle about ¼ inch thick and slightly larger than the baking pan. Drape the dough over the top of the pan, pressing it along the sides to snugly cover the filling. Brush the dough with melted butter and sprinkle it with the sugar. Bake for 1 hour, or until the crust is golden and the filling is bubbly. Serve warm with your favorite ice cream.

# Coconut Milk Panna Cotta with Passion Fruit Curd, Blackberries, and Pistachio Crumble

We trade whole milk for coconut milk in our version of *panna cotta*, a delicate Italian custard whose name translates to "cooked cream." In this recipe, the softly sweetened cream is complemented by a tart passion-fruit curd and roasted blackberries, while a crunchy pistachio crumble adds texture and a slightly savory element.

The panna cotta and curd require several hours of chilling. You can make all the components a day ahead and then assemble the dish the day you plan to serve it.

*Note*: We prefer gelatin sheets, which can be purchased online, over gelatin powder. Passion fruit juice can be readily found at international grocery stores or online. If you can't find coconut cream, scrape the cream from the top of a coconut milk can.

**SPECIAL INGREDIENTS AND EQUIPMENT**: silver gelatin sheets, double boiler, candy thermometer, food processor, 8 individual serving dishes or glasses

**SERVES 8**

## TO MAKE THE PANNA COTTA

Fill the lower pan of a double boiler with 2 inches of water and place it over medium heat. Combine the coconut milk, heavy cream, coconut cream, lime zest, and sugar in the top pan. Add the gelatin sheets or powder and set the pan over medium-high heat. Allow the gelatin to dissolve into the mixture. Once it starts to heat up, give the pot a gentle stir. Do not let the mixture boil; this will reduce the gelatin's ability to set the custard.

Once the gelatin is dissolved, add the salt. Remove the mixture from the heat and let it cool slightly, giving it a whisk every now and then. Transfer the slightly cooled custard to 8 individual serving dishes or a single dish, and chill, uncovered, for 3 hours. Cover the panna cotta only after the custard has completely chilled.

**FOR THE PANNA COTTA**

2 cups full-fat coconut milk

2 cups heavy cream

¼ cup coconut cream

Zest of 2 limes

½ cup sugar

1 ½ teaspoons gelatin powder or 6 ½ silver gelatin sheets

Pinch kosher salt

**FOR THE PASSION
FRUIT CURD**

**4 large eggs**

**4 large egg yolks**

**1 ½ teaspoons lemon zest**

**2 teaspoons rum (optional)**

**1 cup passion fruit juice**

**2 cups sugar**

**1 cup (2 sticks) cold unsalted
    butter, cubed**


**FOR THE PISTACHIO
CRUMBLE**

**1 cup unsalted pistachios**

**6 tablespoons sugar**

**1 cup all-purpose flour**

**¾ teaspoon kosher salt**

**¾ cup (1 ½ sticks) cold
    unsalted butter**


**FOR THE ROASTED
BLACKBERRIES**

**2 cups fresh blackberries**

**½ cup light brown sugar**

**Juice of 1 lemon**


## TO MAKE THE PASSION FRUIT CURD

Fill the lower pan of a double boiler with 2 inches of water and place it on the stove over medium-high heat. In the top pan, add the eggs, yolks, lemon zest, rum, passion fruit juice, and sugar. Whisk gently until the mixture begins to thicken and reaches 165° on an instant-read thermometer, about 5–7 minutes. Remove the pan from the heat and whisk in the cold butter, a little at a time, until it is fully incorporated. Allow the curd to cool slightly, then pour a layer on the chilled panna cotta. Chill for 3 more hours.


## TO MAKE THE PISTACHIO CRUMBLE

Preheat the oven to 350° and line a baking sheet with parchment paper.

Pulse the pistachios in a food processor until they are coarsely chopped. Add the sugar, flour, and salt, and pulse a few more times. Transfer the mixture to a bowl. Grate the cold butter into the bowl. Use your fingers to toss and squeeze the mixture together until it resembles coarse sand.

Spread the crumble in a single layer on the prepared baking sheet and bake for 15 minutes. Stir the crumble with a heatproof spatula to break up any large pieces, then return it to the oven for 8 minutes more, or until it is a golden brown. Cool and store in an airtight container.


## TO ROAST THE BLACKBERRIES

Preheat the oven to 450°. Toss the blackberries with the brown sugar and lemon juice. Spread the berries on a baking sheet lined with parchment paper and roast for 20 minutes, stirring with a heatproof spatula every 5 minutes, until they soften and the juices are reduced to a jam-like consistency. Cool completely.


## TO ASSEMBLE

Remove the chilled panna cotta from the refrigerator. Spoon the cooled blackberries over the top and add the pistachio crumble. Serve immediately.

# Lemon Bars

Every summer in Matunuck, Rhode Island, my grandmother treated us to her famous lemon bars. She would have them waiting when we arrived for her standard four o'clock tea service. They were simple—sweet and tart, enough to make our lips pucker before grabbing another. She wrote her recipe down years ago, and it's been a family treasure ever since.

**SPECIAL EQUIPMENT:** food processor

**MAKES 1 (9½ × 13-INCH) BAKING SHEET**

Preheat the oven to 350°.

### TO MAKE THE CRUST

In the bowl of a food processor, pulse 3 cups of the flour with the confectioners' sugar, butter, and salt until the butter is incorporated. The mixture should be loose and have the texture of wet sand. Line a baking sheet with parchment paper and spray the paper with nonstick spray. Transfer the contents to the baking sheet and firmly press the mixture to form an even crust. Bake for 15 minutes, or until lightly golden. Meanwhile, make the lemon filling.

### TO MAKE THE FILLING

In a large bowl, whisk together the eggs and sugar. In a separate bowl, whisk together the remaining flour along with the lemon zest and juice and baking powder. Add this to the egg mixture and whisk thoroughly. Pour the filling over the par-baked crust and bake for 25–30 minutes, or until the top is set. Let the squares cool for 1 hour before slicing. Dust with confectioners' sugar and serve. The lemon squares will keep, covered, in the refrigerator for 1 week.

**FOR THE CRUST**

3 ¼ cup all-purpose flour, divided

¼ cup confectioners' sugar, plus more for dusting

1 cup (2 sticks) cold unsalted butter, cubed

1 teaspoon kosher salt

Nonstick spray

**FOR THE FILLING**

6 large eggs

3 cups sugar

Zest of 4 lemons

1 ½ cups lemon juice (from about 8 lemons)

2 teaspoons baking powder

# Cinnamon Buns

Cinnamon buns are a weekend breakfast treat for most, but we've turned them into a decadent dessert at Barrington's, complete with Brown Butter Pecan Ice Cream (page 279). We go for a classic style, filling the buns with plenty of cinnamon, sugar, and butter and then topping it with whipped cream cheese icing. Serve them at breakfast or as a sticky-sweet finish to supper.

**SPECIAL EQUIPMENT:** stand mixer with paddle and hook attachment, food processor

---

**MAKES 12 BUNS**

.............................................................................

## TO MAKE THE DOUGH

In a stand mixer fitted with a paddle attachment, cream together the butter, sugar, and vanilla for 5 minutes on high speed. Add the eggs, one at a time, fully incorporating each one. Add the salt.

In a small saucepan over medium-low heat, gently warm the milk to 100°, about 3 minutes. Remove the pan from the heat and add the yeast. Let the yeast sit for 1 minute, then stir to dissolve it fully.

Switch the mixer attachment from the paddle to the dough hook. Add the yeast mixture plus the flour, and mix on low speed. Once the flour starts to incorporate, increase the speed to medium. After 5 minutes, feel the dough. If it is tacky, add more flour, 1 tablespoon at a time, and mix for 2–3 minutes more. It should still be slightly tacky and readily pull away from the sides of the mixing bowl to form a ball. At this point, continue to mix for another 10 minutes. The finished dough will be smooth and elastic.

Spray a nonreactive bowl with nonstick spray. Turn the dough on a floured surface and knead it into a ball by tucking and crimping the edges underneath. Place the dough in the bowl. Spray the top and cover with plastic wrap, then set the bowl in a warm place (about 80°). Allow the dough to double in size, about 90 minutes (the time may vary depending on the temperature of your working environment). Meanwhile, clean and dry the mixer and switch back to the paddle attachment. Set aside for the cream cheese icing. Once the dough doubles in size, punch it down and let it rest for 15 minutes more.

### FOR THE DOUGH
⅓ cup unsalted butter, softened
½ cup sugar
1 teaspoon vanilla
3 large eggs
1 teaspoon kosher salt
1 cup plus 2 tablespoons whole milk
2 teaspoons active dry yeast
4 cups all-purpose flour
Nonstick spray

1 cup (2 sticks) cold unsalted
   butter, cubed

1 cup sugar

½ cup ground cinnamon

2 teaspoons kosher salt

¼ cup all-purpose flour

1 tablespoon cornstarch

1½ cups sugar

2 tablespoons light brown
   sugar

1 teaspoon vanilla extract

FOR THE CREAM CHEESE

ICING

8 tablespoons (1 stick)
   unsalted butter, softened

1 cup (8 ounces) cream
   cheese, softened

2 cups confectioners' sugar

1 teaspoon vanilla

## TO MAKE THE CINNAMON FILLING

Combine all the ingredients in a food processor and pulse until the butter is pea-size and the filling is crumbly. Refrigerate until use.

## TO MAKE THE CINNAMON BUNS

Turn the dough on a floured work surface. Dust the top with more flour. Roll the dough into a large rectangle, about 20 × 15 inches. Spread cinnamon filling on the dough, leaving 1 inch of space around the edge. Starting from the bottom of the rectangle and working left to right, roll the dough tightly toward the top, shaping the log as you go. Slice off the ends of the log to form clean edges. Cut the roll in half, then cut the halves in half again. Cut each quarter into 3 equal pieces to yield 12 buns.

Place the buns in 3 rows of 4 in a 9 × 13-inch baking dish, arranging them cut-side up. Cover the dish with a towel and let the buns rest in a warm place (about 80°) for 25 minutes.

Preheat the oven to 350°. Cover the baking dish with foil and bake for 30 minutes. Remove the foil and bake, uncovered, for 15 minutes more. Meanwhile, make the cream cheese icing.

## TO MAKE THE CREAM CHEESE ICING

Combine the butter, cream cheese, and confectioners' sugar in the bowl of a stand mixer fitted with the paddle attachment. Mix on medium speed for 2 minutes, or until the ingredients are fully incorporated. Add the vanilla and mix 1 minute more. Scrape down the sides.

## TO SERVE

Allow the buns to cool slightly, then spread cream cheese icing on top of them. Serve immediately.

# Zeppole with Salted Caramel Sauce

Nearly every culture has its own version of fried and sugared dough. Originally, zeppole were Italian confections served in honor of Saint Joseph that could come either baked or fried, filled or unfilled. But it was the fried version that became popular with Italian Americans. At Stagioni, these airy, light pillows of dough meet a hot fryer before being dusted with confectioners' sugar and served with a salted caramel sauce.

You will be left with plenty of extra caramel. Use it to drizzle over ice cream or French toast, or stir it into a latte. It will keep in the refrigerator for three months.

*Note*: Fresh farm eggs are the best eggs for this recipe. Try to find some at your local farmers' market.

**SPECIAL EQUIPMENT:** stand mixer, fryer (optional), candy thermometer (optional), 1½-ounce scoop

---

**SERVES 8**

................................................................

### TO MAKE THE SAUCE

Prepare an ice bath and set aside. In a large pot, combine the sugar and water and bring the mixture to a low boil. Scrape down the sides of the pot and watch carefully; the liquid will slowly begin to turn color. Let it deepen to a nice amber color, about 320°–350° on a candy thermometer. Add the heavy cream and whisk carefully (the cream will bubble and spit), then add the salt and immediately put the bowl into the ice bath. Stir the sauce every few minutes until it has cooled to room temperature.

### TO MAKE THE ZEPPOLE

In a medium saucepan, bring the butter, salt, confectioners' sugar, and water to a boil over medium-high heat.

While the mixture comes to a boil, add the egg whites to the bowl of a stand mixer fitted with a whisk attachment and whip them on medium-high speed until stiff peaks form. Switch to the paddle attachment.

**FOR THE SAUCE**

2 cups sugar

½ cup water

2 cups heavy cream

1 tablespoon kosher salt (we prefer Diamond Crystal)

**FOR THE ZEPPOLE**

1 ⅛ cups (2 ¼ sticks) unsalted butter, cubed

½ teaspoon kosher salt

¼ cup confectioners' sugar, plus more for dusting

3 cups water

4 large egg whites

2 ½ cups all-purpose flour

8 large eggs

Canola oil, for frying

Add the flour to the butter and sugar mixture and stir with a wooden spoon until there are no lumps. Add this mixture to the egg whites and mix on low speed. Add the whole eggs, one at a time, and incorporate them.

Preheat the fryer to 350°. (If not using a fryer, fill a 3-quart pot with 3 inches of oil and heat to the same temperature.)

Working in batches, use a 1½-ounce ice cream scoop to portion the batter and drop the zeppole into the hot oil. Fry for 8–10 minutes, or until golden and cooked through. Use a slotted spoon to remove the zeppole and place them on a plate lined with paper towels to drain. Remove any fry bits from the oil between batches. If not using all the batter, cover and refrigerate for up to 48 hours.

TO SERVE

Dust the warm zeppole with confectioners' sugar and serve immediately with salted caramel sauce on the side.

# Queen City Reflections

I t's been almost two decades since I landed in the Queen City, just as green as the city was, a business owner and chef at the beginning of his journey with a city that had just as much growing to do. Looking back, it feels as if I've grown up alongside Charlotte.

When I first got here, there wasn't a climate for independent restaurants. Uptown Charlotte, the booming financial center of North Carolina, was a ghost town after business hours, and those of us who were making a go of independent restaurant ownership were few.

As new business owners, we spent most of our waking hours in the kitchen, leaving little time for camaraderie and collaboration. It felt as if those of us who ran independent restaurants were competing for the same small percentage of customers interested in composed, chef-driven plates. Expanding the palate of a meat-and-three crowd and educating customers on the merits of local food was an uphill battle. There was much work to be done. In the family of southern cities, Charlotte was easily the red-headed stepchild of the group, passed over for rising culinary scenes in Charleston, Atlanta, and Nashville.

The arrival of Johnson & Wales University in 2004 brought some optimism to our culinary aspirations. I hoped that our labor pool would improve and that some of the young people who received their culinary education in Charlotte would stay. Some of them have, and some haven't. But many chefs who work in the city today have spent time in our kitchens.

As the city developed, there was little room for independent restaurants to flourish. Landlords were interested only in tenants who could build 250-seat restaurants and sign twenty-year leases. This was impossible for the independent restaurateur on a tight budget. Since uptown wasn't an option, neighborhoods began to hold potential for the little guys. Still, shopping centers were cautious about leasing to restaurants, and most of the neighborhoods that now house many of our best restaurants were only starting to transition.

By the time I opened Good Food on Montford in 2009, Charlotte's culinary sensibilities were visibly changing. Chefs were tapping into the region's bounty and beginning to become more creative on the plate. Though the Good Food concept struggled for a few years, diners warmed to it eventually. A 2010 James Beard Foundation nomination for Best New Restaurant in the country was testament to that and, we hope, momentum for Charlotte's ever-growing culinary scene.

With each restaurant opening, I feel my own growth in time with Charlotte's evolution. By the time Stagioni opened in 2013, local food critics were praising the city's culinary scene, and word on the street was that we had "turned a corner." A number of veteran chefs opened new concepts, and the next generation of young chefs was waiting in the wings. One look around town, cranes stretching their necks high into the sky and new development everywhere, and it was hard to deny Charlotte's bona fide status.

Take a walk down the streets of uptown today and you'll find a city teeming with a dynamic, young population and a lively culture that populates the city center well after banking hours. Charlotte chefs have come together in ways I could have never imagined in my early days here. Organizations like the Piedmont Culinary Guild have forged a spirit of collaboration among chefs. Young chefs like Joe Kindred, Clark Barlowe, Ashley Boyd, Chris Coleman, and others push the bar ever higher for our culinary scene. New talent like chefs William Dissen and Craig Deihl and cocktail connoisseur Gary Crunkleton have found a second home in Charlotte, and the list keeps growing.

In addition, our farming community has evolved, our diners have become savvier, and Charlotte has started to make space conducive to independent restaurateurs. Every time there is a new successful restaurant on the scene, it encourages other chefs and restaurateurs to be a little bit braver. I didn't think I would take as much pleasure in our collective growth as I have, but as a Charlottean, and a resident of this New South city, I couldn't be more proud.

# Lemon Poppy Seed Ice Cream

**FOR THE SIMPLE SYRUP**

1 cup sugar

1 cup lemon juice
(from 7–8 lemons)

**FOR THE ICE CREAM**

1 quart heavy cream

1 quart whole milk

Zest of 1 lemon

¾ cup plus 1 teaspoon sugar, divided

12 large egg yolks

¼ cup poppy seeds

This ice cream showcases the bright essence of lemon, thanks to a citrus-infused simple syrup and ample lemon zest. Poppy seeds add visual and textural appeal, similar to the pop of caviar. At Barrington's, we pair this ice cream with our Blueberry Bundt Cake (page 263) for a winning combination.

**SPECIAL EQUIPMENT:** 2-quart ice cream maker (if you have a smaller ice cream maker [1.5 quart], cut this recipe in half to make 1 quart of ice cream instead of 2 quarts, or process the recipe in 2 batches), Microplane, thermometer

**MAKES 2 QUARTS**

**TO MAKE THE SIMPLE SYRUP**
In a small saucepan, combine the sugar and lemon juice. Bring the mixture to a boil and stir until the sugar dissolves, then remove from the heat. Set aside.

**TO MAKE THE ICE CREAM**
In a large pot, combine the cream and milk, then add the lemon zest and ¾ cup of the sugar and stir together. Place the yolks in a bowl, and sprinkle them with the remaining sugar. Bring the cream mixture to a boil, then remove it from the heat.

Temper the yolks by slowly pouring 2 cups of the cream mixture into the yolks while whisking. Once the cream is fully incorporated, whisk the yolks back into the remaining cream, then return the mixture to the stovetop and heat to 185°. Use a wooden spoon to stir the mixture until it thickens enough to coat the back of the spoon. Strain, then whisk in 1 cup of the simple syrup. Chill completely and then strain once more. Stir in the poppy seeds and freeze according to the manufacturer's instructions.

# Brown Butter Pecan Ice Cream

This is quite possibly our favorite ice cream at Barrington's. It has a velvety texture, a nutty flavor, and a burst of caramelized sweetness. We found that using actual brown butter made the ice cream grainy, so we traded in toasted powdered milk to mimic its flavor. As if this ice cream couldn't get any better, we pair it with warm Cinnamon Buns (page 271) at the restaurant.

**SPECIAL EQUIPMENT:** ice cream maker with a 2-quart bowl (if you have a smaller ice cream maker, cut the recipe in half and use 1 teaspoon of vanilla for 1 quart of ice cream; you can also make this recipe in 2 batches), candy thermometer

**½ cup powdered milk**

**2 cups chopped pecans, divided**

**1 quart heavy cream**

**1 quart whole milk**

**1 teaspoon kosher salt**

**1 teaspoon vanilla**

**1 cup light brown sugar**

**½ cup plus 1 teaspoon sugar, divided**

**12 large egg yolks**

**MAKES 2 QUARTS**

Preheat the oven to 325°. Line 2 baking sheets with parchment paper. Spread the powdered milk on one sheet and the pecans in a single layer on the other. Place both sheets in the oven and toast the powdered milk for 7 minutes and the pecans until fragrant, about 5–7 minutes.

Combine the cream and milk in a large pot over medium heat. Add the toasted milk powder and 1½ cups of the toasted pecans to the mixture, along with the salt, vanilla, brown sugar, and ½ cup of the white sugar. Whisk vigorously to incorporate the powdered milk.

While the mixture heats, sprinkle the egg yolks with the remaining sugar. Once the mixture comes to a boil, turn off the heat and steep for 30 minutes. Strain, discarding the pecans. Slowly temper the yolks by adding the warmed milk a little at a time, whisking constantly.

Return the mixture to the stovetop over medium-high heat and bring it to 185°, stirring constantly with a wooden spoon. Remove the pan from the heat and transfer the mixture to a bowl. Refrigerate until completely chilled, at least 1 hour. Strain again, then freeze according to the manufacturer's instructions, folding in the remaining toasted pecans halfway through. Return to the freezer for a firmer texture.

# Biscoff Ice Cream

12 large egg yolks

1 quart heavy cream

1 quart whole milk

1 cup sugar

1 cup Biscoff spread

Biscoff, a warmly spiced cookie from the Belgian *speculoos* family of short-crust biscuits, made a name for itself as the "airplane cookie." At Good Food on Montford, we pair the equally famous Biscoff spread with housemade Biscoff ice cream and our Dark Chocolate Brownies (page 259). Enjoy this ice cream with your favorite cookie, brownie, or cake—or just top it with crushed Biscoff cookies for a treat. You can find Biscoff spread or speculoos cookie butter in the grocery aisle with the nut butters.

**SPECIAL EQUIPMENT:** ice cream maker with a 2-quart bowl

**MAKES 2 QUARTS**

Gently whisk the egg yolks to break them up a little; set aside.

In a medium saucepan, bring the cream, milk, and sugar to a boil over medium heat. Remove the pan from the heat and add the Biscoff spread; whisk until it is fully melted. Gradually pour the mixture into the egg yolks, whisking constantly until blended.

Return the mixture to the stovetop over medium-high heat and bring it to 160°, stirring constantly with a wooden spoon. Remove the pan from the heat and transfer the mixture to a bowl. Refrigerate until completely chilled, at least 1 hour. Strain again, then freeze according to the manufacturer's instructions.

# ACKNOWLEDGMENTS

I would like to acknowledge Catherine Carter for her hard work and editorial help and chefs Jason Newman, Larry Schreiber, and Drew Dodd for their contributions to menu development.

I would also like to express my gratitude to my staff over the years. Without them I wouldn't have made it one week.

# INDEX

*Italic page numbers refer to illustrations.*